SO, WHAT'S A NICE GIRL LIKE YOU DOING IN A PLACE LIKE THIS?

SEOUL TO SAIGON

Personal Essays

By

Dr. Sandra Lockney Davis

With
Illustrations by
Terri Zuber

Copyright 2011 by Sandra Lockney Davis
Copyright ca. 1968 "The Story of a Special Services Girl in Vietnam, by Terri Zuber
Copyright 2004 for "War Zone Diversions, An Overview of Women Volunteers in Civilian Staffed Recreation Programs in Vietnam," by Ann Kelsey.

ALL RIGHTS RESERVED. THIS BOOK, OR PARTS THEREOF, MAY NOT BE REPRODUCED IN ANY FORM WITHOUT PERMISSION FROM COPYRIGHT HOLDERS

EAST BAY PUBLISHERS
3650 Ebb Tide Lane
Gulf Breeze, Florida 32563

Printed by CreateSpace

LIBRARY OF CONGRESS CATALOG CARD NUMBER:
pending
ISBN 9781466426030
First Printing 2011
PRINTED IN THE UNITED STATES OF AMERICA

This book is dedicated to U. S. Army Special Services,

and

to all the men and women of the U. S. Military who have served and are serving to protect America, and their families who endure(d) their absence,

God bless you,

and

Thank you.

Service Club Recreation Specialists, Program Directors and Supervisors
VietNam, ca. 1970

Some names have been changed to protect the innocent and the guilty.

Table of Contents

	Foreword by Ann Kelsey	3
	Introduction	5
	Acknowledgements	10
	Maps of Korea and VietNam and My Assignments	12
Chapter 1	Guts, Glory and Lipstick[1]	14
Chapter 2	My Welcome to Korea	24
Chapter 3	The Service Club and Learning the Ropes	46
Chapter 4	The Belle of the Ball	64
Chapter 5	Boredom, Tedium, and The Stalker	76
Chapter 6	Amusements and Other Pastimes	86
Chapter 7	Profiles of the American GI, My Heroes	104
Chapter 8	Hello, VietNam	114
Chapter 9	Mortar Attacks & Me	134
Chapter 10	Almost My Worst Nightmare	148
Chapter 11	I've Been Kicked Out of Better Places	162

Chapter 12	Memories of Long Binh	182
Chapter 13	Tay Ninh and Tet	196
Chapter 14	R & R, Rest and Recreation	216
Chapter 15	My Knights in Shining Armor	236
Chapter 16	Epilogue: Life in the Real World	260
	"What Did You Do in the War, Grandma?"	276
Illustrations	The Story of a Special Services Girl in Vietnam by Terri Zuber	282
Endnotes		291
Bibliography		293
Glossary		296
Index		301
Appendix	"War Zone Diversions, An Overview of Women Volunteers in Civilian Staffed Recreation Programs in Vietnam" by Ann L Kelsey	

FOREW0RD

Morale and recreation programs for members of the United States military traces its roots to the beginning of the twentieth century. In 1903 Congress authorized the Army to build, operate, and maintain various types of recreational programs. Both the Army and non-governmental organizations such as the Red Cross, the YMCA, and the American Library Association sponsored morale and recreation activities during World War I.
In 1941 the Army programs were centralized under the Special Services umbrella, joining the USO, established in 1940, and the Red Cross in bringing morale boosting recreation programs to the troops in World War II. These programs expanded during the mid-twentieth century Cold War, and became important components of the United States military presence in Korea and VietNam, often staffed by civilians, many of them women, both on the home front and overseas.
While the USO and its contributions are well known, and many veterans remember the Red Cross Club Mobiles in World War II and Korea, and the "Donut Dollies" in VietNam, the Service Clubs, libraries, craft shops, and entertainment programs sponsored by Army Special Services frequently go unmentioned and unrecognized.

This is what makes Sandra Lockney Davis' memoir so special and compelling. Her stories and memories of her tours with Special Services in Korea and VietNam provide a vivid, spellbinding window into the Army's Special Services morale and recreation programs from the viewpoint of a young civilian woman. Men also worked for Special Services and not all the women were young. Nevertheless, the majority of those who served in Korea and VietNam were young female college graduates, and it was a life-changing experience for them, just as it was for the mostly young soldiers who came to the clubs, libraries, and craft shops.

Dr. Lockney Davis brings the experience of serving with Special Services alive and gives recognition to a program that then and now seeks to bring soldiers a respite from war and the loneliness of being far from home. In telling her story, she tells all of our stories—the librarians in library services, and the recreation specialists in the service clubs, craft shops and entertainment. Thanks to her memoir, Army Special Services and those who served with it are no longer a footnote in the history of recreational services to the military.

Ann Kelsey
Army Special Services Libraries, Vietnam
1969-1970

INTRODUCTION

Marching down Constitution Avenue behind our U. S. Army Special Services banner, on Veterans' Day, 1993, I joined many of my former colleagues to celebrate the unveiling of the Vietnam Women's Memorial in Washington, D. C. and receive recognition for our service in VietNam[2]. We gathered in groups at the National Mall behind banners identifying our organizations, the Red Cross, the USO, and U. S. Army, Air Force, Navy, and Marine servicewomen and nurses. The streets were lined with people. Men, women and children applauded and cheered as we passed. Veterans wearing parts of their old jungle fatigues and their "go to hell" hats showered us with roses and called out, "Thank you. Thank you for your service." I felt weak, my hands shook, my throat tightened and my tears were uncontrollable. Memories of the closeness, the depth of friendships, the bond we experienced during the war overwhelmed me. I expected the experience to be emotional but I was shocked at my physical reaction as my body relived the intensity of emotion that I felt in VietNam. It was a peak life experience. Finally, it was all right to say that I was proud to have served and humbled to be recognized with the courageous men and women VietNam veterans.

Above: Special Services Ladies gather behind our banner to begin the march.

Below: Riki Coll and I march with our roses.

At age twenty-three in 1964, I went to work in South Korea for the U. S. Army Special Services Program. Korea was a primitive country recovering from the war that had ended eleven years earlier with an enemy a few miles to the north always threatening to attack. American and Allied forces stayed in South Korea to keep the peace and to protect the South from another invasion by the communist forces in the North. American military, civil service and government contractors occupied bases, camps, and missile sites throughout South Korea.

An assignment to South Korea was a one year unaccompanied tour of duty. Unaccompanied meant without family. It was also considered a hardship tour because of the backward living conditions and lack of adequate housing or infrastructure, but for a young girl it was a potentially dangerous and exciting adventure. Chapters One through Five describe what it was like living among our American soldiers in Korea, an isolated country, learning my job with Special Services, experiencing a different culture, and becoming an advanced student of human nature.

Three years later, in 1967, I accepted a job in South VietNam at the height of the VietNam War. The North Vietnamese fired on U. S. ships in August of 1964, an event known as the Gulf of Tonkin incident. Congress passed the Gulf of Tonkin Resolution giving President Lyndon Johnson authority to send ground troops to VietNam in March of 1965. Other allies like Australia and South Korea joined the U. S. to aid the South Vietnamese and to prevent the spread of communism from the North. The allies fought the well trained and dedicated forces of the North Vietnamese Army and the ill trained and ill equipped, but effective Viet Cong from 1965 to 1975.[3] The turning point or the beginning of the end of war was the Tet Offensive, January 31, 1968 which occurred while I was there.

Again, the assignment to VietNam for military, civil service and government contractors was a one year unaccompanied tour of duty. This time it was not an adventure for me, but the most intense, frightening, emotional experience of my life. Chapters Eight through Thirteen recount some of my experiences learning about myself and coping with fear, frustration, stress and the roller coaster emotions of living in a war zone.

When I returned home no one was interested in what I'd experienced. If I said, "When I was in Korea...," I got a mildly quizzical look. If I said, "When I was in VietNam...," people looked around the room, shuffled their feet, and searched for another conversation to join. So, I stopped mentioning it. It wasn't until I met my husband who was curious about the VietNam War and interested in my experiences, that I talked about Korea and VietNam. My inspiration for writing this memoir is my husband's thirty-year campaign of gentle but constant nudging to "write your stories just the way you tell them." His vision of the importance of recording my experiences as history, his faith in my ability to write them, and his encouragement, have been total and unwavering. Another powerful influence and motivation for writing my memoir was my experience at the unveiling of the Women's VietNam War Memorial in Washington, D. C.

The title of my memoir came to me in the middle of the night. It means something to the women who worked with the U. S. Military on any hardship tour. It's safe to say that every American woman who served either in Korea or VietNam was asked at least once, if not once a day, "So, what's a nice girl like you doing in a place like this?" It's also probably safe to say that 90% of the men who served on a hardship tour asked that question at least once.

Writing this book has been, for the most part, a joy. It has been revisiting old friends in my mind, laughing at the situations we got into, like the time we were stranded on a flight line that was mortared regularly with no vehicle and no place to stay. Some of my memories are humorous, like the conditions we endured, namely, sand in our sheets, outside toilets and cold showers. Others are not, like the night I faced the soldier who broke into my hootch while I slept. Some have been a catharsis, like finally telling the story of getting kicked out of the 1st Infantry Division, the legendary "Big Red One." Other recollections are about the eccentric personalities I met who were not amusing, like the Sergeant-Major who didn't think we needed a bunker or the Senior NCO, Non-commissioned officer, who was a stalker.

Fortunately, and most importantly, my best memories are of the young men I met who were brave and polite and funny and helpful and wonderful. They made everything worthwhile and for them, I would do it all again.

An emotional moment for me was receiving my Commendation from a representative from the Secretary of Defense, Les Aspin, November, 1993.

ACKNOWLEDGEMENTS

Many people contributed to this book and I wish them all to know how grateful I am for their advice, time, and effort, reading chapters, giving me thoughtful, critical feedback and positive comments.

To the members of the West Florida Literary Federation and the talented leaders of the Writers' Guild Critique Group, Ms. Andrea Walker, the Memoir Critique Group, co-chairs Jack Beverly and Ora Wills, and the gracious, capable critics, Ron Tew, Tom Johnson, Joan Henderson, Shirley Hage, Nita Freeman, and Darlene Tunker, thank you for helping me polish my prose and clarify my descriptions.

To my former colleagues who reviewed the chapters to help me with names, places, shared memories, and photos, Kay Strasberg Bardsley, Riki Coll, Ann Kelsey, Judi and Harry Purcell, Carol Law, Judy Jenkins Gaudino, Nancy Grove, Susan Selig, and Frankie Milligan; and those who contributed anecdotes, Cathleen Cordova, Renee Coulter Capouya, and Barbara Jay, you made the book better than I thought it would be. I am also grateful for the enthusiasm and encouragement from my fellow Special Services colleagues Marcy Stennes, Mary Carol Shannahan, and Gail Goriesky who joined me, Ann Kelsey, Riki Coll, Judy Jenkins Gaudino, Renee Coulter Capouya, Barbara Jay, and our husbands at an informal, mini reunion in Washington, D. C. on Veterans' Day, November 11, 2010.

A special note of appreciation goes to Terry Zuber whose amusing, perceptive illustrations describe our VietNam experience better than words.

Thanks to George Baskin and Linda Reinauer, each of whom reviewed the whole manuscript in record time and made invaluable suggestions and corrections.

Finally, I could never have finished this book without the encouragement and constant assurances of my husband, my partner, and my best friend, Charlie Davis.

Our mini Reunion Veterans' Day 2010 in Washington D. C.

Ann Kelsey

Riki Coll

Judy Jenkins Gaudino

Marcy Stennes

Renee Coulter Capouya

Barara Jay

Gail Goriesky

Mary Carol Shannahan

Terry Zuber, Illustrator

Maps of Korea and VietNam and My Assignments

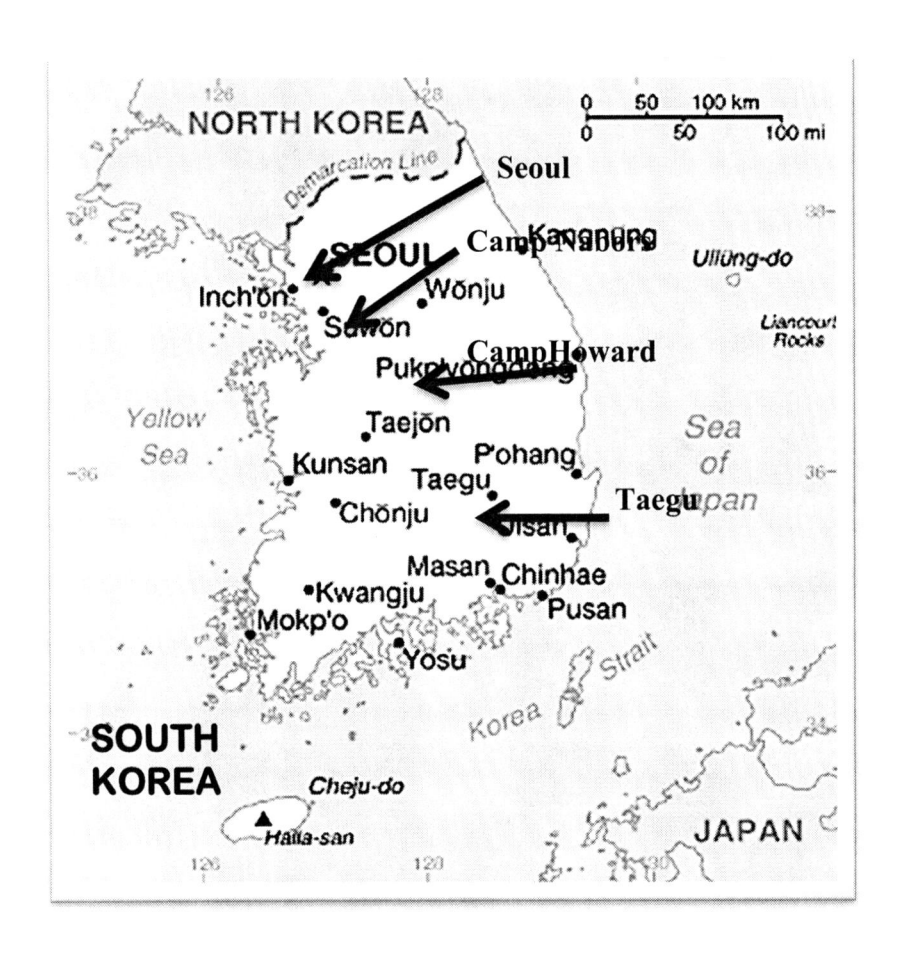

The approximate location of my assignments in Korea from 1964 to 1965 are marked by arrows on the map: Camp Howard (SuWon), Yongsan (Seoul), Camp Nabors. When I returned to Korea in 1970 to 1971 as a librarian, I spent my whole tour in Taegu at Camp Henry, KORSCOM Headquarters.
Courtesy of the UT Austin map collection.

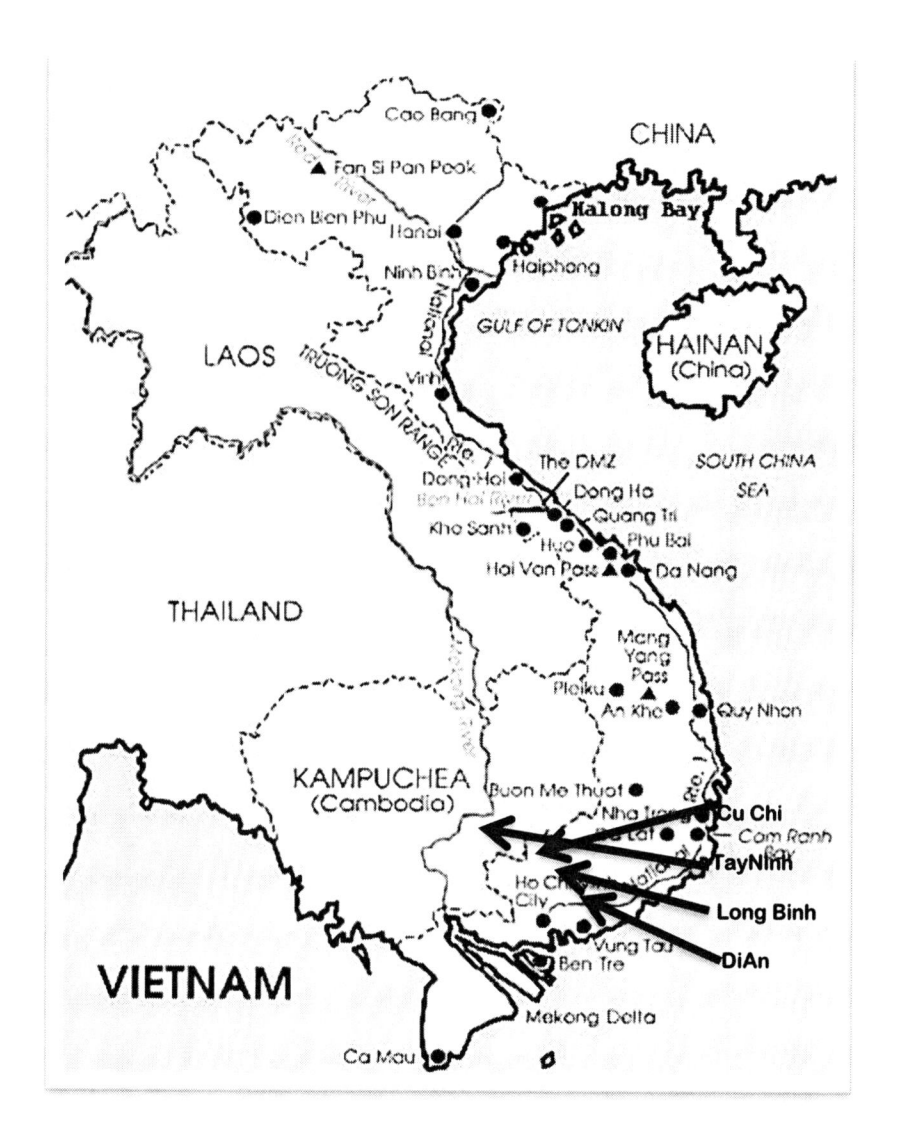

The approximate locations of my assignments in VietNam from 1967 to 1968 are marked by arrows on the map: CuChi, TayNinh, LongBinh and DiAn.

Courtesy of the UT Austin map collection.

1

GUTS, GLORY, AND LIPSTICK

The chaplain who spoke to the troops about to leave Vietnam to go home after a year's tour said, "As you leave on this plane there is one last piece of advice I want to give you to bear in mind always. There's only one difference between a 'fairy tale' and a war story. A fairy tale starts out with 'Once upon a time' and a war story starts out with 'No shit! There I was."[4]

Korea was like a fairy tale, a Grimm's fairy tale, sometimes magical, sometimes scary. VietNam was just like the chaplain described. In the past, when I thought about the times I lived in Korea and VietNam, the good times and the bad, it's as if it happened to someone else. It's hard to believe I survived, but I probably did because the "good Lord takes care of drunks and fools" and I've been one or the other on occasion.

My adventures began when I met a recruiter for U. S. Army Special Services in Washington, D. C., in the fall of 1964.

South Korea, 1964

"In Korea, you'll be one of only a few 'round eyes' in country, among thousands of men! That's what they call American girls," she added. "You'll be the center of attention, the Belle of the Ball!" She was young, petite and full of energy. She wore the blue Special Services uniform and made even the uniform look attractive.

Were Graduated

"I lived in Germany as a dependent and I'd really like to go back to Europe. Are there any openings anywhere in Europe?" I asked.

"Not at the moment, but if you go to Korea for a year you'll have all the training you need so that when there is an opening, you'll be qualified. We always try to fill the slots with people from other commands rather than hire new people." I told her I would think about it.

FATHER AND DAUGHTER -- Miss Susan Lockney congratulates her father, Maj. William J. Lockney shortly after they were both graduated in ceremonies at Arizona State University recently.

My father and I graduated from Arizona State University in 1963

A year earlier I had graduated from Arizona State University with a B. A. in Political Science, a major in International Relations, and two minors, German and Geography. My goal was a career in Foreign Service, to travel and see the world. I moved to Washington, D. C. to find that career. A letter to one of my favorite aunts describes some of my thoughts at the time and my struggle to decide whether to go to Korea or not.

August 7, 1964
Dear Aunt Deanie,
...Everything is going "almost" well here. Have two prospects for jobs. One with the Department of Commerce, which is what I came to D. C. for—a GS-5, Administrative Assistant position--in

a new building and branch located 17 miles from D. C. proper, which means a less expensive place to live and avoiding the traffic, which is practically the best part. It's with a publications section but that's all I know about it. (except the job might become a GS-7 in the near future.)

The other job is fascinating. It's with the Department of the Army in "Special Services." It means I'd be a recreation director or social director and work at the Service Club. Being a social director is not the fascinating part...the catch is that it would be overseas, probably Korea! There is a very good chance that I could make it a career (if I could stand planning games and entertainment all my life) and go back to Europe after a one-year "hitch" in Korea. The career part is not definite; as it stands now, it would be for one year only, unless I extended at the base or post I am assigned.

I've really been in turmoil about the two jobs because Commerce is supposed to let me know if I'm hired next week and the Army can't tell me for approximately a month (or more). So, I must decide quickly if Commerce says "yes." whether I want to accept a "sure thing" now (permanent, career-type, Civil Service job for which I came to D. C.) or travel around the world to parts unknown! (which is what I want, although Korea is a hardship post and may be uncomfortable, to say the least!)...

August 11, 1964
Hi again!

I had the best intentions to mail this but...

Well, Commerce offered me the job and in a moment of weakness, I accepted. Now, I'm disappointed 'cause I really wanted to go to Korea. Haven't called the Department of Army yet. I think if they did call tomorrow and asked me to go I'd refuse the Commerce job (which would be unethical since I accepted) and leave immediately. Oh well, maybe next year after I'm established in Civil Service.

Thought I'd get to go home for a week between jobs, but I found out that if I have a break in service from my current job with the Library of Congress, I lose all annual and sick leave. Besides, I do need the extra pay check.

Will let you know how it works out....

Another part of my decision making process concerned my family. My mother, a homemaker, wondered why I didn't settle down and get married. Her lifelong career was raising four children, oftentimes by herself when Dad was overseas. She was a helpmate and partner with the love of her life, my father, who was a career U. S. Air Force Officer, a jet pilot, a decorated veteran of World War II and Korea, and my first hero. I was the oldest of four children with two sisters and a brother. Having grown up "a military brat" I felt comfortable with the structure and bureaucracy of the military. We lived in Europe for four years during which time I felt protected and secure. With my dependent's I. D. card, I could walk onto any military installation and get help if I needed it. Dad's experience living in hardship conditions and in war zones dictated that he discourage me.

Bill and Gracie Lockney in 1965

My father was a soft-spoken man and, like many military men, he was a protector not a warrior. I never heard him swear or raise his voice in anger. A terrific Dad, he was patient, always interested in what his children were doing. He often asked our opinions to get us to think. No matter what our age or what the problem, he spent as much time as each of us needed to talk about it and solve it. His advice included the pros and cons of any problem but he never dictated to us or forbade us to do anything. He would take time to explain why we should or shouldn't do something and subtly convince us to make the right decision. Self-reliance and responsibility were of utmost importance to him. We were encouraged to make our own decisions.

LTC. William J. Lockney

When he and I discussed the job in Korea, he simply said that he would prefer that I not go. He felt it was not a comfortable or safe place for his daughter to be. That was the strongest protest he had ever made, but his discouraging comments didn't dissuade me. Travel, seeing the world was the most exciting thing to me. I hadn't been to Asia yet, and I might never have another opportunity. I made a list of the pros and cons. The positives were: travel; adventure; the salary; (a Level GS-5 was $5000 per year); being on my own which was important at age 23; the possibility of eventually transferring to Europe; and, last but not least, all the men I'd meet. The only negative I could think of at that time was that my dad didn't want me to accept the position. As much as I loved him and wanted him to be proud of me, I wanted to go.

The Special Services recruiter offered me the position and I declined the Department of Commerce position. After all my deliberating, my final thought was, "Let's see,..hummm....I've never been to Korea, so why not?" I told the recruiter I would go.

EIGHTH UNITED STATES ARMY

Welcome to Korea

Instructions to prepare for Korea
Courtesy of Judi and Harry Purcell

Korea was hot and humid in the summer, freezing cold and miserable in the winter. It was 1964, and the country that had been devastated by war was attempting to recover. The fighting of the Korean War ended in 1953, but a peace treaty was never signed and a large contingent of the U. S. Army remained in place to protect South Korea. The Special Services Program was the recreation and welfare program of the U. S. Army. The Program, which included Service Clubs, Libraries, Crafts Shops and an Entertainment Division, maintained a presence in Korea after the fighting ended and every base or camp had, at minimum, a Service Club. The clubs were operational, the club events and activities were routine, and the Army was accustomed to supporting these programs. At least two Special Services girls were assigned to each club. There was no training or drills to teach us what to do if the North Koreans decided to attack again. As far as danger was concerned, the prevailing attitude was that if the North attacked, there would be enough time to get civilians out of the country. If all else failed, I was told, because of my small stature and dark coloring, I could blend into the population, if I could fake being a deaf mute. Amusing, but not necessarily consoling. In Korea, our other enemy was boredom.

South VietNam, 1967

Deciding to go to VietNam was a different struggle. Two years after my tour of Korea, when I applied for a job in Alaska, the recruiter asked me, "Would you consider going to VietNam instead?"

My father was strongly against it this time. He'd been to war and he knew it was dangerous just to be there, no matter how hard the Army might try to protect me. Still, he would not forbid me or threaten me with disfavor.

I'm the "Korean lady" on the right.

As was my habit when I had an important decision to make, I listed the pros and cons. On the positive side, it was my patriotic duty, a family tradition. If I had been born a boy, I would have followed in my father's footsteps, joined the U. S. Air Force and probably be stationed there already. I knew I could do the job; it was the same as the one in Korea. The hardship tour wasn't a problem for me; after all, I'd survived Korea. The travel would be exciting. The salary was even better this time; I would be a GS-7, with a salary of $7,500 a year, which in those days was managerial level. It would satisfy my curiosity about war; I might never have another chance to see a war up close.

This time the negatives were tough. Unlike Korea, the adventure would be dangerous; I could be wounded or killed. Death was not so far removed from my world as an Air Force brat. Pilots in my father's squadron were killed sometimes during training missions. My father went to war in Korea when I was ten years old and I was vaguely aware of the possibility he wouldn't return. Once I overheard our neighbors whispering how dreadful for "that poor little Lockney girl" that her father might be killed in the war. Since he did return safely, death was still an abstract concept to me. Like all young people, I felt invincible and it was hard for me to imagine that I could die at twenty-five. But what if I were captured? That was my worst fear. My counter thought to all the negatives was that the U. S. Army would not put a civilian in harm's way. Dad wasn't as sure of that as I was. In retrospect, he was right.

Again, I told the recruiter I'd think about it. I did, long and hard. In the end, as cavalier and flippant as it sounds, I thought, "Let's see,...hummm...I've never been to a war, so why not?" I was naïve, idealistic, and patriotic, with a high threshold for excitement and adventure.

VietNam was hot, humid, and dusty when it wasn't hot, humid, raining, and muddy. Our enemy was alive and well and shooting at us. My job in VietNam was similar to my job in Korea. Officially, it required learning to design, as well as supervise, and maintain facilities, to create recreational programs to promote the morale of the American soldier, to give him something constructive to do after duty hours, and to provide a diversion from either the boredom or terror of his circumstances. Unofficially, it required developing negotiating skills to barter, "comshaw," and "midnight requisition" supplies that weren't available through normal channels, learning to think on our feet, and making do with what we had.

In the war zone, some commanding officers considered civilians, especially women, liabilities. Under those circumstances we had to be self-reliant and resourceful, because it was sometimes difficult to get the support we needed to build and manage our clubs. Unlike today, the military of the 1960s was like an exclusive men's club except that a large number of the enlisted men were drafted and didn't want to be there. In spite of that, the servicemen, our GIs, our guys, as we called them, always appreciated us.

When I arrived in VietNam in March, 1967, there were fewer than a half dozen Special Services women in country and only one operating Service Club, with a second Club under construction. Other organizations with female personnel already in country were the Red Cross, known as "Donut Dollies," USO club personnel, and military nurses. Other female military support and clerical personnel were stationed in the Saigon/Long Binh area.

It was somewhat reassuring to me that I was not the only one who had willingly chosen to go to the VietNam War. All the Special Services girls, the Red Cross girls, USO people and many of the nurses and support personnel, like me, volunteered to go to this strange, beautiful country on the other side of the world and live in places we had never heard of, under conditions we never imagined. If there had been a survey to ask why, I'm sure the answers would be pretty much the same: the desire to serve our country, to do something positive for our men in uniform who were forced to be there, the desire to travel and see the world, and to satisfy a curiosity about the war. No one I met there was a patriotic fanatic. We were all young, idealistic, enthusiastic, energetic, college-educated women who gave up a year of our lives to do something for a cause greater than ourselves. The year in VietNam did not advance our careers or make us a lot of money; it was a year of service. It was also a year of growing up, a year of accelerated maturing.

Combat veterans and nurses, who suffered far more than I, have written about the tragedy of living in the war zone and of the horrors of the war. I admire them all. They are my heroes. I've chosen to remember mostly the foibles, follies, the humor, and the irony of living under some of the most adverse conditions and making the best of it.

Like many of the soldiers and many women, I experienced something like survivor guilt while there and since then. My guilt was that I couldn't carry a weapon and go into the jungle to fight alongside our soldiers. I couldn't protect them or keep them safe, and I survived while many of them did not.

In VietNam, I learned that the effects of long-term stress on the human being result in some pretty bizarre behavior, sometimes comic, sometimes not. As a non-combatant female in a war zone, my stress did not come from dodging sniper bullets or fear of stepping on a booby trap like many of our soldiers. My stress was knowing that I was in a dangerous situation, pretending I wasn't, and forcing myself to smile. I called Bingo, served coffee and birthday cake, checked out playing cards and musical instruments, and judged pool tournaments as if there wasn't a war going on. Like everyone else, I lived with the stress of being a helpless target of an enemy who could not be distinguished from the barber who cut our hair or the laundry girl who washed our clothes. The Vietnamese, who was a friend during the day, might be found dead outside the camp perimeter, armed with a weapon after a nighttime firefight with our GIs. It was hard to wrap your mind around, but somehow we all did it. Like my fellow Special Services colleagues, I smiled no matter what. I laughed and joked so "our guys" would forget for a few minutes, about the primitive, uncomfortable, sometimes barbaric, unreal world that they lived in every waking minute.

    We made smiling and small talk an art form.

2

My Welcome To Korea

The sounds of the Drifters' "Under the Boardwalk" or the Beach Boys' "I Get Around" will always remind me of my first tour in Korea.

From the day I stepped aboard the military plane at Travis AFB, California, bound for the Republic of South Korea, I was treated as if I were knock-down gorgeous. It was an exhilarating experience because growing up, I was the fat kid on the block. When I reached puberty the weight dropped off and although I was called cute by some and even pretty by others, I could never shake my self-image as the little fat girl.

I will always remember the feeling entering the plane when I looked up to see more than 200 sets of male eyes staring at me from a sea of U. S. Army green uniforms. The laughter and conversation stopped and the silence was deafening. I was the only female on the flight. The recruiter had been right. I was the center of attention.

When I found my seat the hubbub resumed. For the first few hours, I did nothing but answer questions, like, "Where're you from in the States?" and "So why is a nice girl like you going to a place like Korea?" After the guys who were seated close by had the chance to get answers to their questions or just overhear my answers, everyone settled down to watch the movie, catnap, read or play cards. I slept most of the way.

After about twenty hours, we finally arrived at Kimpo International Airport in Seoul, Korea. Stepping off the plane in Korea at that time was a shock to all the senses, especially the olfactory. The stench was overwhelming. I described it as a combination of open sewage, dirty socks, and Kimchi (a national dish of fermented, spiced cabbage and vegetables). It was so bad that when I returned from Korea, my mom wouldn't let me open my trunk in the house for the smell that lingered on my clothes. I finally had to burn everything.

It was November, cold, wet and dreary. Kimpo International Airport at that time was like one big hangar with grime-covered windows facing the runway on one side and equally grimy windows facing the parking lot on the other. The inside of the hangar was cold, dusty, colorless, and naked. No soft chairs to sit in, no polished floors, no shops, nothing. It was bleak and drab. It had been 11 years since the end of fighting of the Korean War and the recovery was very slow.

I followed the men in line through the gates where the Military Police and a Korean Official wearing a black uniform-like suit with white gloves directed us to a counter where we were asked some preliminary questions, given forms in duplicate to complete, most of which we'd completed before we left or on the plane. Our luggage was opened and checked, after which we were led to a bus to take us to Eighth U. S. Army Headquarters in Yongsan, a suburb of Seoul. The bus looked like an old school bus painted Army green and it was just as uncomfortable. The bus driver wore the same black uniform as the Korean who had checked our luggage. As soon as we left the airport, the paved road ended and we drove all the way into Seoul on a narrow dirt road.

My regional supervisor, Millie Daniels, met me at the bus stop in Yongsan. I was thrilled to see a female and someone in the Special Services uniform. Millie reminded me of someone's eccentric aunt. She had a well-rounded figure and white hair all piled in a small bun at the center of the top of her head which couldn't be seen until she took off her hat, which she rarely did. Her blue eyes sparkled and she rarely stopped talking. She had an official car with a Korean driver to take me to the Transient Bachelor Officers' Quarters, or BOQ, where I would be staying.

The BOQ was an old Army Quonset hut left over from the Korean War. I entered the Quonset into a small living room. A couch, several chairs, and a coffee table filled the room. The Army issue furniture was large wood-framed pieces with worn, leather seats of either a dark nondescript green or brown. The curtains were some kind of heavy dark material that also served as blinds to cover the windows at night. The floors were a drab vinyl and added nothing to the décor of the room. At the other end of the Quonset was a community bathroom called a latrine, with two toilet stalls, two sinks, and two metal showers with heavy white plastic curtains. Everything looked clean and smelled of disinfectant and detergent.

The BOQ rooms were each about ten by ten feet in size, and as bleak as the living room. Each had a single bed, a night stand with lamp, a small chest of drawers and a chair, all too big for the room. I was so tired I didn't even mind showering in the community latrine. The water was hot, and after living in my uniform for almost forty-eight hours, it felt like the most wonderful shower I'd ever had. Even though I was exhausted, it was still exciting to think, "Here I am, halfway around the world in just 72 hours from the time I left Florida." I slept soundly for eight hours.

The next morning, Millie picked me up and we went to breakfast at the Kimchi Kabana, one of the Officers' Messes, which was like a small restaurant with an extensive menu for breakfast, lunch and dinner. Except for the mess halls, all the food on the base camps whether at a club or a snack bar was cooked by a Korean chef who had probably never eaten what he was cooking before he was hired to cook. It always tasted similar to what it was supposed to be, but never exactly the same. After breakfast we took a base taxi to the Special Services Headquarters Office, another Quonset hut. I saw only a few real buildings, as I called them: the Eighth U. S. Army Officers' Club, the PX, and the Yongsan Service Club.

Miss Vera Vincent, the Director of Service Clubs, was a gracious southern lady whose makeup, coiffure, and uniform were immaculate. She was tall, slim and spoke very softly. She greeted us warmly and made a quick inspection of me and my uniform. Fortunately, I remembered to wear the uniform hat and made sure my gloves were spotlessly white. I felt like I passed her inspection because she seemed pleased.

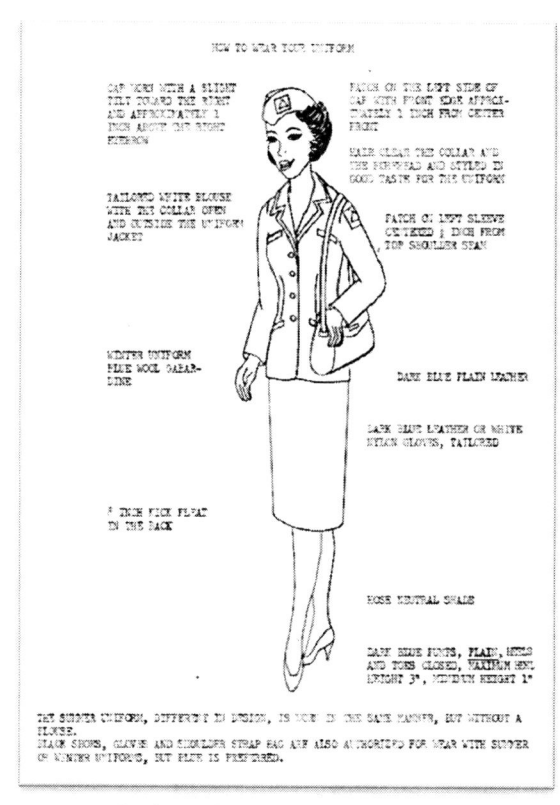

Our conversation was formal, but pleasant. She discussed important rules and regulations, most of which were a repeat of the literature I'd been sent to prepare for the trip. Millie sat without speaking, nodding her approval from time to time. Miss Vincent explained it was mandatory to wear the uniform properly, always with hat, gloves, and heels. Of equal importance was to act in a professional manner at all times. It seemed odd at the time to make such a fuss about the clothes, but she made it clear that the uniform made us official; it was an outward expression of our reason for being there. It protected us. My civilian rating was equivalent to a first lieutenant which meant my behavior should be professional at all times. I listened carefully and thought that nothing I heard was different from what I expected. After our discussion, she took me

Our instructions to wear the uniform.
Courtesy of Judi Purcell

on a tour of the offices to introduce me to each of the other Directors of Libraries, Crafts Shops, and the Entertainment Division. Then it was lunch time and we all went back to the Kimchi Kabana.

"Millie will ride with you to Camp Howard Monday morning to introduce you to your Club Director, Kay Strasburg, and see that you get settled," Miss Vincent explained. "So, you'll have Saturday and Sunday to look around Yongsan and maybe do some sightseeing in Seoul.

"Your assignment, Camp Howard, is a small camp, a supply depot about five hours south of here. It has a very small Post Exchange or PX, but it's only a couple of hour by jeep to Camp Humphreys which has a larger PX and more facilities. And I'm sure we'll be seeing you again here in Seoul soon. This is where the girls come to shop and sightsee on their days off when they can get away. We have Program Directors' meetings here from time to time and you'll be required to attend those. It's always a pleasant experience to get together with the other program directors to visit and exchange ideas." I told her I was looking forward to it.

After lunch as we were leaving the Kimchi Kabana, Millie said, "My house girl is getting married Saturday. Would you like to see a Korean wedding?"

"I'd love to. What does one wear and shall I buy a gift?"

"No gift necessary, I've already given her something. Just wear something you'd wear to church. I'll give you my address and you can get a taxi to my house and we'll leave from there."

On Saturday, I took a base taxi to Millie's house. It was an apartment in downtown Seoul on the second floor of a three-story building. It was quite modern compared to the Quonset hut where I was staying. Just like Millie, the apartment was bright and cheery. It overflowed with beautiful treasures she had accumulated during her travels and living overseas: wall hangings from Japan, lacquer ware chests and tables from Korea, woodcarvings from Thailand and beautiful, colorful carpets from India. Every surface in the living room was covered with statues and figurines. I could have spent a week just looking at everything, but we had to leave for the wedding.

We arrived at the Wedding Hall, a large two-story block building in downtown Seoul, just in time to enter with the few other

A Korean Wedding Party included western and Korean dress.
. Courtesy of Judi and Harry Purcell

American guests. Korean couples booked the Hall by the hour. There was a constant flow of bridal processions with eager young bridegrooms waiting outside for their turn to join their brides to be married. Inside the hall were rows of seats like pews separated by a wide aisle much like a church. I don't remember an altar, but there was a stage several steps high at the front of the hall where the person who conducted the ceremony stood. In the front there were some colorful wall hangings but the Hall was mostly very plain and without decoration. Some of the couples were Christian, as was our couple, but others were Buddhists or Confucianists. The couples walked down the aisle on a long narrow strip of paper. Each time a couple was married the paper was rolled up and replaced with new paper. It was like a red carpet, except the paper was brown wrapping paper.

    An organ played softly in the background until the couple appeared at the entry way to start down the aisle. It all seemed somewhat familiar and not at all as foreign as I expected it to be. Then we were signaled to stand for the couple's entrance. The volume of the music swelled and to our surprise, instead of hearing the wedding march we heard, "Beautiful, Beautiful, Brown Eyes." We Americans exchanged glances and smiled. While it was unusual, it was very touching. I learned later that it was typical in those days for young Koreans to emulate all things American. However, since they had no actual experience in America, they reproduced things as they thought they must be. That was the reason for a vague sense of familiarity at the ceremony. It was a perfect example of an event that was planned by someone who had read about it but never experienced the actual event.

After the ceremony, as we left the building we were each given a rice cake as a gift from the couple for attending their wedding. The rice cake was pink, moist, and a little sticky, but quite tasty. It was altogether a delightful experience and I was pleased to have had the opportunity so early in my tour to learn something of the culture and witness such a private event.

On the way back to the BOQ, the taxi stopped at Millie's apartment first.

"Would you like to try a Korean meal?"

"Sure. With all the restrictions in our instructions about where we can eat, I wasn't sure when or if I'd be able to try some Korean food."

"Okay, meet me at the Kimchi Kabana tomorrow about 4:00 p.m. and we'll have a traditional Korean meal."

My instructions from the Department of the Army to prepare for a tour in Korea described very uncomfortable consequences if I ate outside the military installations. The Army Health authorities issued a list of Korean establishments where Americans could eat safely. At that time I think there were very few places on the list even in Seoul which was the most westernized city in Korea. The water wasn't potable anywhere off the base and the local vegetables were allegedly grown using human fertilizer. Dysentery and other intestinal disorders were common problems among the Americans. Somehow the Koreans were immune. In any case, I was happy to have another opportunity to learn more about the culture of my new temporary home and to experience the cuisine safely.

The next day I met Millie at the Kimchi Kabana. We were escorted to a table and attended by several waiters who treated us as if we were VIPs. Millie knew all of the waiters and had an easy, familiar relationship with them. They seemed to enjoy her good nature and high spirits, or at least happily tolerated them. I found out later that she was also a big tipper. Since I was new in country, the Korean waiters all wanted to help us select some traditional Korean dishes. The entrée they recommended was a beef dish called "Bulgogi." It was strips of beef sautéed with shredded green vegetables, onions, and spices served with rice. It became an instant favorite of mine. I was to find out later that the Koreans didn't have much beef, so to order Bulgogi outside the military installations might mean it would be dog meat. Needless to say I was careful where I ordered it.

Millie insisted that I try the national traditional dish, Kimchi. It was winter, so the Kimchi was the hottest seasoned version. The summer Kimchi is not as highly spiced as the winter, because it is not fermented as long. Kimchi is a combination of cabbage, radishes and other similar vegetables shredded or chopped and marinated in highly spiced seasonings, then fermented for a specific period of time, usually in a large clay pot buried in the ground. I timidly tried the Kimchi, because I was not fond of highly spiced food. The taste was truly a shock in spite of the fact that I was expecting it to be spicy hot. After the second bite I realized that blisters were forming on the roof of my mouth. Millie insisted Kimchi could not make blisters. I didn't disagree with her, but I never ate the winter Kimchi again. The summer Kimchi I liked and ordered it from time to time at approved restaurants during the summer.

The dessert was a crispy, deep-fried banana. It reminded me of the candied apples we used to get at the State Fair and became one of my favorite desserts.

The next morning early, Millie picked me up in the usual black sedan and we headed south to my new assignment, Camp Howard. The sedan was so old; it was hard to tell if it was a Chevy or Ford. It was worn, but clean. The driver, a Korean, was dressed in one of those plain black uniforms with white gloves. Finally, my curiosity got the best of me and I asked Millie about the prevalent uniform. Millie explained that the Koreans liked the "official-ness" of a uniform. It made them feel important and everyone wanted to wear one. It was also a matter of economy. Koreans were poor so money was not wasted on clothes.

Driving through the city, there was much to see. The only automobiles I saw were tiny Japanese models that looked as though they were parts of different cars glued together, and they had been patched up several times. Bicycles were all over the place. It was amazing to see how much stuff they could pile onto a bicycle.

Even the pedestrians were uniquely resourceful in the load they could balance on their heads. The two-bucket yoke was fascinating to me. It was a wooden yoke worn across the person's shoulders with a rope attached at each end of the yoke and with a bucket filled with something tied to the end of each rope. The buckets sometimes held human fertilizer for the fields and were dubbed by Americans as "honey buckets." Sometimes instead of buckets at the end of the ropes there were baskets piled high with dry goods or vegetables. I took pictures whenever I saw one until I'd seen so many and taken so many pictures of them, they ceased to amaze me.

A drunken pig transported to market on a bicycle.
Courtesy of Judi and Harry Purcell.

Above: Mama-san carrying a heavy load.
Below: Honey buckets.
Courtesy of Judi and Harry Purcell.

Judi Purcell was a Recreation Director in Korea the same time I was. Recently, she shared a letter with me she had written to her friends at home after arriving in Korea. I thought her description was the best I had ever read.

> Seoul is a city of contradictions. People wearing both western and traditional clothing, houses jammed together, ritzie hotels and hovels with no floors nor running water, buses jamming the main streets, mobs of people crowding the narrow alleyways, old men leading ox carts and women with babies on their backs. The center of town in Korea's capital is a mass of people during the day and a ghost town at night. (The people have a curfew imposed by the US Army.)
> Men run around downtown with 50 to 78 pounds of goods on their backs. Man is truly a beast of burden in Korea. These are just a few rambling impressions of fascinating Seoul.
> Two things about Korea shocked me the most though. One is women washing their families'
> clothes in creeks, rivers, or even drainage ditches. They really do pound their clothes on stones in the creeks—and this is the way at least 90% of the Korean people get their clothes washed!! The second thing that still shocks me is to see people (of all ages and both sexes) going to the john on the sidewalks and roadsides. Some of the villages that happen to have sidewalks have special slits in the cement for just such a purpose. Since the children to age 12 run around naked all summer—I guess no one could have modesty.[5]

Above: The modern part of Seoul. ca. 1964.

Below: Mama-sans washing clothes in a small stream of water.

Courtesy of Judi and Harry Purcell

We drove through the city and into the country. The countryside was stark and gray in November. For a long time all we saw in between villages were the dry, tiered rice paddies which were just rows of dirt. Villages were usually small clusters of thatched-roofed huts, made out of mud bricks. In front of a hut sometimes I saw a Mama-san, a married lady or an older woman, beating rice with a long wooden-looking rake. It seemed odd harvesting food in the front yard. Another interesting site was a Mama-san sweeping the dirt in her front yard with a very short-handled broom. The broom resembled long stems of dried grass tied together at one end around a short mop or broom handle. The Mama-san stooped to sweep and it looked very uncomfortable.

Papa-sans, as older gentlemen were called, dressed in their white coats and full white pants, wearing their tall black horsehair hats, or white western-style straw hats, sat alongside the road, usually smoking an unusual long-stemmed clay pipe. Sometimes there were two or more Papa-sans, just sitting and smoking. They looked very old and because their skin was deeply tanned and wrinkled, it was hard to determine their ages. Later, I heard the GIs laugh and say they were probably only thirty years old, but they'd lived hard lives.

Papa-sans in their traditional white suits.
Courtesy of Judi and Harry Purcell.

A farmer in his field with an ox drawn plow or taking his goods to market in an ox cart were common sights, but unusual to me.

Above: Mamasan beating rice in her front yard.

Below: A farmer and his tools: an ox- drawn plow and A-frame.

Courtesy of Judi and Harry Purcell.

Since it was very cold, there were few people in the paddies, but every now and then I would see men working on the road or in the fields. The most unusual sight was the "three-man shovel." One man held the shovel handle, while a man stood on each side of the shovel holding the end of a rope tied around the shovel handle at about the middle of the handle. Swinging in unison, they could dig a ditch or spread dirt or manure. Another interesting contraption designed by the Koreans to carry heavy loads was the A-frame which was strapped on one's back. It was hard to imagine how it could be very efficient, but it didn't take long to learn that Koreans did many things differently from the way we did things in the States. The term "there's more than one way to skin a cat" often came to mind.

Looking out of the car window was like watching a movie. I kept pinching myself to make sure I was really there.

Incredibly, the highway from Seoul like the road from Kimpo International Airport was a dirt road. Sometimes an asphalt road would appear when we came to a town bigger than a village, but generally it was a bumpy, dirt road.

An Ox cart was common transportation.
Courtesy of Judi and Harry Purcell

Two workers with A-frames to haul dirt or carry produce. Courtesy of Judi and Harry Purcell.

    There were no service stations or restaurants or rest stops along the road. I learned very quickly that when I traveled, my route and timing would depend on which camps had facilities for women. My trips were always planned around bathroom breaks.
    Finally, about 10:30 a.m., Millie said we should make a rest stop.
    "We'll stop for a break at Osan AFB. Since your father is Air Force, I thought it might make you feel more at home to see an Air Force base. Besides, it's not too far from Camp Howard for you to visit and shop at the Base Exchange."
    The driver left us at the door of the Osan AFB Officers' Club. It was a permanent building and even had an awning over the walkway to the entrance. We entered through a lobby with a hat check window reminiscent of nightclubs in 1940 movies. At the end of the lobby was a large ballroom. The room was filled with tables covered with bright white tablecloths, each with a small bouquet of artificial flowers in the center. At the far end of the ballroom was a stage with dark velvet curtains. The Air Force always had the best of everything because they could fly in supplies when the other military branches could not. The big room was bright, sunny, and well decorated, a pleasant change from the some of the Army

facilities I'd seen so far. Across the room, four or five Air Force pilots in their flight suits sat around a table drinking coffee.

We selected a table near the door and took off our coats. As soon as we settled in, a waiter appeared and took our order for coffee. I pulled a cigarette out of my cigarette case and while I searched my bag for a lighter, a sudden crashing noise and loud laughter came from the other side of the room. I looked up just in time to see a tall, raw-boned, slightly awkward, handsome, blond pilot in a flight suit with shiny silver Captain's bars on his shoulders, leaping over chairs, dodging tables, arm extended, holding a lighter with an open flame in his hand. He lighted my cigarette, smiled proudly, and introduced himself.

"Hi there, my name is Larry Dover. I'm from Texas, and where are you lovely ladies from?" he asked, paying special attention to Millie.

He looked like the movie star Dan Daily, but he was even more handsome. Millie giggled. She was so pleased to be a "lovely lady" that she seemed a little flushed. I was still awed by the attention. I thought things like this only happened in the movies. At this point I appreciated Millie's gift of gab.

"We're pleased to meet you. My name is Millie Daniels and I'm the Regional Supervisor from Special Services Headquarters in Seoul and Sandra, here, is being assigned to the Service Club at Camp Howard, just south of here. She just got in-country this week," Millie explained.

He turned his big blue eyes to me and said, "Welcome to Osan. I hope you enjoy your tour in Korea." He was irresistibly charming and he entertained us until it was time to leave, with stories and jokes about the rough roads, the "aroma" of the countryside, and the "slicky boys," who reputedly could dismantle a jeep and disappear with all the parts within eight minutes. His friends at the table across the room watched, with admiration, but didn't join us. When the time came to leave, he escorted us to our car and said he'd look forward to seeing us again.

"You'll be seeing him again and probably soon," laughed Millie as we drove off. "This is just the beginning for you. You'll be meeting lots of dashing, handsome young men." It was like the recruiter said, I felt like the Belle of the Ball, even though it wasn't much of a Ball, so far.

Camp Howard, Korea, 1964.

    We arrived at the gate of Camp Howard just as a Medevac chopper was taking off from an improvised helipad just off the dirt road which was the main street of the camp. The gate was a little wooden guard post about the size and shape of an outhouse I remember seeing in the back hills of West Virginia. The chopper blades threw up a huge dust storm and only after the dust settled could I see the little camp. It was all dirt and smell. Outside the gate was a farming village which had grown to include some bars, nightclubs, and brothels when the camp was built. A pond separated the village from the camp on one side. The water was brown and muddy and not at all picturesque. The sewage was not well controlled, and the stench was overpowering. We suspected that the pond was the sewage system.

Typical village outside the base camp.

    Kay Strasburg, the Camp Howard Service Club Director, came out of the Quonset hut quarters to meet us and Millie introduced me.

"I guess you were held up at the gate by the Medevac chopper," Kay said. "Sad thing, sad thing. The Education Director is being rushed to the 8th U. S. Army Hospital in Seoul. He was partying down in the village last night, and apparently got a hold of some bad whiskey. The medics here think it's started eating his brain."

It was a "sobering" welcome to my new home.

Millie wanted to get back to Seoul before dark, so she wished me well, said goodbye, and left me with Kay to begin my orientation.

We unloaded my luggage in the "hootch," as our living quarters were called, and Kay took me on a little tour of the Quonset complex of Officers' Mess Hall, where we ate and the "O" Club, where we drank. We didn't meet any of the officers on our tour because everyone was on duty. Kay described several of them by characteristics I would certainly recognize as soon as I met them. One officer had a major problem with the smell of Korea. Kay said I could recognize him by the handkerchief soaked in aftershave that he carried to cover his nose to mask the odors. Another always kept a cigarette in his mouth. He never lighted it, just kept it in his mouth. He'd promised his wife he would quit smoking before he came home and it was his way of quitting. Some of the officers liked to party and play pool well into the night. Others rarely went into the Officers' Club bar.

Typical Quonset hut hootch.
Courtesy of Judi and Harry Purcell

All the buildings on the camp were Quonset huts from the Korean War. It took all of five minutes to walk through the complex. We walked back to our hootch which was at the end of the

Quonset that housed the Officers, but separated from them by a wall. We had our own private outside entrance that opened into our small living room. It was small because a corner of the living room was a bathroom. Sheets of plywood that didn't quite reach the ceiling formed the third and fourth walls of our little bathroom. It had a toilet, sink, and metal unit shower. The full-size, lockable door opened discreetly toward the front door. While we had hot and cold water, we couldn't enjoy a leisurely shower, because the chorine made our skin a pasty white. Another reason we took quick showers was the smell. When one of us showered our little hootch was filled with the smell of chlorine which lingered because of poor ventilation. The windows were all taped shut to keep the cold out.

All the water on the camp came from local sources. I visited the water treatment plant once and saw the tea colored water enter the plant; I watched the chlorine added, and the clear, heavily chlorinated water exit the plant. For weeks I couldn't drink the water.

Our little living room was furnished with the usual Army issue, large heavy blond wood frame sofa and chairs with worn leather cushions. We each had a bedroom, furnished with an oversized blond chest of drawers that dwarfed the room, a small twin bed, an end table and lamp. The downside to our location was that the thermostat was located in the officers' latrine at the far end of the Quonset and separated from our rooms by the walled hallway. The rooms nearest the latrine got all the heat in the winter and the officers who lived in those rooms would turn the heat down preventing the heat from reaching us at the end of the Quonset. We were always cold in the winter, and often called one of the officers to ask him to turn up the temperature so we wouldn't freeze. It worked for awhile until another officer in one of the rooms next to the latrine turned the thermostat down again.

On the bright side, we had a house girl, Mama-san Lee, who worked six days a week. She laundered and ironed our clothes, washed our towels and linens and cleaned our rooms. She was a wonderful lady, who was very conscientious and efficient. I was amazed to come home one afternoon to find her ironing my nylons and underwear! We each paid her about $12.50 a month for all her work and caring attention.

Camp Howard was a supply depot of about 700 men, 70 officers and two American females: me and Kay. I couldn't possibly have asked for a better place to learn the job or a more competent and caring Club Director for my first assignment in Korea. Kay was a no-nonsense, matter-of-fact, yet easy-going sort. An attractive, fashionably tall, slim Midwesterner from Nebraska, she had short dark brown hair and piercing brown eyes that could see through you. The men adored her for her common sense, warm heart and her "don't sweat the small stuff" attitude. She was a wonderful influence on me. While I tended to panic when something didn't go exactly as planned, nothing surprised or rattled her. She was so laid back, one of the GIs who frequented our Service Club described her to me:

"If the Club were on fire, Kay would start a conga line and dance everyone out of the building making them think it was part of the program."

A favorite saying of hers which I have quoted on many occasions was, "Ninety-nine percent of the world's problems can be solved by a hot shower." One of her special gifts was her ability to encourage a person. If Kay said you could do it, you were convinced you could. But she wasn't a pushover. Kay could neutralize a rowdy audience of young GIs within minutes with little effort, with or without a microphone. She was a wonderful role model.

As soon as we finished our little tour of the Quonset hut complex, we walked down the dirt road to the Service Club to begin my "on the job" training.

Above: Judi and Harry Purcell fell in love in Korea and married when they returned to the States.
Below: The romance is still alive, Judi and Harry in 2010.

3

THE SERVICE CLUB AND LEARNING THE ROPES

Hearing the Beatles makes me feel twenty-three again and back in Korea.

Camp Howard, Korea, 1964
    As Kay and I approached the old green Quonset hut that was our Service Club, I could hear the Beatles crooning "She loves you, Yea, Yea, Yea." We stepped through the door and I heard pool balls clicking and ping pong balls smacking. The building smelled of brewing coffee and floor wax and the aroma made it cozy and pleasant. The sounds blended together and became muffled and rhythmic. Somewhere down the hall someone was plucking a guitar, trying to figure out a melody, while someone else was beating drums like he wanted to kill them. I followed Kay to our offices through a large room of worn furniture and faded drapes Kay called the

program room. Card tables and chairs were in neat rows, and a small stage dominated one corner. A bookcase half filled with library books stood in another corner of the room. Our offices overlooked the program room and entryway through a large window, allowing us to see anyone entering or leaving the club or in the program room.

One of our enthusiastic muscians.

"Your job is Recreation Specialist and Program Director and when I'm gone you're acting Club Director. But don't let that worry you, I can show you everything you need to know this afternoon." We both laughed. "Let me show you where everything is," said Kay.

"You know the Special Services Program includes service clubs, libraries, crafts shops, and an entertainment division, right?" I nodded. "Of course, we're so small here at Camp Howard, you and I are the service club, library, and entertainment division all rolled into one. We do have a crafts shop that's run by one of the Korean civilians. It's just a woodworking shop with some models that the guys can buy. Oh yes, there's a room for developing film that we call the photo lab. That's part of the crafts shop, too."

A young soldier poked his head in the door, "Kay, you got time for a pool game?"

"Not now, Doogan, I'm busy. Sandra, this is Doogan, he's the driver for Capt. Norton, the CO of the Supply Company, and a very important person because he can get us stuff when nobody else can. Doogan, this is Sandra Lockney, our new Recreation Specialist. Come back later and you can tell her all your war stories." She laughed. Doogan smiled at me, tipped his fatigue cap and vanished.

"How do I handle requests like that?" I asked. "Do they take precedence over work?"

"My dear, that is our work. As long as you have the program ready for the evening, you're free to play cards or pool or visit with the guys. There isn't a hard and fast rule. You'll get the hang of it pretty quick."

Kay continued, "The service club is the living and family room for the younger enlisted men, but some of the older GIs come around too. Anyway, we program for a broad age group. The younger guys like the competitive stuff, like the quiz games and tournaments. The older guys come for the Movie and Popcorn Night, the refreshments, and Bingo. No alcoholic beverages are allowed in the club, but we serve coffee, punch and cookies or cake on special occasions."

We walked out of the office to the checkout desk, where there was a line of young men leaning on the counter. "Okay, Guys, you were all doing something else before we came out of the office. I know you're here to meet the new girl." She smiled and said, "Jeff, Smitty, Jonesy, Gary, this is Sandra Lockney, our new Recreation Specialist."

"Hi everyone," I said. My response was a little lame, but I didn't know what to say. They smiled at me and I smiled back. I was embarrassed, a little uncomfortable, but flattered. How in the world would I ever get to know them all, I wondered?

Kay interrupted my awkward moment. "She's busy now, but she'll be out to meet you later. Mr. Lee will check out whatever you want."

As we left the checkout desk, Kay continued, "One of our Koreans is at the desk at all times. He checks out the games and musical instruments for use in the Club. The electric guitars and amplifiers are the most popular," Kay explained. "We have a banjo, an accordion, trumpet, trombone, and saxophone. I've tried to get a band together, but can't find musicians except the guitar players and drummers and most of them are 'wannabes.' As men rotate in and out of country we may get one together yet. That's a project you can work on."

Our cook, Mr. Cho, makes program refreshments for us," she explained. The kitchen was small, but had a sink, stove and full-size refrigerator. "Sometimes we use the kitchen for programming when we plan a Chef's Night; that's when the guys do all the cooking. Cookies and pizza are their favorites."

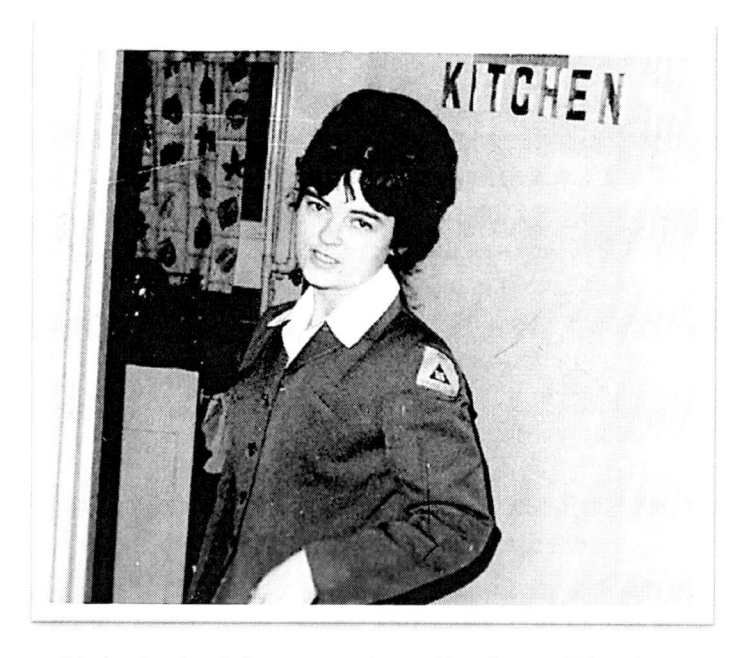

Much as I protested, the guys were always taking pictures which made me feel like a celebrity

We didn't have to open the music room door to hear what was going on inside. "The guitar amplifier is never set at anything but maximum," Kay said loudly so I could hear her over the music. "The rooms aren't soundproof so it's tolerable when there is only one player, but when there are two or three, it's deafening."

A drum set was permanently assembled in the music room to the right. Fortunately, whoever had been playing earlier had left, so Kay opened the door to show me the small, crowded room. "We keep the drumsticks at the checkout desk so anyone who wants to play the drums signs the log first."

Last on our tour were the pool and ping pong rooms. Both rooms were as drab as the rest of the club and only large enough for two tables in each room. "We have to keep a list of names at the checkout desk, so everyone has a turn, otherwise it gets ugly. When you take the hourly headcount, if you see any money, just tell them that the house keeps it. That usually gets their attention. They don't know if we're kidding. Gambling is always a problem in the pool room, but the guys are usually good-natured and stop, if we catch them."

We returned to the office. "Here's a copy of the program calendar for this month. One of the most important things to learn and learn quickly is to plan your programs at least a month in advance. Props, prizes and anything you need for a program have to be ordered from the States and it takes four to six weeks for an order to get here. I'll show you the storeroom and some of the standard program props that we use over and over. You just have to be sure to order replacements as things wear out or run out. We don't dare run out of playing cards or allow the roulette wheel to break. The guys would be furious," She said jokingly.

Someone just outside the office window shouted, "You got that right!"
A young face grinned at us. He looked like he was about twelve years old, but he must have been eighteen. "What's the program tonight?" he asked Kay.

"Connor, you know it's Monday and we always have Game Room Tournaments. Have you been practicing your ping pong serve? Last week you almost won."

"Yeah, I know, but I been busy. Don't know if I'll play. What's to eat tonight?'

"Cho, is making cookies and punch. The tourney doesn't start until 8:00 p.m. so you've got time to practice and get to the mess hall. Come back later."

"Maybe." Connor turned and shuffled back to the ping pong room.
Kay looked at me. "Connor is one of our younger GIs, and one of our 'regulars.' He just wants someone to tell him what to do. You'll see him at least once a day."

The storeroom was packed with decorations, posters, and equipment: a Bingo machine, a popcorn machine, a 16mm film projector, a roulette wheel, and some other things I couldn't identify. I was overwhelmed. "Don't worry. You don't have to know how to operate all the equipment right away. Mr. Lee, our secretary, knows how to run everything and he usually helps set up."

Kay described Mr. Lee as a genius. He could fix anything, find anything, or have anything built; and he knew where all the bodies were buried. A well-educated, soft-spoken gentleman who wore glasses, he probably didn't weigh 100 lbs. wringing wet, but he was a heavyweight in the community and well respected on the base camp. The Koreans that worked for the U.S. belonged to a clique that shared a grapevine of information and materials and Mr. Lee was one of the leaders.

As we walked back to the office again four young soldiers entered the Club. I heard an appreciative wolf whistle. Without thinking, I turned, smiled and said, "Thank you." They looked surprised and smiled sheepishly.

Our secretary, Mr. Lee, Kay, and our cook, Mr. Cho,

Kay and I sat down to look at the calendar. "If it's Sunday, it's Coffee Call in the morning and Bingo at night. If it's Friday, it's either Poker or Casino Night. We play for prizes not for cash, by the way. Some other regular programs that the men expect each month are a Hail and Farewell Party, a Birthday Party and weekly film nights. Otherwise it's up to you to plan whatever you think the men will like. Programming includes planning menus for daily and special or holiday events. I have to warn you, finding the food or ingredients for the menu isn't easy. We'll take turns taking a truck to Seoul for supplies at the Commissary, but it's a day's trip, another reason why we have to plan in advance. If we can't get it there, or you forget something, then you have to make friends with a mess sergeant."

A noise made us look up at the window. There were three handsome young men smiling at us. Kay sighed and said, "Hi guys, whatcha need?"

"We heard there was a new girl," one young fella offered.

I decided it was time to take the initiative. "How nice of you to come to meet me. My name is Sandra, what's yours?" I had heard so many names, after five minutes it was impossible to remember any of them. After they left, I asked Kay how she remembered everyone's name. She laughed and said, "Just read their name tags. It's rare that anyone uses first names."

"But what about that Jeff and Gary you introduced me to?"

"Jefferson and Gary are their last names."

"Okay, back to business...the budget." Kay began to describe the tedious drudgery of the budget process. All purchases had to be requested on a Purchase Order in triplicate, justified in detail and approved by our Special Services Officer and our headquarters.

"Like everything else with the military, the fill-in blanks on the forms never seem to be long enough to describe whatever you want to order. It's a challenge that requires considerable creative writing skills. To make it even worse, every item is scrutinized by our Special Services Officer who sometimes acts like we're spending his money." Kay sighed, "But you get used to it."

Learning to program and order supplies became the easy part of my new life. It was adapting to my unique circumstances and new "society" that was the hard part. Sights, sounds, smells and people were all cultures, the Army culture and the local culture, to absorb while learning my new job. Working long, irregular hours, wearing a uniform all the time became normal for me.

Flying off to an isolated radar site or

Here I am in my winter uniform keeping scores for the ping pong tournament.

hopping on an Army truck to drive for ten hours to pick up supplies once a month became routine. Conducting tours of Buddhist temples or the DMZ for a bus load of servicemen became one of my favorite monthly activities. Everything was exhilarating and exhausting.

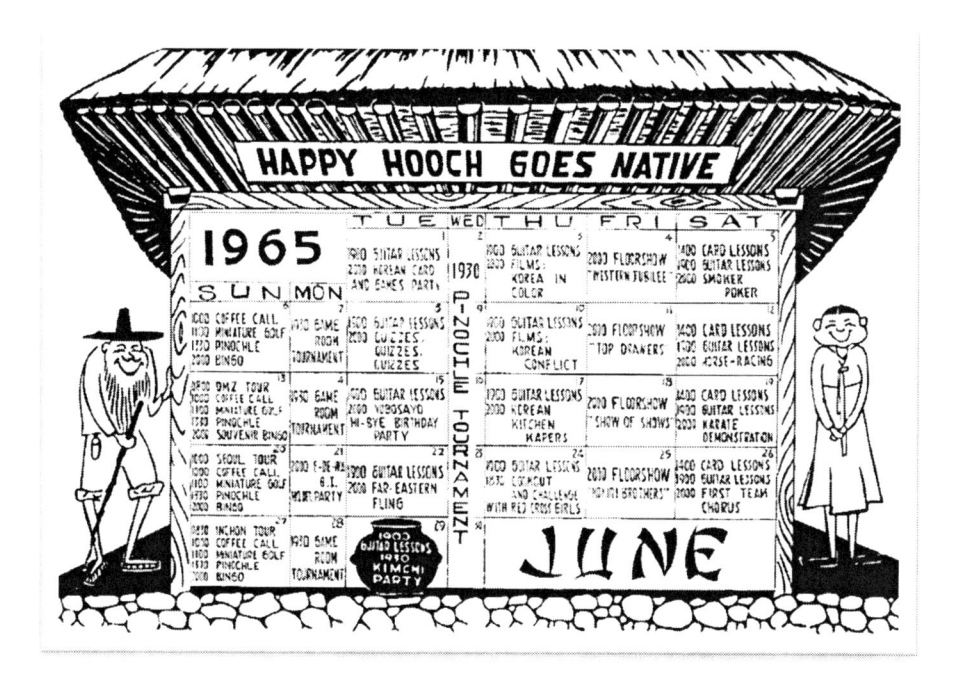

A sample of a Service Club Monthly Program.
Courtesy of Judi Purcell

I worked five days a week including Saturdays and Sundays with two days off duty. The schedule changed every week and the daily schedule could be a morning shift to open the club or an evening shift to conduct the evening program and close the club. Sometimes it was a split shift which meant I opened in the morning, took a few hours off in the afternoon, worked the evening program, and closed the club. The Service Club was open fourteen hours a day, seven days a week.

I wore my uniform at all times unless it was my day off or it was my turn to take leave. In the winter my uniform was a dark blue suit with long sleeves and a white blouse with collar flat over the suit jacket collar, a blue hat, white gloves, nylons, and black pumps. In the summer the uniform was a lighter weight, lighter color blue suit with a short-sleeved jacket, a blue hat, white gloves, nylons, and black pumps. The hem of our uniform skirts had to reach below the knee. The Special Services patch was sewn to the sleeve of each uniform and on the hat. The material for both uniforms was absolutely indestructible. I don't think it could be stained, torn, or burned. It was amazing stuff. The regulation handbag was made of real leather and had a pocket for everything. It was large, expandable and also indestructible. It doubled as an overnight bag on many occasions.

We were often asked to visit company areas to conduct programs or serve refreshments in locations that were accessible only by chopper. I welcomed those opportunities because, to me, it was an important part of the job to take our smiles and small talk to men who were unable to come to the Service Club and who needed a diversion more than anyone else. These times were memorable because the men were always appreciative, grateful and happy to see us.

Kay and I serve Birthday cake at our monthly Birthday Party while our part-time NCO and Mr. Cho look on approvingly.

Kay and I served Coffee and sweet rolls on Sunday morning.

    At the isolated sites the men were always spit-shined and on their best behavior in anticipation of our visit. These sites had no separate recreation facilities or civilian personnel. If they were lucky, their company day room had a pool and ping pong table, dart board, and a supply of cards and board games. Someone always mentioned what a treat it was to see someone not wearing OD, olive drab, or Army green.

    One of the first questions was always, "So what's a nice girl like you doing in a place like this?" There were always more men than we could talk to during the time we had to visit. So, the short answer was, "We're here because you're here."

    Another popular question was, "Where are you from in the World?" It meant "Where is your hometown?" It was a great ice breaker because no matter where you went, someone from your State was in the group. It established a friend in the audience and created a bond with the group.

Familiarizing myself with Korean wasn't the only language I had to learn. The Army has a jargon of its own. Even having grown up a military brat, I didn't know terms and abbreviations like: DEROS, date of expected return from overseas—KATUSA, Korean Army troops assigned to U.S. Army--Midnight Requisition, to scrounge or borrow supplies—R&R, rest and recreation leave.

The GIs and the locals devised a "pidgin" English that was almost a separate language. For example, "Number One" meant good, great, first class, or thumbs up. On the other hand, "Number Ten" meant that it was no good, bad, don't do it, or thumbs down. "Bally bally" meant hurry or move quickly. "Et-e-wa" meant come here. When the GIs referred to their "Yobo," they were referring to their girlfriend or a village prostitute. The term was apparently derived from the Korean phrase, *Yobo sayo,* which is a Korean greeting, as in, hello. "Moose" was another word for girlfriend, but I never learned where it came from.

To describe our day to day living to anyone who has not lived in a Third World country is difficult. Wal-Marts, Walgreens, McDonalds, Macys, or Winn Dixies didn't exist. We did have inside plumbing but no potable water, no bathtubs, no kitchens and little privacy. There were no places to buy clothes, personal hygiene items or groceries except at a few large military installations, like the one in Seoul. We ordered most things from the States and waited the four to six weeks to receive them. Sometimes we waited until we went on leave to buy necessities.

Entertainment during off-duty time was non-existent except for the Special Services Program or the Officer, NCO, and Enlisted Men's Clubs. AFN TV, Armed Forces Network Television, was the only American TV station and I don't remember any Korean TV stations. Programming didn't start until 5:00 p.m., or 1700 hours, Army Time, ended at midnight and included newscasts anchored by a serviceman in uniform, taped sports shows, and re-runs of old sitcoms. The only television sets were located in the clubs and sometimes the company day rooms. I never had a TV in my hootch. Korean radio stations existed but I didn't listen to them because I couldn't understand Korean and the music was unfamiliar. AFN Radio was the only American radio station. Broadcasts were news, disc jockey music programs, taped and sometimes live sports events, and re-runs of old radio shows. Each camp had a theater that showed a movie every evening at 7:00 p.m. and a matinee on Sunday.

Our only form of communication was a military land line phone. It was only allowed for in-country calls. Long distance calls were strictly illegal, although sometimes if you befriended the operator and it was late at night, you might get to call home, if the weather conditions were right and you didn't get bumped by an officer or a more important call.

A day off could mean spending time at the crafts shops, learning woodworking, or in the photography lab, learning to develop photographs. The library, when there was one on the camp, stocked best sellers and provided a quiet place to read or write letters. At Camp Howard the library was the bookshelf in our program room. But a real day off was only possible if I stayed in my hootch where no one could find me, or if I left the camp.

Every day was a duty day, in the sense that I lived and worked on the same base camp as the men. I met them everywhere, at the mess halls, at the PX, at the post office and at the movies. It was necessary to have some "down time" and essential to go somewhere away from home base where I was incognito.

We kept our passports with us at all times. The military command issued us blanket orders authorizing us to use any military ground or air transportation. Like Civil Service employees, I earned annual leave at the rate of one day a month and I could take a day or two off when the work schedule permitted. With two days off, I could catch a ride with a military vehicle--a jeep, ¾ ton or deuce-and-a-half-ton truck or chopper--to Seoul and spend a weekend to shop, rest, or just get away. The in-country R & R (rest and recreation) center, located near Seoul, was known as Walker Hill. It was a compound of separate hotels for officers, NCOs and other enlisted men. Restaurants, a gambling casino, swimming pools and movie theaters were other featured attractions. I visited Walker Hill only once for a special dinner for our EMAC, Enlisted Men's Advisory Council. It was a first-class resort compared to anywhere else in country, with first-class service, food and entertainment.

Above: The Enlisted Men's Advisory Council (EMAC) for Camp Nabors Service Club dinner at Walker Hill. ca. 1965.
Below: Walker Hill, the in-country R&R (rest and relaxation) area in Korea. ca. 1965. Courtesy of Judi and Harry Purcell.

Seoul, Pusan, and Che Ju Island were my favorite places to visit in country. Seoul was an ancient walled city with sightseeing attractions: the East Gate, the last vestige of the wall, Buddhist Temples, Shinto Shrines, and a city park. There were few retail stores or products for Westerners to buy. Most Americans in Korea purchased carved wood chests, lacquerware armoires and tables, oil paintings, and brassware.

Above: One of the Buddhist Temples in Seoul. Courtesy of Judi and Harry Purcell. Below: the East Gate

When I returned to Korea in 1970, Pusan, a large city on the southern coast had become a beach resort with several American-approved, beachfront hotels. Che Ju Island, a beautiful rustic fishing village off the southernmost coast was also designated as an approved vacation site. The island's population of fishermen and farmers tolerated tourists who were drawn by the picturesque landscape and quaint fishing village atmosphere. If I had more than a weekend off, my favorite holiday spot was Tokyo. There was a flight every day from Seoul to Tachikawa AFB to pick up our only daily American newspaper, <u>The Stars and Stripes</u>, which was published in Tokyo. My blanket orders authorized me to fly free if there was an available seat and I did as often as I could.

While the Special Services Program was created to provide wholesome entertainment, leisure activities and manage the recreational facilities to keep the servicemen on the military installations, the program was never 100% successful.

Stories were told and re-told about other recreational activities. Some were true, or at least had a grain of truth to them, and some were a figment of someone's imagination. One story of legend proportions was about a Special Services girl who spoke to an auditorium filled with uniformed soldiers in Oakland, California, preparing to leave for their one-year tour to Korea. She walked on stage to the podium, faced a sea of thousands of GIs, smiled, opened her arms, and said, "This blue Special Services uniform covers all of the recreational facilities that you'll ever want." The male audience erupted into tumultuous laughter, hoots, hollers, foot stomping, and noisy applause. I've often wondered how she recovered and if, later, she ever told that story to her grandchildren.

The Army did its best to keep the men healthy and to take care of the natural "urges" that made them want to leave the military compounds. For example, the camp bus regularly picked up the village prostitutes to bring them to the clinic for weekly check-ups to make sure they had no "social diseases." The girls carried a health card stamped by the clinic when they passed their physicals. Drinking beer and meeting the village girls, although discouraged, was a popular recreation. All soldiers were instructed to check the girl's card to make sure she was healthy before they engaged in any "friendly" activities. In case they forgot, the MPs, Military Police, patrolled the villages, visited the bars, and randomly checked the girls' health cards.

Every man who went to Korea was forced to see films about the dreaded social diseases, syphilis and gonorrhea. It was a sobering experience for them. One character everyone knew was "Bloody Mary," a poor soul who lived in the village outside of Osan AFB. She had been a prostitute who had syphilis. Without treatment for the disease, the condition worsened and affected her mind. She lived like an animal crawling on all fours, begging for money, in the streets of the village. When GIs walked too close to her she attacked them. I saw her once. Her hair was matted and dirty; her clothes were rags. It was a shock to see she existed and her condition had not been exaggerated. It was a sad and frightening sight.

The morals of the Asian people were not less than ours, but they were different. Young women were often forced into prostitution or their families would starve. The country was beginning to recover from a war that ended eleven years earlier, but there were no opportunities for young women like there are in Korea today. Even marriage was sometimes not an option because many of the young men had been killed in the war. Since they had few options they did what they had to do.

Our servicemen affectionately called us "round eyes" and treated us with respect and affection because we reminded them of their sisters, girlfriends, and sometimes their mothers. We were the objects of their affection, rather than sex objects, and the center of attention. For a while it was wonderful, but in most cases, we were ready to go home by the time our tour was over ...and sometimes even before.

Above: Camp Howard Service Club Staff, Christmas, 1964.

Left:

A Fillipino musical group booked by the Entertainment office in Seoul to tour the base camps to entertain the troops.

Korean Girls' College Choir visited the Service Club and sang Christmas Carols. Our commanding officer sits in the center with Santa and me on the left and Kay in Korean dress on the right.

4

THE BELLE OF THE BALL

I can't hear Gale Garnett sing "We'll Sing in the Sunshine," or "My Guy" by Mary Wells without remembering Camp Howard and Osan.

Camp Howard and Osan AFB, 1964

A week after I arrived at Camp Howard, Capt. Larry Dover, the Air Force pilot Millie and I met at Osan AFB enroute to Camp Howard, phoned me.
"How do you like your new home and how's your new job?"
"Well, thanks for asking. Everything is interesting and everyone is so nice and helpful, I'm really enjoying myself."

"I know it's not even Thanksgiving yet, but I wanted to call and invite you to our New Year's Eve party before you got another invitation. Are you free?"

"The holidays are a busy time for us at the Service Club, but I'll check with my director about the schedule for New Year's Eve. I'd love to come if I don't have to work. I can let you know later this week."

"Great. I'll call you later."

Kay and I discussed the holiday schedule and we agreed that neither of us would take any time off for Christmas, but I could take off on New Year's if I wished. This was my first party and I was looking forward to visiting Osan AFB, the largest U. S. Air Force Base in Korea at the time, and seeing Larry again. He had called several times after his initial call just to chat, so our relationship had developed as telephone buddies. He was amusing and I was sure I'd have a fun time.

It was suddenly Thanksgiving. Kay and I visited, served, or ate in each of the three mess halls, then returned to the Club to conduct a quiet film night as the evening program. It was my first Thanksgiving and would be my first Christmas away from my family. In a Christmas card to my aunt I wrote:

Dear Aunt Deanie,

...Couldn't begin to tell you about Korea and my job in so short a space. Suffice it to say: I'm having the time of my life!! Tomorrow I'll be taking a helicopter to some isolated posts to bring a little Christmas cheer. It's my first helicopter flight. Already had my first rides (and then some) in a jeep, three quarter ton truck, and a 2 1/2 ton truck! What experiences!...

The guys were always inviting me to see their world.
Above: I'm on my way to the Firing Range in a jeep, the typical mode of transportation.
Below: Although I'm posing with a rifle, I actually qualified with a .45 handgun.

Korea & Kimchi—
They Go Together
Like Bacon & Eggs

By FOREST L. KIMLER
Pacific Stars and Stripes Staff Writer

I CAUGHT A PHILADELPHIA STREETCAR the other day and rode to Yongdongpo.
After the first few blocks, I realized that sending streetcars to Korea as part of the foreign aid plan was a brilliant idea to help Koreans understand America—at least why Philadelphia is known as the City of Brotherly Love.

With passengers jammed so tight in such a tiny conveyance you have to exercise brotherly love—there isn't room to fight.

I wanted to take a train, but my guide thought I said A-frame, and I spent the rest of the day telling practical jokers to get off my back.

An A-frame is a boon to traveling newsmen who need a portable typewriter stand and don't mind backing into a story (see photo).

But alas, it is fading out of the picture as one of the most ingenious ways ever devised to lift that barge and tote that bale and still have your hands free to get a little drunk and land in jail.

THE REPUBLIC OF KOREA has become so mechanized these days that, if you throw away a beer can, some mechanically-minded free-enterpriser will start making a bus out of it.

Henry Ford would have loved the ROKs. He made a fortune out of building "Tin Lizzies" that ended up as beer cans when the vehicles were scrapped.

He could have retired earlier if he had thought of reversing the cycle and started out with the cans.

My West Virginia countrymen would have loved the ROKs, too.

I stood on a hill outside Seoul the other day and looked at a range of mountains in the distance that looked just like the Cumberland Gap, where moonshiners for years plied their hobby and fought off revenuers.

Those same West Virginia hillbillies would kick themselves if they could see how the ROKs made the whole thing more civilized by bringing Mohammed to the mountains—they installed kisaeng houses instead of stills in the hills.

Kimler demonstrates how the A-frame is useful to itinerant reporters in the field. Helping is Sandy Lockney of the Moyer Service Club.

Another exciting experience to write home about was having my picture in the <u>Stars and Stripes</u>. I just happened to be on duty when the journalist asked for an American girl to pose for a photo in his article.

    Holidays were lonely times for most of the men and busy times for us. The men had only two ways to contact home; they could make a radio call using licensed amateur radio operators or mail a letter through the U. S. mail. To make a radio call home, you would wait in line during designated times at the MARS station, until the radio operator contacted a ham operator near your home. The local operator would dial your home number and connect the telephone to the radio so you could talk to your family and loved ones. You made your call in a room with other people waiting for their turn, so your conversation was overheard by others. The connection might be weak and you might not be able to hear or be heard. At the end of every response you had to say "Over" so that the party you were talking to would know it was their turn to talk. It wasn't an easy way to communicate and definitely not very romantic if you wanted to talk to a loved one. The most common communication in those days was by U. S. mail. A letter could take seven to ten days and a package would take four to six weeks normally, up to eight weeks during the Holidays, to get from the U.S. to Korea and vice versa.

Kay always had plenty of help unpacking and decorating at Christmas.

I programmed as many activities and opportunities to win prizes as I could for Christmas to keep as many of the guys busy and entertained as possible. In addition to the usual programs, there was a night for trimming the tree and making ornaments and Christmas cards, an evening for baking cookies, a hayride and caroling. All of our

Our "Chefs" for either pizza or cookie baking were always supervised closely by Mr. Cho and Mr. Lee.

prizes during December were wrapped like Christmas presents. In addition to the programming at the Service Club, Kay and I always had invitations to eat at the mess hall with the men. Every company and almost every office on the camp had some kind of Christmas party and we were invited to them all.

Before New Year's Eve, and my first formal party, I had much to do. I didn't have a cocktail dress or a formal dress. We were allowed to bring only two suitcases with us on the flight to Korea, plus we were allowed to ship one footlocker-size trunk, called "hold baggage," which arrived about two or three weeks later. I hadn't thought to pack any dressy clothes or anything that I could possibly wear to a formal Air Force Officers' New Year's Eve party. As with all my dilemmas, work-wise and personal, I went to Kay for advice. There were few if any retail stores even in Seoul that sold western-style women's clothes. It was too late to order from the States and too risky to take a chance that it wouldn't fit or arrive on time. The only viable option was to have an outfit made especially for the occasion. Kay told me where I could shop in Seoul.

In Korea, there was this "anything goes" atmosphere because there were no norms. It was a pretend world, like it wasn't real life. To me, this party would be like playing dress up. I decided my costume must be something spectacular.

The shopping trip would be my first adventure to travel by myself to Seoul and find my way around downtown, exciting but a little scary.

Posing for pictures while watching the guys bake Christmas cookies

My next two days off I caught a ride with the supply company jeep. It wasn't hard to get to Seoul or another camp, because there was only one road to Seoul and it passed by all the base camps between Camp Howard and Seoul. To hitch a ride, you simply mentioned that you needed a ride during a meal at the mess hall and someone was always going in that direction. If there was an empty seat, you had a ride. If all else failed, there was a military courier bus to Seoul that stopped at every base camp along the way. There might not be ladies' facilities when the bus stopped at each of the base camps along the way, so it was a long five-hour bus ride, but doable. I preferred hitching a ride, because the GI drivers were always nice enough to stop where I could "powder my nose," if I asked. We used lots of euphemisms like that.

I arrived in Seoul late Thursday afternoon and stayed at the same transient BOQ where I stayed when I arrived in country so there was a familiarity that made it comfortable. The next morning after breakfast I called a taxi to take me to the Bando Hotel. Between the Bando and Chosen Hotels were a myriad of stalls, each occupied by a vendor selling wares. There was no rhyme or reason to the location of the stalls. They weren't in any kind of order so I just had to wander through the market until I found vendors that sold cloth for dress making. It took a while, but I finally found the stalls filled with mountains of bolts of cloth as plain or fancy as you can imagine.

Each stall was run by a family who stayed in the stall all day long. If you shopped early in the morning at lunch or dinner time, you would smell the family's cooking or see them eating just behind the display of their wares in the stall. All three meals smelled the same to me. The usual meal was vegetables, in the form of the traditional Kimchi, over rice. Ramen noodles were another favorite meal. At any time, the family welcomed your visit, dropped everything, and devoted themselves to helping you find what you wanted.

After spending hours rummaging through piles of bolts of materials in all the stalls and trying desperately to communicate with the Mama-san vendors who spoke a pidgin English, usually much better than my almost non-existent pidgin Korean, I finally found the perfect fabric: shiny gold and gaudy. "I'll either look like a member of the royal family or a Halloween character," I thought. It didn't matter; it was going to be fun.

At the hotel I found someone to recommend a tailor who could not only make my dress and shawl, but could make shoes from the same fabric to match. I designed the dress: a floor length, empire waist, straight line gown, with a wrap-around shawl. The shoes were simple pumps covered with the matching gold fabric. The tailor said he could finish the entire outfit in two weeks. Fourteen days later, I caught a ride to Seoul and back the same day to pick up my new outfit. The dress and shoes fit perfectly.

I couldn't wait until New Year's Eve. Fortunately, the holidays were so busy that the time passed quickly, and before I knew it, an Air Force car arrived to take me to Osan AFB. I arrived about 2:00 p.m. with only time to get to the hair dresser then to my quarters to shower and dress. The Korean hairdressers were all very talented and especially good at working with long hair like mine because many Korean girls wore long hair. Within an hour the hair dresser had washed, curled, and piled my hair up on top of my head with a lock of long hair sweeping down my shoulder. Like a dark brown version of Marie Antoinette's powdered wig, it looked elegantly gaudy and matched my gown perfectly.

The festivities started at 5:00 p.m. with a cocktail party at the home of the Commanding General of Osan AFB. The General's house sat up on a hill above the base, overlooking the Officers' Club where the New Year's party would be held. A long, winding circular drive led up to a huge parking area next to the house at the top of the hill. We were to be there for the reception at 5:00 p.m. and then go to the Officers' Club for the party.

Larry called me at 4:30 p.m. He seemed a little agitated.

"Look, I hate to tell you this but I haven't found a vehicle to take us to the General's reception yet so I'm running a bit late."

"No problem, it'll give me more time to get ready."

He arrived about 5:15 p.m. looking even more handsome in his dress blues. I opened the door and was thrilled to see that his eyes widened and his jaw dropped as he breathed a, "Wow, you look terrific."

We walked out of the BOQ down the walk where he stopped, turned to me and said, "I'm so sorry, but the only vehicle I could borrow was a truck," as he pointed at a blue van-like truck.

I had to laugh. How perfect. The carriage for my magical evening was an Air Force blue bread truck!

He offered me his arm, escorted me to the passenger's side of the truck, helped me maneuver a high step up into the truck, and led me to the side bench inside the door. He ran around to the driver's side, jumped in and pulled the crank to close the folding doors. Fortunately it ran well enough to negotiate the driveway to the hilltop house, but with the muffler missing, it sounded more like a West Virginia logging truck.

There were no windows in the vehicle, so it wasn't until he came to the rider's side to help me out of the truck that I saw we were surrounded by a crowd of military brass, more Generals, Colonels, and Majors, than I could count! As I exited the bread truck in my solid gold dress and high heels, there was the sound of a large inhaling of breath and conversations stopped midsentence. It wasn't the entrance I planned, but the effect was outstanding. It was as if I were the star of a Gene Wilder movie.

We went through the reception line and I met the General and his wife who were as charming and friendly as they could be. Larry introduced me to his immediate boss and to as many other people as he could find.

After making the rounds at the reception, we boarded the bread truck again, and headed for the Officers' Club. The party was in full swing by the time we got there. The Club was brightly decorated, complete with strobe lights, just like a disco. It was so crowded that Larry and I had to turn sideways as we made our way across the floor. We sat with Larry's friends who were all pilots. Some of the single men had dates with Korean girls so, fortunately, I was not the only girl at our table or in the room, but I was one of only four round eyes in the whole club.

The Korean band played popular and big band American music. There was something unique about being in Korea. The Koreans tried to re-create what they thought it must be like in America and it always resulted in something like a caricature of the real thing. They didn't know what the real thing was, but I always appreciated their efforts, and enjoyed it as a different experience.

Larry loved to dance and was good at it, so we danced almost every dance. Just before midnight, we made our way to the front door in time to kiss, wish each other a Happy New Year and leave. Larry had said earlier that we'd better leave before midnight. With so many unattached males in the club he didn't want to hang around to fight them all off, to protect me from being kissed to death.

It was a clear starry night and the walk to the transient quarters was refreshing after the noise and smoke of the party. Larry kissed my hand gallantly and told me what a wonderful time he'd had.

"I'll pick you up for a champagne brunch in the morning and then, I've got something exciting planned for you before you have to leave." What could be more exciting than my New Year's Eve, I wondered.

The next morning the Club was miraculously transformed from the disco the night before to an elegant restaurant serving a champagne brunch. The Eggs Benedict, the fruit, the champagne, everything was delicious, but I couldn't wait for Larry's surprise.

"Have you ever flown a plane?"

"No."

"Would you like to?"

"Would I!"

It was a small-fixed wing two-seater plane, like a Cessna. The day was gorgeous, cerulean blue sky with a few puffy white clouds and air that was clear and cold. We took off and climbed higher than the surrounding mountains, soaring around and between the clouds.

"It's all yours," he said as he took his hands off of the controls. I wasn't expecting it and was too flustered to know what to do.

He said, "You better do something quick because the plane won't fly itself," and laughed.

I grabbed the controls. The plane tilted to the right and I tried to correct it by turning to the left. The plane banked to the left and I tried to adjust again. The controls were so sensitive that every time I moved, the plane moved too. It took a while to get the feel of it so I practiced banking to the left then to the right. If I'd been just riding, I'd probably have gotten airsick, but the excitement of being at the controls and the thrill of piloting the plane dominated all my senses. Soon, we were flying smoothly and I began enjoying the view. It was an exhilarating feeling of power and thrilling to look down where everything was small and up at the endless sea of blue sky. There was no other feeling like it. "I could really become addicted to this," I remember saying. For the first time I understood the reason my father had stayed in the U. S. Air Force as a pilot. He had given up trying to explain the thrill and excitement of flying because there was nothing to compare it to, that we earthbound beings could understand. Now, I understood words were inadequate.

Too soon it was time to go back. Larry handed me the radio and told me to request permission from the tower to land. He told me what to say, and I repeated his words exactly. There was a long silence. Finally, the voice from the tower said slowly,

"Could you repeat that?...Over."

My first flying adventure.

I repeated the request to land exactly as Larry had told me to and said,

"Over."

The voice from the tower paused again, then gave me permission to land and the number of the runway to use. Larry, muffling his laughter, returned the radio to the dash and took the controls. We landed and Larry's friend, Jeff, who had been with us at the party the night before, met us as we climbed out of the plane. Jeff said that Larry was needed in the office, so Larry suggested that Jeff take me to the Officers' Club for coffee until he could join us. They were so casual about it; I didn't give it another thought.

I was a little giddy from the flight and couldn't wait to talk about my adventure, so I was happy I could tell Jeff all about it. We went to the Club where we joined several of Larry's fellow pilots I'd met the evening before. I was well entertained and the time passed quickly before Larry rejoined us. It was time for me to return to Camp Howard, so Larry escorted me to the Air Force car he'd secured to take me home. On the way, I found out the startling reason for his sudden "call to the office."

Larry was the duty officer of the day or AO and he left his duty with Jeff to take me flying. Another plane that landed about the same time we did, on another runway, had a minor accident. It rolled off the runway and damaged a wheel. No one was hurt, but an official accident report was required according to regulation procedure after any accident. The AO was supposed to investigate the circumstances of the accident immediately and make this official report. Part of the investigation was to replay the radio calls prior to any accident. Not only was Larry missing when the incident occurred, but my voice was on the radio requesting landing instructions. According to Larry, it doesn't get much worse than that.

The happy ending was that Larry convinced the radio operator to "erase" the last radio communication, my voice, and Jeff had covered for him well enough that Larry could make the report, so no one was the wiser.

While Larry's memory of that New Year's Eve weekend was a little tainted, by the near Court-Martial escape, mine was not. I had seen the world from a different perspective, felt the thrill of flying through clouds, and I'd been "the Belle of the Ball."

5

BOREDOM, TEDIUM, AND THE STALKER

The GIs played "Under the Boardwalk" by the Drifters over and over and we recorded Barbra Streisand and Nancy Wilson albums.

Camp Howard, Korea, 1964.

  After three months, the training part of my job was almost complete. The regulars at the Service Club had become my friends. Kay introduced me to the hierarchy of officers and acquainted me with whom to see about supplies and repairs, so I knew almost everyone in our little camp. At a meeting in Seoul, I met some of the other Program Directors and made friends. I was planning programs and learning to stand in front of the men to conduct programs successfully, which meant my knees didn't shake and my voice didn't quiver when reading the game directions or calling Bingo.

Our guys, who came to the Service Club, were wonderful, always ready to help us or participate in our programs, if only to please us. They appreciated everything we did to make the Club a comfortable and friendly place for them.

I was feeling pretty good about my new career and comfortable with my living conditions. That was about to change as I learned how boredom and the stress of a hardship tour sometimes affect soldiers.

Boredom fueled their imagination and no subjects escaped the soldiers' irreverent sense of humor. The stories about life with the Army in Korea ranged from the improbable to the unbelievable, but were mostly amusing. One story was about an ambitious, efficient company clerk who often had nothing to do at work. One day when all his reports were completed, he decided to have some fun and see if anyone ever read the voluminous paperwork sent to Headquarters every month. He prepared an Army form and titled it "Paperclip Report." It included columns to fill in figures for the paperclips on hand, used that month, ordered from supply, unaccounted for, and finally the totals of each category and a "year to date" column. He sent it forward as part of his monthly report and waited. There was no response. In spite of his disappointment, every month the clerk included the paperclip form with his monthly report. After six months in country he went on his mid-tour R & R leave. When he returned, the monthly report was due and in his rush to complete it on time, he forgot his paperclip report. Two weeks later, he received a memo saying:

"Paperclip report not received, please submit as soon as possible."

Some men spent off duty-hours at their Clubs, either the Non-Commissioned Officers, NCO, or the Enlisted Men's, EM Club which like the Officers Club, served alcoholic beverages for ten to twenty-five cents a drink. Others spent their time in the "vill" or village where they befriended the locals. Some men had a Yobo, a

Using a microphone was an accomplishment for me

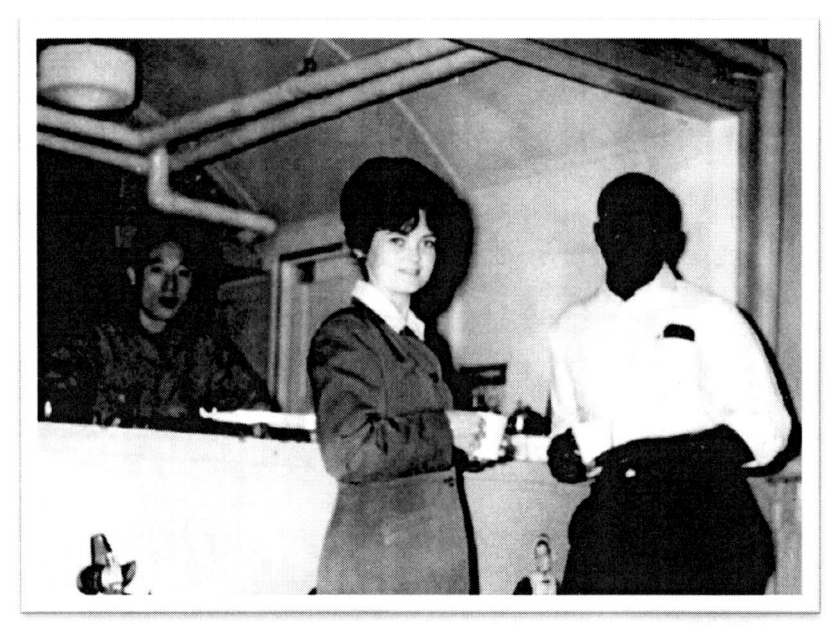

Coffee break with one of our NCO part time employees and, our cook, Mr. Cho.

regular girlfriend. One seasoned sergeant, who, like many of the men, had his paycheck sent home to his wife every month, wrote home, "Please send me some extra money for razor blades and stuff." By return mail, his wife replied, "Here's $5.00 for razor blades. You'll get your stuff when you get home."

    The boredom/stress syndrome affected us at the Service Club when we encountered obsessive or unreasonable individuals in the line of duty, like when the Office of the Inspector General, or IG, made an unannounced visit to our camp. The inspection was unannounced, so the inspectors could see how the units operated before they could hide mistakes and make everything look good. For us, there were never any unannounced inspections because the company clerk grapevine included the Service Club and we always knew which rumors were true and which weren't. Official announcements were always old news. We didn't change anything for the inspection because Kay understood the military regulations that applied to us, and she made sure we did everything the Army way, always.

    The IG Officer arrived about mid-afternoon and I was assigned to escort him through the Club and answer any questions.

Mr. Cho, our cook, had just washed and dried the dishes from the coffee service, when Mr. Lee, our secretary, asked Mr. Cho to help unload some supplies and put them in the storage room. At that very moment, the IG Officer and I walked into the kitchen. He looked around Mr. Cho's spotless kitchen. He had not found any problems in the whole Club. Just as he turned to leave he noticed the dishwater in the sink and scribbled a note on his clipboard.

    The next day, Kay received a formal report in the usual Army jargon in triplicate basically saying that the kitchen did not pass inspection because of dirty dishwater in the sink. Attached to the report was an equally long form with a cover memo directing that corrective action be reported immediately. Kay completed the top of the form, TO: and FROM: and in the space to describe the violation, she typed: "Dishwater in sink." In the space to describe corrective action she typed:

    "Pulled the plug."

    We never heard any more about it.

    I also learned some scary effects of the hardship tour syndrome. One afternoon, after supper as I walked up the dirt road to the Service Club to work the evening shift, I noticed someone standing in the doorway of the NCO club which was located directly across the road from the Service Club. His frame filled the doorway. As I got closer, I could see that he was in fatigues and wearing a sidearm, which was unusual. The stripes on his arm identified him as a sergeant. It looked like he was staring in my direction. I waved, but he didn't respond. He just stared. I didn't think too much about it. When we closed the club at 10:00 p.m. and headed down the road to the hootch, I saw him standing in the same doorway. Mr. Lee and Mr. Cho, our Korean staff members routinely walked us to our hootch after work. On this evening, I appreciated the staff escort whereas before I thought it was just a nice time to visit with them off the clock.

    Walking to work after dinner the next day, I noticed the same sergeant standing in the same doorway, again, staring in my direction. This time I didn't wave. After work when the staff walked me home, he was there. It was as if he hadn't moved. I didn't mention to the staff that the sergeant had watched me twice before

    It made me nervous so I described the sergeant's regular appearances to Kay. It was odd that this NCO should be standing in the same doorway watching each time I came or left the Service Club two days in a row. Kay said he must be too shy to introduce himself. He might be new in country and surprised to see another round eye on our little compound. That made sense, so I forgot about it.

The next few days we both walked to work as usual and there was no sign of the mysterious sergeant. It was my turn to work split shifts for a couple of days to allow Kay to go to Seoul. We took turns working split shifts every so often so we each could get away and pretend we didn't live in a fish bowl. Years later, when I saw M*A*S*H on television, I swore they filmed it at Camp Howard. We had the same terrible P.A. system operated by a GI with a monotone voice who announced the evening movie and everything happening in the camp, and the driver for the supply company CO could have passed for Radar's twin.

The first day Kay was gone I didn't see the sergeant, but the second day as I returned to work for the evening program, he stood in the NCO Club doorway again. It made me nervous, knowing I was working alone, but I put the thought out of my mind and conducted the evening program as usual. When Mr. Lee and Mr. Cho walked me home he was there as usual.

The next day Kay returned and I took a day off. I decided to walk to the PX to buy something to read. There was no one near the magazine section when I walked in. As I browsed through the titles, I suddenly had the feeling that someone was watching me. When I looked up, there was the sergeant. Up close he appeared even bigger. He was over six feet tall with weight lifter's shoulders. His baby face and freckles made him look younger than he probably was. He stood close enough to touch me, posing as if he were standing at attention for inspection, with his chest out and shoulders back. Concentrating on a magazine, he pretended not to notice me. I was uncomfortable but didn't know what to do. He glanced up from his magazine and looked me in the eye. It was only an instant but his look was frighteningly intense. My gut tightened and I felt more like flight than fight. I quickly left the building and started back to the hootch. His combat boots made a crunching sound on the dirt road as he followed only a few steps behind me.

I ran into the hootch and locked the door. Trembling, I sat quietly on the couch to regain my composure. This couldn't be happening, I thought, but it was. Kay was due home for lunch, so I waited to tell her that the sergeant was back and his behavior was getting bizarre. This time she thought it was strange too. One of the camp personnel clerks was a friend of a friend of Kay's, so she decided to ask some questions. Through her sources she discovered that the sergeant had been in country almost eight months and was the senior NCO in the Provost's Office which was the Military Police.

"He's the senior NCO and the head of the police department. He outranks most of the sergeants on the camp and who would believe a sergeant of his rank and position would behave so erratically? That's just great. I can't go to the police because he is the police." I blurted out, incredulously.

While I was feeling a little panicky, Kay was still calm. She said that he was probably a jerk playing a practical joke. She thought the best thing would be to ignore him and that would probably make him lose interest. It sounded like a good plan at the time, while I was sitting safely in our little living room. Our hootch was located on the perimeter of the base camp which was marked by a ten foot steel fence. A Korean guard patrolled the perimeter and walked by our hootch regularly all night long. I felt a little more secure since we had a guard and lived in the same building as the officers in charge of the camp.

The next day at the Service Club, as I sat at the desk in my office, I looked up to see that the side door was propped open. In the parking lot, leaning against one of the Army trucks staring at me, was the sergeant. I ignored him. When Kay returned to the office he was gone. Before I could tell her that he had been watching me from the parking lot, she told me that Mr. Lee had taken her aside to tell her that there was "a sergeant watching Miss Sandra" and he was concerned. That evening after closing the Service Club, the staff walked me and Kay to our hootch. The sergeant was watching us from the NCO Club.

By this time the word had reached our friends that someone was harassing me. In those days no one used the term "stalker." Two of these friends, a young Lieutenant, Dave Weston, and a young civilian engineer, Jack Lake, came by our hootch one evening to tell me they were aware of the sergeant's bizarre behavior and were concerned for me. Both were like my big brothers. Dave was tall, handsome, and blond. He was an outgoing, charming young man, and very attractive to women, especially Korean women, who rarely if ever saw a blond-haired man. Early in his tour, he had indulged himself during his off-duty hours and visited the village frequently until he discovered he had acquired a social disease. He became very wise, very quickly for his young age. For the time that I knew him, he was content to stay at the camp and enjoy safer pursuits like playing pool, reading, and tape recording music. Jack, an engineer for Hughes Aircraft, was an adorable man, square built and prematurely gray. He was attractive too, but Jack was like an innocent little boy who was interested in and enthusiastic about everything and everyone. Always smiling with something nice to say about everyone, he was a delight to be around. It was reassuring to me that they were concerned and I appreciated their protective attitudes.

    I explained that someone on our staff was with me at all times and always walked me back to the hootch in the evenings. Unconvinced of my safety, they checked on me every evening. Either Dave or Jack invited us for a drink after work or offered to come over to our place and bring a new album or tape to record.

    One afternoon when I was in my office at the Service Club, I answered the phone as usual. The voice on the other end of the line was deep and gruff.

    "I've been watching you and I know what you're up to," he said.

    I laughed, thinking it was a joke, and said, "And what am I up to?"

    "At 15:23 hours, I saw you mail that package and I know what was in it."

    This time I didn't laugh because I realized it was the sergeant. I froze. My silence angered him and his voice grew louder and even more threatening.

    He said, "I know you're mailing black market drugs back to the States. I'll be watching you. I'm going to catch you in the act and then you'll pay."

    It made no sense. I didn't know anything about black market drugs. I hadn't been to the post office nor had I mailed a package. A chill ran through me and I knew I was talking to a crazy person. I hung up.

I told Kay the "ignoring-him plan" wasn't working. Since we couldn't contact the police on our Camp, Kay decided we should call the Criminal Investigation Division, CID, at Camp Humphreys, the nearest Army camp. Two days later a Sgt. Jones called to set up an appointment to meet us at our hootch. He said he didn't want to meet us at the Service Club because the subject, the sergeant, might see him and realize he was being watched. After hearing the whole story, he said that he would have someone watch me, ostensibly to protect me. He kept calling the sergeant "my friend," as if he needed a code name. Sgt. Jones apparently had a flare for the dramatic and he took this opportunity, while he had the undivided attention of two young ladies, to impress us.

"As soon as 'your friend' does something, I can arrest him."

Not good news for me. There was nothing to be done except go to work as usual and try to pretend everything was all right.

The next Friday night, I was scheduled to take a bus load of servicemen in the evening to see a talent show at Camp Humphreys' Service Club. After dinner at the mess hall, I walked back to the Service Club to meet the men and the bus. I could see the patio behind the NCO club from the road and the sergeant sitting with his fellow NCOs drinking beer.

Good, I thought. He won't be bugging me. We boarded the bus and rode about 30 minutes to Camp Humphreys. The Service Club was busy, but not crowded, so there were plenty of seats for the show. The men went their separate ways, some found seats in the audience, some checked out the pool room, while others looked for the refreshments. From my seat, at the back of the room, I could see the Club entrance and just before the Master of Ceremonies introduced the first act, I looked up to see the sergeant and his cronies swagger into the club. In an instant, my hands felt like ice and the hair on the back of my neck stood up. I hurried to the Club office to call Sgt. Jones.

"Sgt Jones, this is Sandra Lockney from Camp Howard. I'm here at the Service Club at Camp Humphreys and the sergeant who keeps following me just appeared out of nowhere with some of his buddies. I saw him before I left Camp Howard, sitting on the patio of the NCO Club. He really had to move fast to get here when he did. What do I do now?"

"I'll be right there."

When Sgt. Jones showed up, he took me into one of the offices. "Did the Sergeant approach you?" he asked.

"No."

"Has he said anything to you?"

"No."

I guess he was disappointed that "my friend" still hadn't done anything. Sgt. Jones sat with me for the rest of the show and escorted me to the bus. To him, nothing had changed. He couldn't arrest the sergeant for attending the talent show. Everything had changed for me; I felt vulnerable and totally unprotected. I wasn't safe anywhere.

The bus drove into Camp Howard before the Service Club closed, much to my relief. The whole trip back I kept thinking, What will I do now? I can't live looking over my shoulder wondering when and what this crazy sergeant is going to do. The authorities were no help. I was trapped.

Dave had called Kay earlier to tell her about this great new Al Hirt tape from the States that he and Jack wanted to bring over to record for us. It was a relief to have friends around to help me regain some sense of security. They arrived while I was describing the evening's events to Kay. Dave was incensed that this sergeant could get away with harassing me. He ranted and raved, but came short of suggesting a solution. As a lieutenant he was subject to military protocol, and to step out of the chain of command would be detrimental to him and probably not help me. I understood his position and was simply grateful for his concern for my safety and his vigil when he was off duty. Nothing could be done until the sergeant actually did something. Jack was particularly quiet, but I didn't notice until later that he said nothing while Dave dominated the conversation.

That night I dreamed I heard the Sergeant outside my window. He was breaking into my room. In my dream, I could see his .45 revolver pointed directly at me. He was about to shoot me when I woke up in a sweat. The perimeter guard had just walked past our hootch on his routine patrol around the base camp.

The next morning at breakfast there was a hum of conversation until I walked into the mess hall. Then it got quiet. When the conversations resumed, I found out that the night before, my friend Jack had walked into the NCO quarters and asked for the sergeant. Jack found him sitting on his bunk and cold cocked him!

Mild-tempered, good-natured Jack had done what no one else could do.

Jack was shipped out before breakfast.

My orders transferring me to Seoul and a car to transport me out of Camp Howard arrived that same day.

My only regret is that I never saw Jack again to thank him.

6

AMUSEMENTS AND OTHER PASTIMES

The refrain from "Hang On Sloopy, Sloopy Hang On" by the McCoys takes me back to Korea, 1965, and Otis Redding's "Sittin on the Dock of the Bay" reminds me of VietNam, 1968.

      Whether it is a war zone or not, the American GI, when far from home, is resourceful, creative, and meets the world with that unique American sense of humor. During a hardship tour, to counteract the boredom, monotony, or the fear and isolation, he creates recreation and hobbies to amuse himself, similar to the ways he had fun at home. However, because of the availability of materials and often, the strangeness of the circumstances, his efforts sometime only vaguely resemble the original activity and his sense of humor, under such circumstances, is oftentimes a little warped.

Camp Nabors, Korea, 1965

Home of the 65th Medical Group Headquarters, Camp Nabors was a small camp outside of Seoul that housed research labs and was home to medical researchers, technicians, and hospital administrators among others. One of their missions was to develop antivenin and poison antidotes to protect soldiers stationed in tropical and sub-tropical places. They sent a unit of technicians TDY, i.e. temporary duty, to Southeast Asia to collect venomous creatures, insects, and plants to bring back to Camp Nabors. In the labs, they would create the antivenin and develop antidotes to poisonous creatures and plants to protect soldiers stationed in Southeast Asia who were exposed to such dangers.

At Camp Nabors, I was the Service Club Director, Program Director, and for the first time, the only female on the camp. The enlisted men were all specialized in some field of science and/or research and the officers were all in the medical research or administrative field. The Club was the easiest I'd ever run, because a large number of enlisted men were active in planning activities that appealed to them and helping me conduct them. Many of them had been to college or were working on degrees, and spent most of their off-duty time on the base camp rather than in the local Korean bars. They found unique ways to amuse themselves.

One Sunday morning at Coffee Call, I was handing out cards and games at the checkout desk. I had to use a small step ladder to reach one of the board games on a high shelf and while perched there, someone called out, "Hey, look. We've got company." I turned to see who it was and standing next to me behind the desk was Tommy, one of our EMAC (Enlisted Men's Advisory Council) members with the biggest boa constrictor I have ever seen wrapped casually around his neck. Tommy was known for his active imagination and overly developed sense of humor. He had this huge grin on his face as he held out the snake's head for me to pet. In my mind I rapidly reviewed all my options: Should I scream as they expected? Should I jump down and run? Or, should I keep my cool and pretend it's just another day at the office?

I chose the latter. I smiled and said, "Why Tommy, how nice of you to bring a guest." Hesitating for just an instant, I bravely reached out to touch the huge creature. The snake's skin was very soft, dry and smooth, not slimy or rough, as I expected. Everyone was a little deflated, but undoubtedly enjoyed my immediate facial expression during my deliberation time before my disappointing reaction. Since I didn't see any money exchanged, I couldn't help wondering which of "my little darlings" won the bet on my reaction, but I never found out.

On another occasion, when a TDY unit had just returned from another trip to the jungle, I noticed a very long line outside one of the labs.

"What's all the excitement about?" I asked Johnson, one of our Service Club regulars.

"Come with me and I'll show you." I wasn't sure how safe a surprise in one of the labs was, but I followed him anyway.

Inside the lab on a counter was a huge, square glass display case. At the bottom of the case was a small coiled snake. Lying next to the snake was a small black furry animal that looked like a pet ferret, but wasn't. Both looked perfectly comfortable. The wager was who would eat whom: the viper or the mongoose.

There was a daily report. The drama intensified each day. Sooner or later hunger would force one or the other into action. The whole idea of a little furry animal in a case waiting to eat the snake or be eaten, was too gruesome for me, but try as I might to avoid it, someone always delighted in coming to the Club to tell me what the two creatures were doing, which was mostly just lying there and that both were still alive. The vigil continued for days.

The end finally came. After about two weeks, Johnson, who delighted to be the first to know everything, came into the Club to announce, jubilantly, "Hey, everyone, there's big lump in the snake and the mongoose is gone!"

Some of the men cheered, hooted and slapped each other on the back, while others sulked and mumbled. It was easy to tell who bet on the snake and who bet on the mongoose.

"EXCUSE ME, MA'AM, BUT DOES THAT BOA CONSTRICTOR IN THE GAME ROOM BELONG TO ANYONE?"

VietNam, 1967-1968

Humorous encounters with animals happened in VietNam, too. My friend and fellow Service Club Program Director, Renee Coulter Capouya, had her own experience with a furry friend. She tells the story like this:

It started out much as any day in Vietnam. There were the obligatory reports and paperwork. There was some scrounging for needed supplies and plans being made to redecorate some of the rooms of the club with some paint I had found.

Being thoroughly entrenched in my quest for redecorating, I was totally unprepared when into my office walked a friend carrying a monkey! He had flown his mission to a fire support base that day and found this poor creature about to be made homeless. The soldiers there were moving and couldn't take it with them. The monkey had ridden in the helicopter inside the crew chief's jacket back to the base, occasionally popping out to take a breath.

Well, so now we had a dilemma! What could we do with this monkey? And did I mention that I've always had a soft spot for animals? So, didn't it make sense that the monkey now had the home it needed with me at the service club? Made perfect sense to me! It was obvious that this animal was domesticated

Renee and her furry friend, VietNam, 1968-69

and couldn't be returned to the jungle.

So the monkey and I started our new life together. What a conversation piece! The soldiers loved it, too. Well, this domestic bliss lasted for about a day and a half. When the officer in charge of the service club heard about it, I received a phone call. His first statement was, "I heard there's some monkey business going on over there!" He explained that we couldn't keep a monkey in a facility where food was served.

Have you ever tried to find a home for a monkey? It's not that easy! I returned the monkey to the friend who had brought it to me. On his next mission to another remote area, he took the monkey with him and found it a new home among the soldiers there. Rumor has it the monkey gave birth soon after!

And the friend who brought the monkey? He's been my husband for forty years.[6]

Renee and Dave on a romantic vacation in 2010.

Renee and Dave Capouya fell in love in VietNam and married when they completed their tours.
Left: Renee and Dave in VietNam, 1968-9.

HOW ABOUT SUBSTITUTING A QUIET
EVENING OF BINGO FOR HAROLD'S CLUB...
THERE ARE TWO TARANTULAS SETTING
UP HOUSEKEEPING IN OUR CASINO PROPS.

Camp Howard, Korea, 1964

The officers also had a sense of humor and were resourceful and creative when it came to recreation. At one of the Hail and Farewell parties at Camp Howard, Korea, the officers decided to stage their own floor show and they rehearsed in secret for weeks. Officers, guests, Special Services and Red Cross girls from nearby base camps were invited to this special party. The suspense and anticipation became intense.

Finally the night came. The lights in the "O" Club dimmed and a spotlight hit the temporarily rigged stage curtain and the strains of "It's been a hard day's night and I've been working like a dog..." blasted the audience. With cutouts of guitars and drums made from crafts shop plywood, and a huge base drum cutout with the band's name, "The Bedbugs," painted on it, four of the younger officers lip-synched songs and mimicked the facial expressions of the Beatles while gyrating to the beat of the music. The audience sang with them, then gave them a standing ovation.

Unidentified officers performed the Beatles music calling themselves "The Bedbugs."

The next performance was a conga line of officers led by the base commander. A full Colonel, a Lt. Colonel, a Major, and several Captains, holding lighted white candles, wearing white shirts, black pants, marched around the room in a squat position singing the seven dwarfs' song, "Hi ho, hi ho, it's off to work we go!" We doubled over with laughter, and some of us literally fell off the barstools.

Unidentified officers formed a conga line parading around the Officers' Club singing, "Hi ho, hi ho, it's off to work we go!"

The final performance was a long line of unrecognizable marching black top hats with faces painted on bellies, humming the music from the movie, "The Bridge on the River Kwai." Laughter turned to tears and the whistles, cheers, and foot stomping were deafening.

Unidentified officers marched around the Officers' Club singing the refrain from the Bridge of the River Kwai.

Korea, 1964 and 1970

Everyone tried to find constructive things to do when not on duty. One popular pastime was photography. The PX, the Post Exchange, stocked or could order the most complicated and expensive camera and electronic equipment in the world for very reasonable prices. I bought a large complicated camera with zoom and multiple attachments. It soon became obvious it was too big to carry with me all the time and I missed some wonderful shots. I invested in a smaller camera which still had too many attachments and was still too big to carry everywhere. Finally I purchased a tiny spy camera that fit in my pocket. Unfortunately the tiny camera took 16mm film slides, or tiny slides, but I took pictures wherever I went.

Most of us photo buffs spent much of our off duty time taking photographs and much of our money on film and cameras. The down side of the hobby was the only way to get my film developed was to send the film in a pre-addressed bag to Hawaii and wait two weeks for it to be developed and returned. To solve this problem, many of the photo buffs spent long hours in the photo lab developing their own film.

The up side of this hobby was that the Korean culture and landscape provided more than enough subjects. Everywhere you looked was something unique to capture in film to take home to show your friends and family so they could see and appreciate where you'd been and what you'd experienced.

During the first six months of my tour, like everyone else, I took pictures constantly: the bicycles with the stacks of baskets tied to the back, the A-frames piled high with wares or sometimes a drugged pig, the men and women balancing huge loads on their heads, and the distinguished papa-sans in their tall horsehair black hats and flowing white garments. The naked hills in winter, the terraced rice paddies in the summer, the gnarled stunted trees, the elaborate Buddhist temples that appeared suddenly on top of a steep mountain or on a road in the middle of nowhere, were sights that just begged to be photographed.

Korean women wore the beautiful and colorful Korean traditional dress which was a feast for the eye in bursts of red, green, blue and yellow. This traditional costume was a full, floor- length gown with a long-sleeved, short jacket, and a huge cummerbund. I've never been able to verify it, but one of the stories I heard while I was in Korea about the origin of this traditional dress was that the style was designed to protect the Korean women from being raped by the Japanese invaders during the Sixteenth Century. The dress was purposely designed to hide the female shape which accounted for the high waist, bulky cummerbund, and full skirt.

Another favorite pastime was to spend hundreds of dollars on what was known in those days as electronic equipment. Reel-to-reel tape deck and amplifiers with speakers were high tech. The PX sold top of the line equipment for half and sometimes a third of the regular price. I spent hours recording LPs, long playing records, and tapes to build a tape collection to impress my friends when I returned to the States. Unfortunately, the reel-to-reel tape decks were obsolete, replaced by the tape cartridges and cassettes, by the time I got home. The boxes of tapes I'd recorded were stored for years before I threw them away.

In 1964, the U. S. Military in Korea did not allow POVs, privately owned vehicles, but some of the younger officers found ways around the restricting regulations. One of the young officers had a pilot friend who flew the daily flight to Japan to pick up The Stars and Stripes, our worldwide military newspaper. Using his influence, whether friendship or something more substantial, he persuaded his friend to bring back parts of a moped from Japan on every run. He would then sell the parts to other officers who would assemble them. I never found out how they got licenses for them, but it was probably by greasing someone's palm, which was the Korean way at that time. Touring the countryside on mopeds became one of the popular pastimes in Taegu. Jim Garber, one of my regular library patrons and good friend, was the happy owner of a moped and spent many pleasant hours touring the dirt roads surrounding Camp Henry. He invited me on occasion to ride with him. On those special days, I'd pack a camera and lunch of fresh fruit, dates, cheese, bread or crackers and nuts from the commissary and Jim would bring wine. It was always a golden opportunity to take pictures that I could send home. Often we would be a group of five or six mopeds when other officers would join us with their Korean girlfriends or one of the other Special Services girls. The roads were never crowded. A large truck sometimes slowed us down or forced us to the side of the road, but that happened infrequently. The bicyclists and pedestrians were usually just curious and stopped to watch these crazy Americans drive by.

Camp Howard, Korea, 1964
	Other hobbies and pastimes only vaguely resembled their stateside counterparts. One such hobby was pheasant hunting.
	One evening after dinner, when I was stationed at Camp Howard, Kay and I walked into the Officers' Club for a drink and to discuss our evening's program. The "O" Club was a room with a bar, a pool table, ping pong table, and a couple of tables with chairs, in the same Quonset hut as the Officers' Mess. Colonel Joe who was the camp's Executive Officer must have been watching for us because he greeted us at the door.
	"May I buy you ladies a drink?" Reluctantly we accepted. It meant that we wouldn't get any time to discuss the program. We rarely paid for our drinks which cost fifteen to twenty-five cents apiece if the bartender was on duty, free if he wasn't. Someone always wanted our attention and would rush to invite us for a drink.

Usually, if we had Service Club business to discuss or just wanted to be alone we could sometimes politely decline. Since this was the second in command of the camp we accepted and joined him and his Adjutant, Major Bailey. Colonel Joe, as he wanted us ladies to call him, was a man about fifty, and bald, who liked to flirt with the ladies.

He commented on the cool November weather. "It must be pheasant hunting time." He turned to his Adjutant, Major Bailey, who wanted to be called Major Bailey. "Let's get some shotguns and go get us some pheasant. Would you ladies like to have pheasant under glass with a little champagne for dinner Saturday night? " He was trying to impress us. We nodded and smiled.

Curious, I asked, "How and where can you hunt around here? All I've seen are rice paddies and a few scrawny trees. Don't you have to have some trees or a forest or something?"

Major Bailey smiled and shook his head. "Well, we make do with what we have; and we have the basics. The Special Services Officer has shotguns that we check out. The Motor Pool gives us a jeep. We drive out beyond the village where there are lots of Chinese pheasants and shoot a couple."

At first I thought he was joking, but since there wasn't much else to do at this isolated base camp, and I had already noticed that the men developed unique pastimes to keep sane and busy, I realized that he was serious. Major Bailey continued, "What we shoot, the cook prepares for dinner. It makes for fine dining."

I had never been hunting, never really wanted to, but since it seemed like such a bizarre idea I said I'd like to go as an observer, not as a hunter. They seemed surprised, but pleased and they invited me to join them.

The next morning was Saturday and my morning off duty. Instead of sleeping in as was my habit on days that I didn't have to open the club at 8:00 a.m., I woke early, dressed warmly in a pair of Army fatigue pants with long johns and went to breakfast at the Mess Hall. My hunting companions were almost finished with breakfast. I grabbed a cup of coffee and we walked outside to a jeep, already stocked with the shotguns from Special Services. Major Bailey drove and Colonel Joe rode "shotgun." I sat in the back. We drove out of the gate into the little village outside the camp perimeter, and so I relaxed to enjoy the view. The dirt streets of the village were busy with street vendors, opening their stalls for business, bicyclists with high piles of turnips or baskets with unknown contents, men with A-frames on their backs carrying all manner of things, and women with piles of clothes balanced on their heads. I presumed most of the men were going to work in the fields. The women were headed in the direction of the lake, maybe to wash clothes. Every once in a while, I saw a woman with her short handled-broom sweeping the dirt in front of a stall.

I wondered how long it would be until we found any pheasants. Eventually, I figured we'd park the jeep and start walking to stalk our prey. No sooner had we driven through the small village than we stopped and both men stepped out of the jeep. KaBoom! A blast from one of the shotguns startled me and I wondered what the heck was going on. Colonel Joe muttered something under his breath. I saw pheasants flying frantically in all directions, trying to avoid the loud, obnoxious noise, dropping feathers, leaving a trail behind them. Major Bailey took his turn firing at the escaping pheasants. He missed, too.

It was unbelievable to me that we were parked alongside a rice paddy and they were shooting pheasant on the ground. Fortunately, neither was a good shot, and the birds escaped. I wasn't a hunter, but even I thought that it was illegal, or at least unsportsmanlike to shoot a bird on the ground.

This same scene was repeated several times, before the great hunters decided to call it a day. Colonel Joe said his sight was off and Major Bailey made some excuse.

"We'll have to postpone our pheasant under glass for a while, but we'll get some next time." Colonel Joe was trying to save face and, because he was almost apologetic, I nodded in agreement and said that sounded like a good plan. It was getting late and Colonel Joe said they had to return to work. I was relieved to return to the camp and go to work myself. The drive and the sights of the early morning village activity had been enjoyable, but it wasn't much of a hunting experience. I politely thanked my hosts and wished them better luck on their next hunt. My curiosity about pheasant hunting was satisfied.

Camp Henry, Korea, 1970

When I returned to Korea as a librarian for KORSCOM, on a second tour in 1970, I was again invited to join a pheasant hunt. This time I was stationed at Taegu, Korea, the second largest city in Korea where the rice paddies and trees were even fewer and farther away than they were at Camp Howard. Several of the lieutenants in KORSCOM command, Jim Smith, Dick Duggan, Joel Parsons, Bill Jenkins, and Mike Lewis, were all good friends and happily married young officers who spent many hours at the Camp Henry Library and the tennis courts trying to keep fit and occupied until their tours were over and they could go home to their wives and families. I became part of the gang as their token female and adopted sister. I was supposed to remind them of home and keep them from becoming too barbaric in their behavior and uncouth in their language. In other words, my job was to keep them straight.

The invitation to the hunt made me recall my first experience which I described to my friends, whose comments were all slightly disrespectful, but made in good humor.

"What do you expect from field grade officers." quipped Jim. "I'm surprised they knew how to fire a weapon."

"Yeah. For a Lt. Colonel, it's probably been ten or twenty years since he had any hands-on training. Don't they just give orders?" jokingly added Joel, whose father was a retired Army officer.

"We'll show you what pheasant hunting is all about," boasted Mike.

"But you have to be one of the guys to hunt with us," challenged Bill.

It was a not-so-thinly veiled dare that I join the hunt as a hunter. They assured me that we would not be hunting from a jeep or shooting birds on the ground. According to them, we were a real hunting party of six.

We all met for breakfast then got into two jeeps to caravan to the hunting place. We drove for about thirty minutes to an isolated spot where the rice paddies were separated by small stands of trees. It still didn't look like a safe place to hunt, but who was I to say? Bill handed me a 12-gauge shotgun.

"Have you ever fired a weapon before?"

"Sure. I qualified with an M-14 and a .45-caliber on the firing range."

I was confident I could fire the weapon, but wasn't sure I could hit anything.

"Could I shoot a couple of practice rounds so I can tell what the spread is and check the sight?" My companions smiled and practically in unison, making fun of my comment, said, "Don't worry, with your qualifications you can't miss."

They pointed me toward the path and they fell in line behind me. I thought, because I was the only girl, they were being polite.

We walked through rice paddies and through trees for about forty-five minutes, but saw no pheasants. Dick suggested we take a coke break. Again, I asked if I could practice with the shotgun a couple of times so I would have confidence firing the weapon. Finally, Bill took pity on me and agreed to throw his coke can in the air as a target. He threw once. I missed. He threw again, I missed. He threw a third time. I missed. That can was thrown a dozen times and with a 12-gauge shotgun I never touched it. To say I was embarrassed is an understatement. Everyone was very polite, but bored with my target practice and eager to continue the hunt. They didn't expect me to hit anything. It was my expectations of myself that frustrated me. I apologized several times and felt miserably silly. By this time some of the villagers and a dog had joined us to watch. At least a half

The shotgun was almost as big as I was.

dozen Korean children of all ages and a dog followed us. I was concerned that they might get in the way when we shot, but Joel assured me not to worry.

"These people always follow us, but they know to stay behind us until after we fire our weapons. They retrieve any birds we shoot for a reward. We give them a couple hundred Won (which amounted to pennies) or a bird to take home to eat if we bag enough birds."

We continued walking in the same formation, with me at the head, and the others behind. I walked through a small stand of trees and just as I came out on the other side into a large rice paddy, I saw a pheasant to my left. He must not have seen me because he took off, flew to the right, crossing directly in front of me. Instinctively raising my shotgun, I looked down the barrel and aimed just in front of him as he flew. There was loud roaring in my ears and everything seemed to be happening in slow motion and sounds seemed far away. I couldn't hear or see anything but the bird. I was conscious only vaguely of the distant, faint shouts of my five friends, "Shoot! Shoot!" Ignoring everything around me, but totally focused on the pheasant, I squeezed the trigger. There was a burst of feathers as the bird fell to the ground. Had I just grazed the poor bird? Stunned that I'd hit anything, I carefully lowered the shotgun and stood there trying to breathe normally so that my companions would not see my shock. I watched the feathers twirling to the ground. It seemed like a long time but it was a split second.

A group of excited Korean children ran toward the downed bird shouting in Korean to each other, scrambling to fetch the pheasant to claim the reward. Chaos ensued. Mike trotted after the youngsters to retrieve my pheasant. When he caught up to them, he took the bird and gave them a couple of hundred Won as their reward. He ran back to where I was standing, holding the bird up high so all could see the beautiful pheasant's colors, shades of blue and rich reddish browns with white and black spots. As he handed me my trophy, he said,

"That's the most beautiful pheasant I've ever seen."

Jim, Bill, and Joel, joined Mike and Dick, gathering around me admiring my kill. They patted me on the back whooping and hollering things like,

"Wow, what a shot!"

"Great shot!"
"That cross shot is the most difficult to make and you did it!"
"You certainly kept a cool head!"

Amazed at my trophy.

The accolades from my companions were overwhelming. They, who a short time earlier, were snickering and impatient with my target practice, were now jumping up and down praising my marksmanship. It was one of those glorious moments that would usually render me speechless, to think of all the witty, brilliant comments I could have made much later. Suddenly I realized why they were all walking behind me all morning. They were afraid I would accidently shoot them.

I have no idea where it came from, but at the height of the excitement, I stepped away, turned slowly to face my companions who had doubted me all morning, and said with the sweetest smile I could muster,

"Well, I didn't come to shoot coke cans."

The rest of the day, I walked anywhere I wanted.

As a postscript, more than forty years later, my stuffed pheasant is resting comfortably in my attic.

7

PROFILES OF THE AMERICAN GI, MY HEROES

Play the The Searchers' "Love Potion #9" and I'm transported back to Korea. Play the Mamas and the Papas' "California Dreaming" and I'm back in VietNam.

      The Service Clubs were hangouts for the young GIs, many of whom had been drafted and were away from home for the first time. They frequented the Club because they didn't want to spend all their time in the enlisted club or village bars, drinking and spending what little money they had. The American GI is smart, resourceful, generous, kind, compassionate, and fun-loving. We thought of them as our guys, some were like our little brothers, others like our big brothers. These young men were part grown-up, part crusty façade with a soft center, and all hero.

Camp Howard, Korea, 1964
The One Hundred Dollar Loan

At Camp Howard, Kay was my Club Director, my supervisor, my roommate, and the only other female in the camp. She taught me programming, club management and how to survive in the world of the military. With her counseling I learned the Special Services cardinal rules, which I don't remember seeing in writing, but were mostly common sense. Don't show favoritism or date any of the men. Don't go down to the vill (village) without an escort. Stay out of Restricted Areas. Never lend money. In some cases one just has to learn the hard way, or at least I do.

In addition to our Korean staff, and some paid servicemen, we usually had plenty of volunteers to help us do whatever we needed done, whether it was build something or find some supplies, set up for an activity or clean up after a program. There were always homesick young men who attached themselves to us by volunteering to help with anything they could. It made the work fun for us and for them.

Sometimes there was the exceptional volunteer, who had some rank and maturity who would make himself available whenever we needed someone to lead or help us organize the audience. One such young man was Donny. From the Midwest, probably in his early twenties, Donny was married and quick to whip out photos of his new baby boy. He was a SP5, or Specialist fifth class, so he outranked most of the other guys who frequented the Club. Donny was unusual because he was there if you needed him, but he was never intrusive. The guys liked him, so in spite of his rank he fit in. He was what we called a regular at the Service Club, he was there often and helped out when needed. One evening, I noticed he was distracted and failed to come into the office to say hello, chat, and ask about the program, as was his habit. He lingered at the back of the room. After the program was over, he helped us clean up and put away the program materials. Finally, I asked what was wrong. At first, he said, "Nothing," but I pursued and, finally, he told me, "Jenny had a fender bender and the car was towed to a garage. She doesn't have the money to get it back and the baby is sick but Jenny can't take him to the doctor because the garage won't let her have the car until she pays for the repair. I can't do anything till pay day." He looked so dejected.

Donny was not one to exaggerate and I thought he truly needed help. My dad always said I was tighter than the skin on an onion, and yet, without blinking an eye, I asked, "How much do you need?"

"One hundred dollars," he said as if it was a most gigantic amount of money in the world.

For a brief second I thought, "Uh oh this is a no-no," but I dismissed the thought and wrote him a check for one hundred dollars.

He couldn't stop thanking me, saying he'd pay me back on pay day which was two weeks away. "Don't worry about it." I said, "Just pay me back when you can." He left the Club before we closed which was unusual for him.

We closed the Club at 10:00 p.m. and the staff walked me back to our "hootch," our living quarters. As was part of our routine after work when we were home, Kay and I discussed the evening's program. I don't remember how the subject came up because I wasn't going to mention my impetuous generosity, but I told her...everything. Though we had never actually discussed Donny, I thought she would agree that he was responsible and dependable.

Kay listened to the whole story as she always did, with all her attention in a non-judgmental way. After a slight pause, she smiled sympathetically and said, "You can kiss your one hundred dollars goodbye."

"Well," I said, "I'll be disappointed if he doesn't come back to the club as usual to help just because he owes me money, but I won't feel bad if he doesn't pay me back. I can afford it."

The next week came and went. I didn't see Donny at all, which was most unusual. He usually came to the club at least every other evening. I thought, "He's probably
working a different shift." The second week came and went. Then, I was concerned that the club and I had lost a friend.

Late in the afternoon on Saturday, the day after pay day, I was sitting at my desk, writing a monthly report, when I looked up to see Donny smiling broadly, striding confidently toward me. He handed me a $100 bill, and asked, "You need any help with the program tonight?"

My faith in my fellow man was restored. I could have hugged his neck. But I didn't.

Camp Howard, Korea, 1964, and
CuChi, VietNam, 1967

The Gang Leader

He was tall, very black and scary. He must have been about six foot, five because when I stood next to him I looked at his belt buckle. Dark sunglasses covered his eyes. His six-foot- five frame looked even taller because he always stood straight and stiff. His demeanor was menacing and I felt intimidated whenever I saw him. He never spoke when I was around, but the other African-American GIs, or Blacks as they were called in those days, seemed to defer to him. In 1964, many of the soldiers were drafted and didn't want to be in the Army or in Korea. They were definitely not the volunteer Army of today. Even Kay, who could size a person up within seconds and handle any adversity with her Midwestern directness and plain spoken logic, was a little wary of him. I don't remember if we ever knew his full name, but we referred to him as the "gang leader."

He and his followers spent all of their time in the pool room, but never participated in any of our programs. Part of my job was to take a headcount at specific times every day which meant I walked into every room to record the number of servicemen in the Club. In the pool room, if there was money on the table, I was to warn the men about gambling. I don't remember ever seeing any money, for which I was grateful. It would have been rude to interrupt, and, I thought, possibly a little dangerous. Fortunately I didn't have to confront anyone, especially the gang leader. The young man was impressive and one of the men I remembered from Camp Howard. That was Korea, 1964.

Three years later, in 1967, I arrived in VietNam, and was assigned to CuChi and the 25th Infantry Division, the Hawaiian division nicknamed Tropic Lightning. The Club was called the Ilikai East and my Director was Riki Coll, an attractive, petite woman who spoke softly and carried a big stick. Ever the professional and leader, she maintained a steady and calm exterior which made the atmosphere of the club friendly and inviting. But this calm exterior was punctuated occasionally by a dry sense of humor and a quirky, delightful sense of fun which endeared her to all the men and all her Special Services colleagues including me. My first day was spent meeting the staff and learning where everything was, the supply cabinets, files, program equipment, and visiting with the volunteers and my new clientele, the servicemen who dragged in at all hours of the day. They were all in dirty fatigues, and usually hot and tired. Riki told me the program for the evening Popcorn and a Movie Night. That made it easy if we had a projectionist and Riki assured me, "Don't worry. We have a nice young soldier who volunteers for us. He's a 'short-timer,' which means he's due to go home in a couple of weeks, but until then he says he'd like to volunteer to help at the Club. In the lingo of the soldier here, it means he'll help us until it's time for him to catch the Freedom Bird home to the world."

    The movie was scheduled at 7:00 p.m. but we had to start making popcorn about 5:00 p.m. so that we'd have enough ready for the men who came to see the movie. At 4:00 p.m. I went out into the program area to make sure the popcorn machine had been cleaned and the ingredients were laid out. Our volunteer had set up the projector and screen and was already making the popcorn. I was stunned when I saw him. It was the same very tall, very imposing young black man I remembered from the Service Club in Korea.

    We recognized each other at once and it was like old home week. We laughed and talked about the old Service Club at Camp Howard and how different it was in CuChi. It was as if we had been the best of friends. He spoke about going home, what he planned to do, and how grateful he was to be alive to make it home. He was so different, pleasant, accommodating, and so polite. It was hard to believe he was the same person. What a change the war had made in this young man.

    I thought of him again, years later, when I heard the story about the young man at a cocktail party who was asked where he was from and replied, "I was born in Mississippi, but I grew up in VietNam,"

DiAn, and TayNinh, VietNam, 1967

The Baker

     At the LongBinh Service Club in VietNam, we took a survey to ask the men who used the Club what they would like to have served at the Sunday morning Coffee Call. The survey was my assignment, as was securing whatever the results indicated we needed. Surprisingly, the majority said they wanted toast, plain old butter and jelly on toast. This simple request presented a few problems. It wasn't like you could run out to Wal-Mart and buy a toaster. We had to order everything from the Sears Roebuck catalog and wait six to eight weeks for the item to arrive. A learning experience on how to plan in advance! That wasn't the only problem. Where would we get bread to toast? There were no grocery stores and the VietNam vendors didn't have bread. I asked one of the mess halls if they would give us some bread on Sunday mornings, but they didn't get loaves of bread on Sunday, they served sweet rolls or doughnuts. I had tasted the sweet rolls and doughnuts and understood why the guys had asked for toast. These tasty sweets were made to last a long time and to fill up a very large soldier who might spend all day digging bunkers. They were not delicacies, but coarse, heavy, full bodied pastries.
    I wasn't sure what to do. One of the sergeants had mentioned that all their baked products came from a bakery on the other side of the base camp, so my plan was to contact the bakery. The phone book was not like a civilian phone book. You had to know the name and unit number of the company you wanted to contact before you could look up the number. Of course, I had no idea of the name of the unit so the only thing I could do was get a jeep and find the bakery. Like everything else in VietNam it was not as simple as jumping in my car and driving there. I had to request a jeep and driver for a specific date and time and estimate how long it would take to get there, talk to someone about providing the bread and return to the Club. Since I had no clue how long it would take, I requested a jeep for four hours. On the designated date and time the jeep driver picked me up. The driver was one of our regular Service Club guys who was most helpful and stopped several times to ask where the bakery was.

We were directed to a huge metal building that looked more like an airplane hangar than a bakery. As I entered the building, a young PFC, with a charming Georgia drawl, greeted me and asked if he could help me. I told him about the survey, the request of the troops for toast on Sunday mornings and our need for loaves of bread. He listened attentively and said he'd have to talk to his Sergeant. A few minutes later a very large, gruff-looking sergeant sporting a cigar that had been chewed down to a small nub, came out to meet me. As one of the few round eyes in country, I was accustomed to being greeted with surprise, shock, or disbelief, but never with rudeness or downright animosity. My instinct was to run, but I couldn't abandon my mission for the guys. I took a deep breath, smiled and in my most charming voice I introduced myself and explained my quest. He just stared at me. He never spoke, but turned and stomped back into his bakery. I wasn't sure what to do, so I just stood there, frustrated. The PFC came back out and with a slightly embarrassed smile said, "It's O.K. If you're here at 0700 hours Sunday morning, we'll have the bread ready.

Every Sunday morning at 7:00 a. m., in my requisitioned jeep I picked up bread. It was always ready, but I don't remember ever seeing the sergeant or the PFC again. Three months later I was transferred.

My Sunday mornings were hard work beginning at 6:00 a.m., picking up bread, making and serving toast, but I got a break too.

I was in TayNinh at Christmas, and although it was a great place to be if you had to be in VietNam, Christmas was still a nostalgic and lonesome time. One day, I received a card with an in-country address. Inside, a simple, "Merry Christmas and Happy New

Year" was written in a large scrawl. It was signed by Sergeant James P. Brown and PFC Clarence Stone, Bakery, LongBinh. I had no idea how they found me. The thought of their efforts, and the sweetness of the gesture, brought tears to my eyes.

DiAn and LongBinh, VietNam, 1967

The 1st Sergeant and His Boys

I was sitting in my office in the Stateside Service Club at DiAn one afternoon about 3:30 p.m. when a 1st Sergeant with a tired sunburned face, and all kinds of camouflaged black stripes on the dirtiest fatigues I'd ever seen, came into my office. He said, "Ma'am, I'd like to ask a favor. My unit just came in from the jungle and I am throwing a little welcome back party for my boys. I've got a tent set up in our company area at the perimeter and I got tubs of ice, beer and sodas. I was wondering if you and any other girls here could come with me to meet them. They'd be so happy to see you and I'd be grateful if you could come."

"Sure!" was my instant reply. I checked with my club director, Joyce Blevins, whose comment was, "Well isn't that why we're here!" She was a cool lady. I rounded up two of the Red Cross girls on the camp and off we went in the Sergeant's open jeep. One cannot adequately describe the volume and density of the dust in VietNam, but I can tell you that we were pretty well covered with dirt by the time we reached the company area. I thought the Sergeant looked whipped, but his guys were walking zombies. We hopped out of the jeep and suddenly they came alive. We were greeted by roaring cheers and whistles. The next two hours we spent pouring beer and sodas into paper cups while chatting with as many guys as we could. They were wonderful. As usual, they didn't know there were round eyes in VietNam, much less at DiAn. They spent all their time in the jungle and when they did return to the base camp they only had time for sleeping and eating before returning to the jungle and their search for Viet Cong or "Charlie," as they nicknamed the enemy. When we finally left, we were thanked by all of them, sometimes with words and sometimes just by their smiles.

Months later when I was stationed at LongBinh, the same 1st Sergeant walked into my office and asked if I had a minute. For him, I had as much time as he wanted. He was one of the special NCOs that truly cared about his men, whom he called "his boys." He had just returned from his mid-tour R & R to Hawaii where his wife met him and they had spent a glorious week away from the war. We visited until his ride showed up to take him back to his unit. Just as he was leaving he handed me a small square, gift-wrapped box. I was so surprised and, initially, couldn't think of anything to say. He told me to open it. In the box was a beautiful blue star sapphire ring.

    I was so flustered I said all the stupid things that you always hope you won't say, but do. He said he had told his wife how we had dropped everything to meet and visit with his boys when they needed cheering up most and how grateful he was. She insisted they shop for a gift for me. I couldn't believe they would spend their precious little time together shopping for me when I didn't feel I deserved anything special. As Joyce had said, we were only doing what we came to do. He went back to his unit and I never saw him again, but I have always treasured the gift and heartfelt gratitude of the Sergeant and the memory of the visit with his boys. I wear the ring with pride.

DiAn, VietNam, 1967

The Soldier I Didn't Know

    I was on duty at the Stateside Service Club in DiAn, the base camp of the 1st Infantry Division, the legendary The Big Red One, when I noticed a particularly somber soldier in dirty fatigues standing at the corner of the checkout counter staring at the reel-to-reel tape recorder. I could tell from his fatigues and his demeanor that he had probably walked straight out of the bush. The Mamas and the Papas' tape was playing. He just stared at it. I walked over to him and asked if he'd like to check out a deck of cards.

    "No, thank you, ma'am," he said so softly that I could hardly hear him. I asked him where he was from and how long he'd been in country. He said he'd come in from the field to go on a week's R & R (Rest and Recreation) to Japan.

He continued to stare at the tape recorder or the floor. He seemed so uncomfortable and it was like pulling eye teeth to get him to talk, so I didn't pursue any more conversation. The stare of that young soldier had a name. They called it "the thousand-yard stare." Men who spent their VietNam tour "humping it in the bush," who had seen much and sometimes done much, who were stripped down to just surviving, and just barely able to hang onto some semblance of reality, developed that stare. It was a good thing he was on his way to a vacation, I thought, when I noticed he was gone.

A couple of weeks later, when I arrived at work at 1:00 p.m. for the evening shift, the Sergeant on duty said some soldier had asked for me. When he was told I wouldn't be in until 1:00 p.m., he said he couldn't wait, and asked the Sergeant to give me a package. He didn't leave his name or a note. I couldn't figure out who it could be. The package contained the most beautiful gold chain and cloisonné medallion I'd ever seen. The box had a Tokyo jeweler's name on it. Almost immediately I remembered the quiet young man who stared at the tape recorder. I am sure that the gift was from him. Since he didn't leave his name, there was no way to find him, so I couldn't thank him. If I could have found him I would have told him how much I loved the thought as well as the gift.

When I wear it, I remember him.

8

HELLO, VIETNAM

"Up, Up and Away" by the 5th Dimension, "Light My Fire" by the Doors, and "Day Dream Believer" by the Monkees are reminders of my early days in VietNam.

March, 1967

At age twenty-five, two years after leaving Korea, I boarded a TWA flight to VietNam. Again, like my flight to Korea, I was the only female on the plane. The men were curious about my presence, but it was not the same atmosphere as the earlier flight. There was not the loud boisterous joking and laughing. Except for an isolated greeting between friends surprised to see each other on the flight, it was quiet with a murmur of conversations. Everyone was subdued and introspective, maybe, like me, thinking about what it was going to be like living in a war zone.

I found my assigned seat next to a tall, blond, handsome, Scandinavian-looking second lieutenant. He introduced himself as Eric and helped me get my overnight bag in the overhead compartment. I was getting settled when a voice from a seat behind us yelled, "Hey, Scotty, what happened to OCS?"

Scotty, the soldier who just entered the plane and was walking up the aisle yelled back, "Man, you crazy? Don'cha know the lifespan of a second louie in 'Nam is about two weeks? I plan to get back home."

Eric and I glanced at one another then quickly looked away. I knew he'd heard the comments and I didn't know what to say. He smiled and broke the silence, "That's an infantry lieutenant, I'm artillery." The comment was unsettling so I changed the subject and we talked about favorite books, movies, songs, and about our families.

"My wife and I built a home on my folk's farm. We're fifth-generation farmers. We just had our first baby, a boy." He proudly showed me a snapshot from his pocket. "I got my orders changed so I could be there when he was born. He's a big baby, already ten pounds."

My part of the conversation was listening and nodding in agreement, because that's what I did best.

"Sorry, I'm doing a lot of talking about me. How about you?" he asked.

"Well...I've been with Special Services for three years. I've been thinking about going to graduate school when I get home, but I haven't chosen a place to go back to. My folks are military and home is wherever they are."

When the stewardess turned off the overhead lights, and we sat in semi-darkness, our conversation took on an abstract quality. We talked about what he'd heard about the war and the classmates he knew who'd been to VietNam, some who returned and others who didn't. As he spoke, I sensed that he was thinking about his own survival. He was obviously comfortable talking to me about private thoughts and fears, because we were strangers. His orders read LongBinh, but he didn't know where he'd be assigned after that. I felt concern for him, but not for myself because it didn't occur to me that the Army would assign me to a dangerous area. The flight was long and I slept most of the time.

When the pilot announced that we could see VietNam from the windows there was a scurry of activity and a rush to see what the war looked like from 30,000 feet. The landscape was lush, green and beautiful.

My thoughts turned to what to do when we landed. If no one met me, I would have to pick up my luggage, get through customs, and find a phone. Of course, the phone number and address in my pocket wouldn't do me much good since I didn't have any Piasters, Vietnamese money, to pay for a phone call or a taxi. I'd lived and worked with the military all my life and, as odd as it may sound, I was accustomed to uncertainty. We landed at about two o'clock in the afternoon. Curfew was seven o'clock in the evening which gave me five hours to get to wherever I was supposed to be, and it might take that long if no one met me.

The attendant opened the plane door and a blast of hot, humid, foul-smelling air hit us. It smelled like decaying foliage, open sewage, dirty sneakers and another strange smell which I learned later was "nuoc mam," a national condiment of fermented vinegar anchovy fish sauce. Eric and I said goodbye and wished each other luck. It didn't occur to either of us to exchange addresses since neither of us knew where we'd be. I never knew what happened to him.

I walked in line some distance to the terminal. It was filled with uniformed soldiers, marines, and airmen. GIs in fatigues with M-16 rifles slung over their shoulders were everywhere. All the weapons made me nervous and even though I knew it was a war zone, it was still a shock to see so many. The GIs in their dress uniforms were either arriving or departing. It was obvious which was which, when a huge cheer erupted from a group of tanned, tired, uniformed men, when boarding call for a flight to the U. S. was announced. Standing with all the men from my flight, I noticed that most of the departing men didn't look at us. If they looked in our direction at all, it was a look that said, "Boy, am I glad I'm not in your shoes." They practically skipped by us to their plane.

In the terminal we were herded through the counters where Vietnamese men who spoke little English rummaged through our luggage looking for who knows what. There were forms to fill out in triplicate and most of them I had filled out before I left the States, and some I had completed on the plane before we landed. The in-processing forms were endless. Finally, I made it to the front of the terminal. There were no phones in sight and that was worrisome.

PROCESSING: PHOTOGRAPHED, FINGERPRINTED AND NUMBERED... EVERYTHING IN TRIPLICATE... ID. CARD... RATION CARD... COMMISSARY CARD... NON-COMBATANT CARD. (TWO-IN CASE YOU GET "CAPTURED"... WHY ARE THEY BOTH IN ENGLISH?) BRIEFINGS: DON'T DO THIS... DO THAT... DON'T FORGET YOUR MALARIA PILL... DON'T DRINK THE WATER ... WATCH OUT FOR LITTLE OL' TAXI DRIVERS ...' DON'T MAKE ANY MISTAKES ...

The paperwork, was endless.
Courtesy of Terri Zuber

I stood for a moment, flanked on both sides by my luggage, debating my next move, when a GI holding up a sign displaying the blue Special Services logo appeared and said, "Excuse me Ma'am, I'm supposed to take you to the transient quarters." He didn't have to

YOU FORGOT TO TELEGRAM YOUR ARRIVAL ... THE TELEPHONE IS BUSY (ALWAYS) ... YOU OWE 17 LITTLE PEOPLE TIPS FOR CARRYING YOUR LUGGAGE 7 FEET ... YOU HAVEN'T CONVERTED YOUR MONEY ... YOU'RE CERTAIN V.C. HAVE TAKEN OVER THE AIRPORT ... AND THE $250.00 YOU BROUGHT ISN'T ENOUGH FOR THE TICKET HOME ... YOU'VE ARRIVED!

Courtesy of Terri Zuber

ask my name, because I was the only American female in the terminal.

"You don't know how happy I am to see you; I wasn't sure what to do."

He smiled at me like he understood, gathered up my bags and led me to an old black sedan.

"I'm Sandra. What shall I call you?" He hesitated and blushed slightly, before he said, "PFC Gary Hill is my name, Ma'am."

"May I call you Gary?" I asked. He nodded and never looked at me again.

We drove in silence through Saigon on our way downtown to the Meyerkord Hotel, which was both transient and permanent quarters for women who worked in Saigon. A set of orders was issued to me authorizing me to stay there whenever I was in Saigon. The orders came in handy because I had to go to Saigon a number of times to report to Headquarters between transfers, to catch an R & R flight and sometimes just to take a hot shower, sleep on cool clean sheets in an air-conditioned room or shop for supplies at the "Big" PX. So it was a home away from home.

It was a beautiful sunny day for a ride through the city of Saigon. After a flight of over twenty hours, adrenalin was the only thing keeping me awake and alert enough to enjoy the view. The French occupied VietNam after World War II

It took a while to adjust to seeing an armed guard in front of the PX where you shopped, and the apartment or hotel where you lived.

until the battle of DienBienPhu in the 1950s. Evidence of their occupation and the remnants of their influence were everywhere. Streets and sidewalks were paved and the French architecture gave parts of the city a romantic European flavor unlike any Asian city I'd ever seen. Saigon was a potpourri of rickshaws, bicycles and horse drawn carts, telltale signs that we were in a poor country in Asia. By contrast, I saw Mercedes sedans, Peugeots, and Citroens, retail stores with sophisticated window displays, stately government buildings and French villas. Hotels and restaurants looked as though they had been elegant in their heyday, but now the entrances were blocked with concrete barriers topped with concertina wire. VietNam was not primitive like Korea, but there was ample evidence of poverty here, too. Without the sandbags and barbed wire, and if I hadn't known there was a war going on, it would have been an enchanting place for a holiday.

    We finally arrived at the Meyerkord Hotel and I thanked Gary for his help.

    "See you at the Service Club," I said. It became my standard goodbye. He nodded and smiled.

    The hotel was surrounded by a four-foot block wall covered with sandbags and concertina wire. At the entrance stood a round, concrete guard shelter occupied by an armed Vietnamese soldier. It was clear that even here in Saigon, it was not safe.

    My room was like an old motel. It was sparsely furnished with twin beds, a night stand and lamp for each bed, and a dresser with a mirror. The furniture was ancient and showed lots of wear and tear. The small bathroom had hot and cold running water, but I was warned to take a shower as early as possible because when the permanent tenants returned from work and showered, the hot water ran out. The nicest part of the room was a window that looked out on the street. It was interesting to watch the people and traffic. A Vietnamese policeman in a white uniform directed traffic from a small round platform in the middle of the intersection. He constantly moved his arms in a rigid formal way and blew his whistle at regular intervals for hours. At curfew the policeman left, and it was quiet and no one was on the street. The white uniform was an odd choice of color for police dress. Later I found out that the Americans referred to the Vietnamese police as "white mice" for that very reason. The desk clerk told me about a snack bar in the basement of the hotel, but I was more tired than hungry so I showered, grateful for the hot water, and went to bed.

The next morning another driver picked me up, and took me to the Special Services Headquarters. The Director of Service Clubs, Miss Ruth Baker, was an attractive lady about 5'4," with short, well-styled, blond hair, probably in her early forties. The tailored uniform she wore gave her a formal, professional air, but her soft voice and kind blue eyes projected the image of a caring person. I immediately liked her.

"Welcome to VietNam, Sandra. We're happy you're here. We have so few girls in country and so many base camps that have requested Service Clubs. We just don't have enough girls to go out there to help design and manage the Clubs fast enough to meet all the requests. Of course, we're doing exceptionally well, considering that the Special Services Program has been in VietNam less than a year." She smiled, and, then asked, "Were your quarters at the Meyerkord satisfactory, and did you sleep well?"

"Yes, everything was fine, thank you."

"Your assignment will be CuChi, the Headquarters of the 25th Infantry Division. Riki Coll is the Club Director and Effie Fairchild is acting Program Director until you can get there. We need Effie to open a club on another base camp as soon as possible. We've scheduled a chopper to pick her up to bring her here today, and take you to CuChi in the morning. You'll have travel orders, so whenever you need to get somewhere you will be authorized to fly. Most places are not safe to travel by road."

We talked about the program and some of the challenges I would face with supplies and transportation. Miss Baker told me about her experiences when she and Effie first arrived in-country three months earlier. Thirty-two years later, in 1999, she wrote an article about it for the <u>Army Special Services Reunion Committee Newsletter</u>.

> We reported to the office the next day after signing all of those papers <u>again</u>, we were briefed on what was awaiting the club directors. Riki had been committed to the 25th Infantry Division, but their living quarters were not ready. The 1st Infantry Division was anxious to establish the first club at 1st Brigade. On Christmas Day our Special Services Officer, Major Whiting, Riki, Effie and I flew to 1st Brigade to discuss our needs. A 40 by 100 foot

facility was being built for a PX. A small one bedroom "hootch" was being built for the Colonel. The Colonel said, "If you'll let us have these two ladies to set up a club, I'll give them my "hootch" and the PX building. We'll make them first priority and have them ready in four days."

We returned to Saigon to arrange for <u>limited</u> equipment and supplies. The Entertainment Director let us have musical instruments. We got two day room kits which had chairs (a total of twenty-four), bingo cards, and numbers, playing cards, table games, an electric coffee maker, a small electric popcorn popper, etc. The Library section had received some paperback collections. They volunteered one for our use and agreed that we could make the books available on the honor system. On 29 December, 1966 1st Brigade sent a plane to pick up Effie and Riki and the 'worldly goods' mentioned above. There were as yet no doors and locks on the club or the hootch and no electricity in the club. That good old Special Services ingenuity came into play, and all was secured and lighted—with two 100 watt bulbs!

1 January 1967 was New Year's Day and Opening Day with coffee call following Sunday services. While Riki went to mass, Effie went across the road, crawled through a fence and went into the weed patch to pick flowers for the table. Unfortunately the weed patch was actually a mine field. Fortunately the soldiers who drove up in a truck remained calm and guided Effie step-by-careful step to safety. [Editor's note: Many of you who were in Vietnam and perhaps elsewhere with Service Clubs will remember Terry Zuber's whimsical cartoon of a blue suited Service Club worker strolling in a mine field picking posies, which memorialized Effie's floral expedition in perpetuity.]

Courtesy of Terri Zuber

    Martha Raye was in command headquarters, and when she was told of the club, she said 'I'll do a show opening night.' When the commanding officer and others on his staff arrived that night they found the club <u>full</u>, the floors and all twenty-four chairs were packed with people. Outside (the building was screened and louvered) troops were lined up five and six deep looking and listening. The Colonel's first words were 'My God, what would we do if 90% of the troops weren't in the field?'

    We were off to a good start. All new employees were told the story of the mine field, and troop commanders who questioned the need for a facility larger than 800 square feet were told to call the Colonel in PhuocVinh.

Postscript: Fast forward thirty some years later. Cathleen Cordova receives a request for help from a student writing a paper on PTSD. It turns out that the student, Becky, is Effie's great niece. Moreover, Effie's Vietnam memorabilia inherited by Becky's mother, created a sensation when Becky discovered a hand grenade in Effie's belongings, resulting in a call to the local bomb squad. According to Cathleen, finding her great-aunt's war souvenir seemed to spark Becky's interest in learning more about the Vietnam War and its veterans. Effie, Cathleen says must be smiling! Oh yes—the grenade was a dud. [7]

    After Miss Baker finished relating her stories, all part of my training, she introduced me to the Directors of Libraries, Crafts, and Entertainment. I spent the rest of the day in the office looking over program descriptions, monthly reports, and requisitions forms. That was the sum of my training. If I'd been thinking, I might have asked if I would be in danger, but I wasn't thinking, so I didn't ask. Her comment about road travel didn't register with me until later.

    The next morning the same driver took me to the flight line and drove me as close to my chopper as he could to load my luggage. It surprised me that the drivers were not friendlier and more talkative than they were, but I was told later that the GI drivers in Saigon frequently saw "round eyes" so I wasn't as unique in the big city. Women in the Army, women Marines, nurses, and MACV (Military Assistance Command VietNam) secretaries, were stationed in the Saigon-LongBinh area. The Special Services, Red Cross and USO Headquarters were also based in Saigon.

    The chopper looked more like the skeleton of a helicopter. It was wide open, both side doors had been removed, and there were no steps to get into it. According to regulations, I was wearing my summer uniform, a suit with a straight skirt. It was obvious immediately that it was not going to be easy to get on board. The crew consisted of a pilot, copilot, and a gunner on each side of the chopper manning machine guns. The two gunners were trying to help me, but were having as much trouble as I, figuring out how to get me in the thing without embarrassing all of us. Finally, they reached down, grabbed my arms and lifted me into the chopper.

> THERE ARE TWO DIRECT METHODS OF BOARDING A CHOPPER... IF YOU ARE A MAN.
> FOR WOMEN, THERE ARE 137 WAYS... NONE HAVE BEEN REFINED FOR GENERAL ACCEPTANCE

We always needed help getting in and out of choppers.
Courtesy of Terri Zuber

It was a bit awkward, but it worked. Inside, canvas benches replaced individual seats. The benches were designed to be rearranged or removed when the chopper's mission was to airlift wounded to hospitals, or combat-ready troops into the jungle. Everything and everyone had to be strapped in or tied down securely. The noise made conversation impossible. One of the gunners pointed to a seat for me. As soon as I sat down, he grabbed the seat belts and fastened me in. It was loud, scary, and exciting.

The chopper lifted off slowly, hovered a second or two, then with a rush of power took off so fast it took my breath away. It was the normal procedure for the pilots to take off as fast as possible and quickly gain altitude to avoid small arms fire and rockets. Likewise they flew at high altitudes to be out of range of most enemy fire. One of the pleasures of any chopper ride was, at the higher altitudes the temperature was cool and pleasant.

The view was spectacular. The wind whipped through the bay, and it felt as if I were flying all by myself. Below me, I could see fishing boats in the river and the villages along the river banks. As we flew farther away from the city, I saw more and more lush green foliage; it was the tropical jungle I'd heard about. The Saigon River snaked through the green foliage and tributaries branched out on each side like squiggly little lines. Occasionally, a cluster of thatched roofs would appear in a clearing. The huts were surrounded by rice paddies and little gardens.

The Saigon River was a familiar site flying in or out of Saigon.

The flight was much too short since I was enjoying myself. One of the gunners touched my shoulder and pointed to a huge cleared area and mouthed the words "CuChi." From a distance the base camp was a desert dotted with frame buildings and roads carved into the sand. What a contrast to the beautiful, luscious tropical forest surrounding it. Black smoke curled up to the sky from several different places on the camp. Later, I learned that the smoke was from the daily burning of human waste drums from the latrines. The GIs called them "shit pots" and did everything in their power to avoid latrine duty. It was a burnt sweet, acrid, oily smell that stuck in your nose for days if you happened to walk by downwind.

We landed on a chopper pad in front of a small tropical building with screened walls and a thatched roof, the terminal. A small plaque next to the front door read "CuChi International Airport," a typical example of American GI humor.

Our "International Airport" in CuChi.

A jeep was waiting to take me to the Ilikai East Service Club to meet Riki Coll, my new boss. The jeep driver was probably nineteen years old, extremely formal, and more than a little nervous.

"My name is Sandra, and may I ask yours?"

"Jerry Munsen," he said. Then he blurted out, "Ma'am, you're the first 'round eye' I've talked to since I got here. Excuse me, if I'm a little nervous."

"Don't worry, Jerry, you're doing fine," I assured him. As we drove along, he relaxed and seemed to enjoy pointing out significant places, like the Chapel, the PX, and the Post Office. I was amused by his tour guide descriptions as we drove across the vast wasteland of a base camp. Jerry stopped talking and stared straight ahead every time we drove by a urinal or a shower, both of which were scattered all over the camp. The urinals consisted of four posts with two or three stringer boards connecting them on all but one side, leaving an opening for entry and exit. Inside the little corral-like structure were several "piss tubes," sticking out of the ground. Anyone using the facility could be seen from all sides. A friend of mine and Special Services librarian who served in VietNam, Ann Kelsey, remembers walking by the piss tubes either to or from work and nonchalantly greeting the occupants with a "Good morning," or "Good afternoon," which struck her even then as one of the quintessential examples of how the totally abnormal became completely normal.

Ann Kelsey, VietNam 1969.
Courtesy of Ann Kelsey

The showers were similarly constructed, but with canvas attached to one or two sides to keep the sand from blowing in while the men showered. The water came out of a fifty-five gallon water drum, mounted on top of the corral structure. The men walked to and from the showers either naked or with a towel wrapped around their waists. It was a little shocking, but I was not nearly as embarrassed as Jerry. "No big deal," I told myself, "I must be prepared for the

Two of our Vietnamese workers pose for a picture at the
Ilikai East Service Club in CuChi, VietNam, 1967.

unexpected." It was one of the many surprises I was to experience in the war zone.

We finally arrived at the Ilikai East Service Club. The 25th Infantry Division was the Hawaiian Division and the men had chosen to name their club after the famous Ilikai Hotel in Hawaii. The Ilikai East was a fragile looking tropical "U" shaped building with a courtyard between two wings. It was as different from its fancy namesake as it could possibly be. The building had screened walls and a thatched roof.

Four months before I arrived in CuChi, my predecessor, Mary K. Jensen, wrote home about her impressions of CuChi, the service club, and VietNam, eloquently and accurately. Too bad I didn't have the opportunity to read her letter before I was assigned there. It would have better prepared me for what I experienced while living in CuChi. She wrote:

Arriving in Vietnam at the end of April, (1966) I was assigned to the 25th Inf. Div. at CuChi for 30 days to open a new Club. When I left at the end of November, they still hadn't even started pouring the pad! The Ilikai East is a 'lovely' thatched roof collapsing building. During the rainy season, May through November, we spent most of our time swimming through the place. Every time a heavy wind came through, the roof practically blew off. Needless to say programming under these circumstances is nearly impossible. Since the building is only temporary, nobody will do any needed repairs. Our whole area is serviced by one 10K generator, which is constantly out of order. We had no power at all for most of the month of October. Even when the generator is working, the wiring is so poor that the voltage is down to 80-85 by the time it reaches the Club. One morning I plugged in a coffee pot and blew the fuse!

The people at CuChi individually are great, and try to do anything for us they can. It's just the command that is so impossible. The thing that really made it so demoralizing for us was that the 9th and 1st Divisions were getting such great support from their commands.

We have been through numerous mortar attacks, but we all take them in our stride. I can get into a bunker in no time flat. I even slept peacefully through the last two attacks. The most difficult thing to get used to is all the dirt and dust. My 'tan' washes away whenever I'm lucky enough to get to Saigon to take a bath. Our hooch, though dusty all of the time, is quite comfortable with an enclosed back yard where we have our shower and latrine. Though there is no hot water, we have found if we shower late in the afternoon the sun has at least taken the chill off.

The soldiers over here are really fantastic! Though there is a wide difference of opinion on whether or not we should be here, every one of them is doing his job with a minimum of complaints. It is saddening to see the youth of the men who are being killed and wounded though. There is a maturity these kids have that is really amazing!

I could go on for days describing the many experiences I've had, but I'll just say that this year has been one of the most rewarding and unforgettable that I've spent with Special Services, and I wouldn't have missed it for anything. I will admit though that I'm looking forward to returning to California in April. Vietnam is very taxing physically and mentally to everybody. [8]

Riki took me to our hootch to deposit my luggage before we went back to the Club to work. Riki was a small, slim girl with dark eyes and wavy dark hair. She wore her hair pulled straight back and tied at the base of her neck. She wore no makeup which gave her a youthful fresh scrubbed look.

Riki and the Vietnamese workers. CuChi, 1967.

Courtesy of Terri Zuber

Our pool room and view of our office. Riki showed our workers how to paint our pool room brighten up the place for our guys. It was a welcome change since everything else was a Army green or sand color. ca. 1968.
Courtesy of Riki Coll

    She greeted me with a big bright smile and said, "Welcome, I'm glad you're here." Riki was a professional and I wanted to learn everything I could from her and she made it easy. In spite of her "iron fist in the velvet glove" modus operandi, she was soft-spoken, generous with her compliments, her encouragement and support, but demanding that the work be done right and on time. Her lighter side was charming and fun loving. The men appreciated her dry sense of humor and her spontaneity. She could beat them at pool, ping pong or cards. They could take their pick.
    Riki and I became best friends and I considered myself fortunate to work with her on my first assignment in VietNam, because I would need her solid, stable influence and balanced perspective when the mortars started flying and the war got personal.

9

MORTAR ATTACKS AND ME

I remember two of the favorites at CuChi were Frankie Valli's "Can't Take My Eyes Off You" and Aretha Franklin's "Respect."

CuChi, VietNam, 1967

"You ladies look as though you could use a break. Why don't I pick you up after work on Friday and take you to the best Officers' Club in CuChi for a drink?" He sat across the table from us in the mess hall. Capt. Don Sanders was a hospital administrative officer and he lived in the medical company area next to our hootch. His company supported the Service Club Program by allowing us to use their mess hall. Since we ate three meals at mess hall, we knew all of the officers well enough to make dinner conversation, but Don was the friendliest and always managed to sit at our table.

"Thanks, I'm on duty Friday night, but you can go," said Riki looking at me. I had been in CuChi less than a week and hadn't seen any of the base camp since my arrival, not that there was much to see according to Riki.

"Sure, I'd love to." My first invitation to go anywhere gave me something to look forward to.

Riki and I went back to work to start the program. We scheduled a "Casino Night" and I had to set up the tables, assemble all the decorations and materials we needed: poker chips, dice, cards and roulette wheel. The prizes had to be selected carefully, even though the guys really didn't care what they were. It was the winning that counted.

Everything happened quickly in VietNam. The day I arrived at CuChi, I dropped my luggage off at the hootch and went to work. Within days, I was accustomed to my new surroundings and the work routine. Every morning, I got up, put on my uniform, went to the mess hall at the Medical Admin Company next to our hootch with Riki for breakfast, and then we went to work at the Club by eight o'clock. We'd go to the mess hall for dinner late in the afternoon before returning to the Club to conduct the evening program. Since I was the Program Director, I was responsible for conducting the program, so I usually closed the Club at 10:00 p.m. If the program required two people, Riki would work late to help me. Often, when I was tired, instead of going to the mess hall, I'd go back to the hootch, eat C-rations and rest before the evening program. The cans of crackers and cheese were pretty good, but most of the selections required a couple of cocktails to make them edible.

Sometimes Riki and I would switch schedules so I didn't work every evening. The schedule was more theoretical than actual. In reality we were both at the Club from morning to evening. There was always work to do at the club: typing requisitions, work orders, reports, planning programs or making decorations and props and there were always men ready to challenge us to a game of pool, ping pong or cards.

After a week of routine, I was looking forward to Friday evening and my first opportunity to see what else was on the base camp. Don was a pleasant looking young man in his thirties with shoulders broad enough to be a weight lifter. He was about 5'10"and blond with a square jaw and wide set, clear gray eyes. He was from Arizona and had graduated from Arizona State, my alma mater, a few years before I was there. We found other things in common when we talked at the mess hall that week. I enjoyed his company and was looking forward to our drink. It wasn't a real date because there was no place to go. A date meant meeting at the mess hall to eat and walking together instead of separately to the Officers' Club for a drink. The important thing was that Don's invitation gave me the opportunity to get out of my uniform, get into some civilian clothes and that made me happy.

Courtesy of Terri Zuber

After work, I rushed back to the hootch, washed off some of the dust, and changed into a simple skirt and blouse. Don picked me up in an open jeep, which was the most common mode of transportation. In an open jeep you were a victim of the elements. During the rainy season you could drown in one; if you were lucky it had a top, but jeeps in VietNam never had any doors. In the dry season you could asphyxiate from the dust and sand riding in a jeep. It was the dry season so it was hot, humid, and dusty. By the time we got to the O Club I was covered with sand from head to foot. I remembered the instructions for preparing to come to VietNam recommended that you wear a short haircut style, so I cut my hair. Now, I understood why.

  This so-called best O Club on the base camp was a tropical building like most of the buildings at CuChi. Like the Service Club and our hootch, the walls were screens. The inside looked like a thatched kiosk on a beach in Hawaii. There was a bar the width of the room with eight bar stools and four tables with four chairs each. A couple of brightly colored Hawaiian beach posters hung on the frame of the screened walls.

  Aside from us, only two officers and the bartender were in the bar. Don got our drinks, and we talked about our good old alma mater. The two, standing at the bar were talking quietly, when I noticed their voices getting louder and louder.

  One said, "It's incoming."

  The other said loudly, "No, that's outgoing."

  They repeated these comments until one of the officers, with drink in hand, walked to the screen door, opened it slightly, looked outside, as if it made any difference since the whole building was screen, and said calmly,

  "Nope, it's incoming."

  I looked at Don.

  "Incoming means the mortars are coming at us," he said. Outgoing means guns are firing at the VC. You'll hear it every night. The big 155mm and 175mm guns fire intermittently. We call it 'H & I,' Harassment and Interdiction." He said it as a matter of fact.

  I took a sip of my Tom Collins and tried to look as calm and sophisticated as I could, while trying to make sense of what I was hearing. It wasn't computing in my brain: the tropical atmosphere of the bar, the pleasant attention of my escort, the soft light of the setting sun and these words, "incoming" and "outgoing." Then a siren sounded shrill and loud. Very calmly, Don picked up my drink and said, "Come with me."

Everything began to get hazy. It was as if I was in a fog and everyone was moving in slow motion. We walked out the back door and into the hospital's Command Bunker, which was a metal cargo container. Inside it seemed huge. On one wall were switches and lights, like a control board. A man worked at the board, flipping switches and talking on an Army radio phone, but I couldn't tell his rank or his name because he was wearing a brightly colored Hawaiian shirt and Bermuda shorts.

Don led me to one of the metal folding chairs lined up against the far wall, and gave me my drink. I could hear the "boom...thud...shudder, shudder, boom...thud...shudder, shudder," in the distance. With each "boom," I could feel the concussion of air. With each "thud," I could feel the ground move. Don was explaining something to me in a calm, quiet voice, but with the roaring in my ears, I could barely hear what he was saying.

"After you've been here for a while, you'll be able to tell whether it's incoming or outgoing."

Someone else came into the bunker wearing Bermuda shorts and carrying a puppy, making the count six people and a puppy. I kept thinking that someone would jump up and say, "April Fool" or something like, "Ha ha, the joke's on you." But nobody did.

Everyone talked in low voices and I couldn't hear anything they said. The roaring in my ears kept getting louder and the "boom, thud, shudder, shudder" in the distance held my complete attention. Everyone seemed so casual and unconcerned, but to me it was unreal.

"They don't have to have this performance for me; I know there's a war going on...," I thought, and immediately realized what a dumb thought that was.

I think everyone wonders whether or not they are a coward and what they will do in an emergency. I never gave it much thought until, VietNam. Suddenly I remembered Riki was working at the Service Club that night. I hoped that the men at the Service Club had taken care of her and had taken her to a bunker. Then I thought, "I wonder where the bunker is?" Finally, there was quiet and we heard the All Clear siren. After an attack, everyone was required to report to their company area, and I was anxious to get back to check on Riki.

Driving back to the hootch gave me time to think about my first mortar attack. All I knew about myself was that I was numbed by the experience. If Don hadn't guided me to the bunker, I would probably have sat there through the whole attack. I was immobilized by fear while conflicting, scattered thoughts collided in my mind.

When we arrived at the hootch, there was Riki curled up in the chair reading a book. The Club had to be closed because of the attack. We could not open it again until the next morning. "If I'd been working alone at the Service Club when the siren sounded," I said to myself, "I'd be busy washing out my underwear about now." To me, Riki was the bravest person I'd ever met because she acted like it was just another day at the office. Someday maybe I would learn to cope as well. Funny, I didn't remember asking her where the bunker was at the Service Club, but I vaguely remembered she said something on my first day about bunkers in the medical company area next door to our hootch, although I didn't know what to do with that information.

"It's unusual to have a mortar attack during the daylight hours," she said. "They usually happen at night." That was not reassuring. One thing for certain, my summer cotton pajamas wouldn't stand up to a night in a bunker.

The next day I went to the PX to buy a robe. My instructions to prepare for a tour of duty in VietNam recommended that I pack a three-month supply of personal hygiene items. Unsaid was, the PXs on the base camps don't stock feminine products. I guess they figured I could get to the Big PX in Saigon that carried that type of item or I could write home and ask for replacements by mail. Army nurses and Red Cross girls lived on the camp and I wondered why the Army didn't stock certain essentials for us at the PX. It was probably because the Army didn't think of supplies for women because there were so few of us, I thought. Later I learned that one of the nurses, Elizabeth Allen, asked a PX sergeant about some feminine items.

One day I'm just kind of talking to Sarg, and I said, 'Couldn't we just please get some tampons?'

He looked at me and he said, 'Well, we've been getting them.'

>I said, 'But they're not in the PX and they're not in any unit.'
>One of the troops setting (sic) behind him said 'Are you talking about those cotton things with those strings on them?'
>I said, 'Yeah, that's what I'm talking about.'
>He said, 'Well, we've been issuing those to the guys in the field.'
>I said, 'Come on, what are they using them for?'
>He said, 'Those are the best things in the world to clean your piece with, your M16, because that little cotton pad fits right into the barrel and then that string, you just drop that down, you just pull that out and that's quick.'
>I thought that was absolutely one of the funniest things I'd ever heard. They were sending them to us, but the guys were using them in the field. [9]

The nurses laughed a long time about it, and no one complained after that, since the tampons were being put to good use.

It made shopping at the PX easy since there wasn't a women's department for clothes or cosmetics. Robes for ladies didn't exist, but one men's small size terry cloth robe hung on the rack. It was huge on me and it was white, but I bought it anyway.

A week later when Riki was in Saigon and I was alone in the hootch, there was another attack. It must have been sometime between 1:00 and 2:00 a.m. The siren screamed and jolted me awake. Fortunately, I had laid out my new white terry cloth robe at the bottom of my bunk. I grabbed it and ran for the nearest exit, the back door. Now, I knew what to do with the comment Riki had made about bunkers in the company area next to our hootch. The back door was just a screen door with a little hook and eye latch. I flipped it open and ran across the yard to the six foot board fence gate that separated our hootch from the Medical Admin Company. The gate latch was rusted and it was stuck. The siren was blaring, it was pitch black, and I couldn't get the gate open. This time I had no thoughts. I felt just plain, unadulterated fear. There was no one to hear me yell for help. I was on my own.

Finally, with pure brute strength I didn't know I had, I forced the latch open, and ran through the gate. I didn't know where to run, I just ran. Someone grabbed me and literally threw me down in a hole. The bunker was just a trench-like foxhole about five feet deep, about four feet wide and maybe ten feet long. The roof was plywood with sandbags piled on top. It was nothing like the nice clean, neat Command Bunker where I "enjoyed" my first mortar attack. This was a long narrow hole just deep enough to sit or squat in and it was so dark inside that I could hardly see. Then I recognized Don crouched next to me and two other guys were in the bunker who must have jumped in first because they were sitting behind me. Don had grabbed me and I thanked him. We were all silent. At first I was glad to be there with some people. Then I realized that I was sitting on a pallet, just inches away from a muddy dirt floor and surrounded by dirt walls. I tried not to think of what creatures lived there. No one said anything, we all just listened.

"How long do you think it will last?" I whispered.

"Not long. Charlie doesn't have enough mortars or rockets to keep up an attack for long. It's usually a hit and run operation," said Don. "Don't worry, they're lousy shots. They can't hit the broad side of a barn door. These night attacks are to make us lose sleep and keep us on edge."

Well, it's working as far as I'm concerned, I thought. My mind was racing through several emotional phases. First, it was a relief to be with someone who knew what to do, supposedly. Fear was the next phase, when I thought of what might happen next. The last phase was anger. After all, no one explained to me what to do during a mortar attack. We didn't even have a bunker. I had no training. It was not my natural inclination to jump into a hole for any reason, at any time. The more I thought about it, the angrier I got. By the time the All Clear sounded, it was starting to get daylight and I was exhausted.

In the hootch, I fell onto the bunk, and was asleep before my head hit the pillow. After a couple of hours sleep the alarm went off. I sat up and swung my legs to the floor and looked down. I burst out laughing. My lovely new, white terry cloth robe was now a two-toned, dirty, clay-colored brown. No matter how many times it was washed, it remained a dirty brown color. I threw it away after my assignment in CuChi.

Riki got in later that day and I told her all about my harrowing night. "Why don't we have a bunker next to our hootch?" I asked.

"It's a good question and I think we should ask it," she said.

The next day, we made an appointment to see the Command Sergeant Major. When we arrived, his clerk offered us coffee and a comfortable chair until the Sergeant Major was free. Before long we were escorted into his office. He was a large impressive man, with a square, clean shaven face and a pleasant expression. His uniform was perfect. He didn't look like he lived in a war zone. After a few pleasantries, Riki told the Sergeant Major that we didn't have a bunker. She turned to me to describe the last mortar attack.

"I was terrified because I didn't know where a bunker was. First, it wasn't easy to get out of the backyard. I ran... not knowing where to run. Then someone grabbed me and threw me into a bunker somewhere in the Medical Admin Company area next to our hootch."

"Why don't we have a bunker?" asked Riki.

He leaned back in his chair and paused for a minute as if he were thinking.

"Well, you know the safest place for you to be? That ditch out in the front yard of your hootch. The next time you hear the siren, just go out there and lie flat in that ditch," he said with a big, wide grin.

His attempt at humor fell on deaf ears. Neither Riki nor I smiled. He agreed to look into the matter and get back to us. We were politely dismissed. I decided that he was not one of my favorite people. After the next mortar attack we found shrapnel in the ditch in our front yard.

I don't remember how many mortar attacks we had at CuChi. I was tired all the time, never got enough sleep, and always dreaded the nighttime. After one attack, a mortar shell hit the base chapel and leveled it. The thatched roof lying flat on the ground was an eerie sight. Two days later, Special Services Headquarters called me to report to Saigon. First I thought how wonderful, a good night's sleep on clean sheets in an air conditioned-room. Then I wondered what I'd done or hadn't done. I caught a chopper ride and reported to the Director's office the next afternoon. Miss Baker was at her desk working when I walked into the office. She looked up, handed me a pencil, paper and envelope, then pointed to an empty desk saying, "Sit down and write a letter to your family. Your father, the Colonel, called the Red Cross to find out why you haven't been writing. He saw a picture of the mortared chapel at CuChi on the front page of the Washington Post and, naturally he was concerned about you. When you finish the letter, I'll mail it and you can leave." In the middle of a war, I felt like I'd been sent to the principal's office.

It didn't take long to understand that the bizarre was the norm in the war. Riki warned me of the dilemma of how easy it was to become desensitized, but how necessary it was. It was important to realize when it was happening to you. She told the story of her first realization of the beginnings of callousness creeping into her psyche. The siren screamed mortar attack one night when she was working at the Ilikai and everyone quickly exited to find a bunker. She and a small group who were last leaving the building found the bunkers full. With no other choice, they stood outside between the buildings. Inside one of the company buildings, they could see through a window, a sergeant and company clerk still working. The sergeant came out to see what was happening and stood next to Riki. After a minute or two, he chuckled and said, "Watch this," as he picked up a hand full of road gravel and tossed it up on the roof creating the sound of gun shots. The reaction was instantaneous. The clerk leaped up and ran screaming from the building as if the VC were hot on his trail. Everyone doubled over with laughter including Riki. She said, "Suddenly I realized what a cruel joke it was for the poor PFC who was frightened out of his wits. I was ashamed of myself."

On another occasion, when Riki was on vacation, Harriet Moore, an Area Director, came to work with me until Riki returned. Harriet, an ex-WAC from WWII and Korea, was probably in her late forties, but her hair was snow white. In stature, she was only five feet five, but she seemed much bigger. The most distinctive things about her were her broad shoulders and a voice that sounded like walking on gravel. I never saw her without a Lucky Strike dangling from her lips. The men loved her like an eccentric grandmother, and she loved them. Her speech was punctuated with Army jargon, and her direct, rough manner of speaking made them feel comfortable with her. She was wonderful to me and she mesmerized me with her stories of WWII and living through the bombing in Europe. She was the most self-reliant woman I had ever met and I admired her.

One night about midnight, the siren blared and it seemed like the world was being blown up. The "boom, boom, thud, shudder, shudder," was deafening and flashes of light were everywhere, like lightning in a thunder storm. I grabbed my two-toned robe and took off for the back door. I didn't even think of Harriet until I reached the back door, but I didn't stop. I yelled over my shoulder,

"Harriet, get up! It's a mortar attack!" and kept running.

When I finally got to the bunker, I realized, "Oh my gosh, I left her in the hootch." I began to feel guilty. About that time, she crawled into the bunker, a cigarette between her lips, her cigarette pack and her lighter in her hand. She must have stopped to light up before she got to the bunker.

I guess I knew from that point on that I was not a hero, but I sure was a survivor!

Years later, I found out from the Special Services girls who served in CuChi after I left, that the Command built a bunker in the backyard of the hootch. It was located right outside the back door and it was so big that the carpenters built benches along the wall so the girls wouldn't have to sit on the dirt floor. When it was completed, the girls persuaded the communications guys to install a telephone with a cord long enough to reach into the bunker. When they had a mortar attack the girls called their in-country friends to give them a real-time description of the action. They also stocked their private bunker with beer, champagne and C-rations!

Wish I'd thought of that.

Our attack instructions.
Courtesy of Terri Zuber

Program interruptions were taken in stride.
Courtesy of Terri Zuber

Humor helped any situation.
Courtesy of Terri Zuber

10

ALMOST MY WORST NIGHTMARE

"Louie, Louie" by The Kingsmen played at the Ilikai East Service Club constantly and the refrain bounced around in my head night and day.

CuChi, VietNam, 1967

My worst nightmare was not being hit by a mortar or rocket, although there were plenty of opportunities for that to happen. It was not being shot by a sniper or sapper. My greatest fear was being taken prisoner by the Viet Cong or NVA. We carried I.D. cards that said in English we were non-combatants, but even the Vietnamese who spoke enough English to work with the Americans usually couldn't read English. Why would we think that the Viet Cong could read it or would honor it? It was just one of the in jokes among us girls. While we all laughed and made light of the possibility, I didn't think I'd survive as a POW.

During my first three months in CuChi I rarely got a full night's sleep because of the mortar and rocket attacks. Lack of sleep and fatigue were common conditions in the war zone causing us to run on automatic pilot much of the time, but Riki viewed life in the war zone with a well-developed sense of humor which made it easier to adjust to our many inconveniences like sand, heat, humidity, cold showers, the outhouse, mess hall food, C-rations, mortar attacks, and running out of water. There always seemed to be a problem with the water supply. Potable water was precious, and sometimes there was even a problem with water for bathing not only for us but for the guys. To counter this problem, signs were posted for the men to see in all company areas and in the men's shower areas saying: "Conserve water, shower with a buddy." We could never catch the guys who kept putting them up in our Ilikai East Service Club.

Six months before I arrived, the command built our hootch near the Service Club located in the medical administration company area. Prior to that time, my predecessor lived with the Red Cross girls and nurses near the hospital and miles from the club. The new hootch was conveniently close to the club, but there were disadvantages that we didn't recognize until later.

The only time I spent in our hootch was to rest and sleep. The place was bare and uncomfortable. It was hot and dusty inside the hootch during the dry season because the wind blew the sand in through the screened, louvered walls. Before going to bed, I had to shake the sand out of the sheets. In the rainy season, it was humid and damp. The hootch consisted of two bedrooms, living room, and a wide spot in the hallway we called the kitchen where a set of cabinets with a counter top was built against the wall. There was no sink, running water, or appliances, but we called it our kitchen because it's where we kept the potable water jug, our C-rations and our booze.

The Army issue furniture was not particularly comfortable and the lighting, except for a bedside lamp, was terrible: too dim to read by and too bright for ambiance. We didn't have any amenities like television, radio, or kitchen facilities. Our potable water supply was a large glass water jug that was re-filled irregularly. One of us had to be at the hootch for the delivery of the potable water and it was always difficult to coordinate our schedule with water delivery truck drivers. One morning getting ready for work I discovered that we had no water in the hootch. The only makeup I wore was a brand of mascara that required a small amount of water. Since there was none, I dampened the mascara brush with some stale beer left over from the night before. No one ever noticed.

    The medical company supported us with mess facilities and other basic services, like water, electricity, bunker access, and what I called outhouse maintenance. The Army called it burning the shitpots. The back door of the building was a screen door with only a hook and eye latch which opened out into a yard of sand surrounded by an eight foot solid board fence. The gate to the fence was located on the side of the yard adjoining the medical company. It was locked with a large rusty bar latch which never seemed to get any easier to open even though it was our well-used path to the bunkers.

    CuChi had been the site of heavy fighting during VietNam's war with the occupying French forces in the 1940s and '50s. The Vietnamese built tunnels throughout the region and made it an underground haven for their fighters. The Americans built the base camp on top of the tunnels not knowing of their existence. We were not aware of the tunnels but were aware of the constant Viet Cong activity around the camp directed at us regularly in the form of mortars and rockets. We ran to a bunker probably three nights a week.

    In our back yard, a boardwalk led to two small buildings which were built against the fence. One was an outhouse or latrine and the other, a shower house. They were located against the fence for a couple of reasons. The latrine had half of a fifty-five gallon drum (the shitpot) underneath each hole. There was a small square hole cut in the wall which was the fence, just large enough to allow the drums to be pulled out from the back of the latrine so that the contents could be burned at scheduled times.

    The latrine had two holes and no toilet paper holders. The shower house was a little shack next to it also built against the backyard fence. It was empty except for a shower head with a pull cord in the middle of the building, and pallets covering the dirt floor.

Our shower and latrine in the back yard.

It was an adventure to enter either the latrine or shower to see what creatures were occupying the buildings, day or night. On the roof of the shower building was a fifty-five gallon drum of water. The GIs, who delivered water, climbed a ladder from outside the fence to the roof of the shower to fill the tank every two or three days. In spite of the heat and humidity, the water was too cold for a shower early in the morning or at night when we got home. During the day, the sun warmed it and by afternoon it was the perfect temperature for a shower. Riki and I took turns returning to the hootch to shower in the afternoons, making sure we weren't showering when the water truck came to fill the tank. It was an odd and complicated schedule, but it worked.

Our front yard was also a sandbox, but it was surrounded by concertina wire or rolled barbed wire. There was a boardwalk from our front door to a small bridge across a drainage ditch. A street light illuminated the front yard and a spotlight lighted the backyard.

The hootch was a football field away on the opposite side of the street from the Service Club, but that was sometimes an obstacle course. We crossed the front yard, walked over the bridge covering the drainage ditch which became a raging torrent during heavy rains,

The front porch and yard of our hootch.

then walked across a dirt road, across another bridge and drainage ditch to the boardwalk, and up two steps into the club. It wasn't a long walk, except during the monsoon season which was about half of the year, when the rain was so hard you couldn't see your hand in front of your face, and didn't dare go out, for fear of being washed away. Otherwise it wasn't a bad walk at all.

    The Ilikai East Service Club was a thatched-roof structure with half walls and screens with shutters propped up during the day, then let down and latched at night. The shutters provided some cover when it rained, but while they were open all day the sand and wind blew through the building. We had fans to keep us cool, when the wind wasn't blowing and we had electricity.

    The Club while very small had the same supplies and equipment as any other club. The guys dubbed a small stage in one corner the "Hole in the Wall," and other than the pool and ping pong tables, it was the most popular spot in the Club. The men played our musical instruments, formed bands, and had jam sessions on the stage often. There was no shortage of talent among our GIs.

The Ilikai East Service Club in CuChi, VietNam in 1967.

    Programming was the same in VietNam as Korea, except the GIs were in and out of combat in the jungle and in and out of the base camp. We had fewer regulars to get to know or to depend on for help. The men were tired, hot and dirty, and while happy to help, it was hard to ask a guy to work who just came out of the jungle. All they wanted was a place to rest and get out of the sun. The Club had no running water or bathrooms. The closest bathroom for me was the latrine at our hootch. The men used the piss tubes or latrine in the nearest company area.

    Our office was located next to the checkout counter at the Club's entrance. It was not a room, but was a row of file cabinets forming one wall and three plywood half walls. It was open allowing the air or sand to flow through, and so we could see everything going on in the Club, but likewise, everyone could see us. Privacy was nonexistent.

Every day was the same for the men, so we tried to make holidays different. For Memorial Day, we decided a cookout would be a special treat for the men after the more serious ceremonies to honor the day. Our friends at several mess halls agreed to give us hamburgers, hot dogs, buns, and all the condiments. One mess sergeant volunteered to bake us a huge sheet cake with red, white and blue frosting. We bought soft drinks, paper plates, napkins, and cups at the PX. A group of guys who formed a band agreed to play for us. It promised to be a fun day.

Memorial Day was bright and sunny, hot and humid, much like every other day, but it started earlier than usual for us. Riki and I decorated the club with red, white, and blue crepe paper and flags. The vehicle we requested to drive me to the mess halls to pick up the food arrived promptly at 8:00 a.m. and it took a couple of hours to get to each mess hall that donated something for the party. I returned to the club in time to direct the guys setting up tables and grills, and to cover the tables with bright colored plastic tablecloths and little flags for centerpieces.

A covered patio was our stage and several other covered picnic tables provided plenty of seating for our hungry GIs. It looked colorful and festive. Our volunteer chefs arrived to start the coals and set out the cooking paraphernalia by 10:00 a.m., so the food would be ready by noon when the crowd was expected. Hungry GIs began arriving at 11:30 a.m. Riki and I spent the next three hours serving hot dogs, hamburgers, potato chips, cake and soft drinks in between running back and forth keeping the condiments stocked. It was exhausting, but fun.

Riki had to leave as soon as the cookout was over to take time sheets, reports, and requisitions to our Saigon headquarters. She caught a chopper late that afternoon in time to get to the temporary

The Memorial Day cookout, CuChi, VietNam, 1967

quarters in Saigon before curfew. I recruited several guys to help clean up. The program for the evening was a movie and popcorn. Volunteers popped the corn and ran the projector, so I wouldn't have much to do.

I closed the club as usual at 10:00 p.m. and the two EMs (enlisted men) on duty walked me to the bridge in front of our hootch to make sure I got home all right. It had been a long, tiring day and was the time of the month that drained me of energy making me feel generally lousy. All I could think of was a good night's sleep. The water in the tank for the shower was ice cold so I just sponged off, put on my pajamas and laid out my robe at the foot of my bunk.

Reading was out of the question because my eyes kept closing, so I turned out the light and fell asleep. During the night, I had the sensation of a feather touching my elbow. It felt like the wings of a butterfly fluttering against my arm. I remember brushing my arm. The second time I felt the touch, l rolled over and looked directly into the eyes of a black man. He was so dark I couldn't see him at first. What happened next cannot be explained except I believe the good Lord was taking care of both of us.

In my half sleep, I thought I was still in the Service Club and swung my legs over the edge of the bed to the floor, took his arm, scolding him and saying, "You know you're not supposed to be here! You're going to be in real trouble if anyone catches you. Come with me and I'll show you how to get out the back way."

"It's your period, isn't it?" he whispered.

Stunned, my mind raced to understand what he said and figure out what I was going to do next. All I wanted to do was get rid of him, so I mumbled something like, "Uh huh."

By this time we had reached the backdoor and I realized that the latch was unhooked. I opened the screen door, pointed to the shower building, "You can get over the fence by climbing on the shower building and using the ladder on the other side so no one will see you leave."

"Yeah, I know," he said softly.

It hit me, that's the way he had come in.

He said something like, "I'll come back in a couple of days," and walked slowly toward the shower house.

Watching him until he disappeared over the roof, I leaned back against the wall and tried to catch my breath. I latched the little hook and eye latch. Dazed and disoriented, I began to realize what had happened. Had I just escaped being raped and maybe murdered in my bed?

It was still dark out and I had no idea of what time it was. I sat down and stared at the phone not knowing who to call or what to say.

The sun was just coming up when I picked up the phone and asked the operator for the Military Police. A voice answered, "Provost's Office," and I said, "A man came into my hootch last night." There was a silence. The operator said, "Is he still there, Ma'am?"

"No."

"Can you hold on a minute, Ma'am?"

It occurred to me that he didn't know what to do either. All I could think of was that old character actor, William Bendix, whose classic line was, "What a revolting development this turned out to be!"

Another male voice came on the phone and said, "Ma'am, someone will be there very shortly."

I dressed in my uniform, ready for work, and waited for someone to come. About 45 minutes later, there was a knock at the door. I opened the door to two CID (Criminal Investigation Division) men in civilian clothes. They stood looking at me uncomfortably for several seconds which seemed much longer to me. Finally, one said, "Did you call the MPs this morning to report a break-in?" I figured out later that they were uncomfortable because they didn't know if I'd been raped or not. They introduced themselves as Mr. Miller and Mr. Connor.

Connor asked me to tell them what happened. "Can you describe the man?"

Miller, said, "Think carefully. Can you remember anything unusual about him?"

"Sorry, all I know is that he was black."

Then Miller said, "I know this is uncomfortable, but it would help us if you could remember any little detail about him. Let's try something. Close your eyes. Now, breathe deeply and think back, breathe, you are at the back door and he's standing in front of you on the stoop. Breathe. Keep your eyes closed and tell me what you see."

In spite of the fact there were two officers with me, I felt lightheaded and weak trying to relive the experience. Suddenly, "white sneakers" popped into my head and I blurted out, "He was wearing white sneakers and how odd they looked with his fatigues." Then I remembered something else, "His hair was parted in an unusual way, to the side but almost in the middle."

Miller patted my hand and said, "Good that helps. You're going to see this man again and when you do, you'll recognize him instantly. When it happens, call me immediately."

I never wanted to see the man again, so I hoped that wouldn't happen. It was impressive that the breathing exercise had helped me remember something, even though I still could not see or imagine the man's face or any other distinguishing characteristics. It made me wonder if Miller might be right about seeing the man again. The interview ended. Miller said "I'll be in touch, and if you think of anything else call me." They left.

I felt alone, vulnerable, and thought, They should have done something. Like, how about a real back door we could lock instead of a latched screen door? And what about taking down the ladder on the outside of the fence to our shower tank, that open invitation to our backyard? How about a guard? I went to work.

Riki returned late that afternoon and got a "blow by blow" description of what happened to me during the night and what happened with the investigators. She was horrified, and neither of us could decide which was worse, the incident or the response by the CID. After work, back at the hootch, we had a couple of drinks before I felt relaxed and safe enough to go to bed.

Every day for the next couple of weeks, I found myself looking over my shoulder, expecting to see the would-be attacker. Every night I was terrified that he would come again. Our friends were concerned for us and one of my friends, Tim Thompson, was particularly worried. Tim was a first lieutenant in the infantry. He was tanned, well built, and had big, soft, warm eyes. A Bostonian, he was a quiet, thoughtful man, with a deep, well-modulated voice that made me feel safe and protected. He called me every evening when he could and always drove by to check on me when he was off duty. One afternoon he called me at the Club, which was unusual. "Can we meet at your hootch?" he asked. I thought it was strange but agreed.

"I'm being transferred and leaving right away. I don't feel good about leaving and I want you to take this for protection." He pulled out a 45mm revolver and handed it to me. It was a scary moment. Not that I didn't know how to use it. My dad had taught me how to fire one when I was a kid; and I had qualified with a 45mm on a firing range in Korea just a few years earlier. Hard as I tried, I couldn't imagine shooting anyone, especially an American soldier. Having a weapon of any kind was a violation of my non-combatant status, my contract with Special Services and grounds for dismissal. "Tim, I don't know what to say. I am sorry you're leaving, but I can't take this weapon. It scares me and I can't imagine using it. I might shoot the wrong person."

While he said that he understood, it didn't make him feel any better about not being there for me. I was sorry to see him go and we promised each other to write, to keep in touch.

Days went by without anything happening. One day Riki and I were having lunch as usual at the medical company mess hall. When we finished, I took my tray back to the window to the kitchen and there, standing in the hallway to the kitchen, wearing fatigues, sneakers, and apron was the soldier I feared. My insides turned to jelly; it felt like the room moved. As soon as I could make my feet move, I left. When we were outside, I told Riki.

We rushed across the street to the club to call Mr. Miller. "The soldier who broke into my quarters works in the Medical Administration mess hall next to our hootch and I just saw him."

He said, "Okay, I'll be right there and we'll go get him."

"What! I can't go back there again. I can describe him now and you'll recognize him." I was panicked.

He arrived within twenty minutes. He had to convince me to go with him. "I know it's uncomfortable for you," he said. "But you have to point him out in person before I can arrest him."

I had no choice. We walked across the dirt road and into the empty mess hall. There was a lot of clanging of trays, loud talking and laughter coming from the kitchen area. The mess hall seemed to have shrunk in size. It was so small and close, it felt like I was walking in a tunnel with no way out.

I stepped through the kitchen door with Miller close behind me and ran right into my would-be attacker. He was just inches away from me when I pointed at him and muttered, "That's him." I turned and ran for the door.

Back at the club, I told Riki what happened and breathed a sigh of relief that the mystery was solved and I didn't have to sleep with one eye open anymore.

I didn't see Miller that day, but the next day, Riki and I were at our desks in the club when he came to see me. Miller sat at my desk with his back to the doorway. Just as he was explaining that the soldier had been arrested, confined to his company area and I would never, with emphasis, ever see him again, I looked up to see my would-be attacker walking along the half wall toward the office doorway. He stopped at the doorway, looked at both of us, then stepped up to my desk.

Miller looked like he'd swallowed a worm. The blood drained from his face. I felt a sort of numbness starting in my solar plexus and spreading throughout my body. I couldn't speak and I couldn't move.

The soldier stood before me, sweat pouring down his face, wringing his hat, and swaying slightly. He said, "I'm sorry if I frightened you. I didn't mean to hurt you."

I couldn't hear what I said or if I said anything. The three of us were frozen in place. We just stood there for what seemed like a long, long time.

Miller jumped up and grabbed him by the arm and dragged him toward the front door. Over his shoulder he shouted, "I'm sorry; I don't know how this happened. I'll take care of it."

Riki and I looked at each other in disbelief. Had it really happened?

Suddenly Riki said, "Did he say that the man was confined to his company area? That's where our hootch is!"

Riki and I went to see the commanding general. I explained that the soldier who broke into our hootch was confined to his company area which was our back yard and his job was at the mess hall where we ate three meals a day. "How can I feel safe knowing that he's there all the time?" The general was not sympathetic to my situation and, showing his irritation, made a comment to the effect that I was being unreasonable, ending our meeting.

Just when I thought it couldn't get worse, it did. Two days later during our monthly Birthday party, I was serving cake at the checkout counter when the soldier and two of his buddies came through the cake line.

He looked me straight in the eye and said, "They're going to transfer me to the 196th Light Infantry to be killed."

I lost my grip of the cake server and dropped a piece of cake on the tray. I didn't know what to say. I didn't want him to get killed, but the fear in my gut wouldn't allow me to be anywhere near him. "Here, have a piece of cake and take it back to your company area. I'm sorry but you can't stay here." He and his friends looked at each other, took the pieces of cake, and left.

It was the proverbial straw that broke the camel's back. I didn't call Miller. I didn't call the police. I did call Special Services Headquarters and volunteered to go anywhere.

My orders to report to Special Services Headquarters in Saigon arrived immediately. I was too tired to be either excited or worried about a new assignment. I just hoped I could get some sleep. My only positive thought was, at least it wasn't my worst nightmare.

11

I'VE BEEN KICKED OUT OF BETTER PLACES

The Mamas and the Papas singing "Monday, Monday" and "California Dreaming" remind me of DiAn's Stateside Service Club

CuChi, VietNam, 1967

    The chopper arrived at exactly 8:00 a.m. to take me and all my possessions, two suitcases, to our Headquarters in Saigon to report to the Director of Service Clubs to see what my next assignment might be. I was tired of being scared and unhappy, and in a hurry to get out of CuChi. The jeep dropped me off at the terminal shack on the flight line and one of the GIs helped me load my luggage on the chopper. As soon as I got on board, I buckled up and anticipated the cool air of the higher altitude. As we took off, I saw the body bags on the runway. I stared with fascination, not wanting to, but unable to look away. My attention was jerked away by the thrust of the takeoff. In seconds we were airborne and too high to be hit by the small arms fire. The image of the black bags was burned in my brain and I couldn't shake it out of my head. The bags were too small for our guys, they must have been Vietnamese, I told myself and tried to forget it. We landed at TanSonNhut where a jeep was waiting to take me to headquarters.

Miss Baker greeted me, "How was your flight?"

"Fine, it's always cooler up there than down here." I managed a smile and didn't mention the body bags. Our meeting was cordial and low key. Miss Baker was one of the most diplomatic people I had ever met, so she didn't mention CuChi or the reason I requested a transfer. It was probably a prerequisite of her GS level position since she worked closely with the Army brass. After some small talk, she said, "We just opened a new Service Club at DiAn. Are you familiar with the 1st Infantry Division? It's known as The Big Red One."

"Not really," I said with feigned interest.

"DiAn is the Division Headquarters. We have two Club Directors, Joyce and Nancy, assigned there now and they're doing a great job, but I need a Director to open a Club in Dong Tam in the Delta. Nancy volunteered, but she can't leave DiAn until we find a Program Director to take her place. We need someone with your programming and in-country experience. I'd like you to accept the transfer to DiAn."

It was the same as when I came in country, we were trying to open as many clubs as possible with the fewest people. Riki and I worked well together, we were friends and I would have preferred to work with her, but I couldn't stay in CuChi any longer, so any place would do. In any case, I didn't think I had a choice. I accepted.

The next day I was on a chopper to DiAn and the Big Red One. A jeep picked me up at the chopper pad and drove me to the Service Club. The roads were just as dusty as CuChi and the weather was just as hot and humid. The landscape was void of any foliage, but it seemed to be a more permanent camp. There were some block buildings on the camp, which was unheard of at CuChi.

The servicemen had named the club the Stateside Service Club. It was a single-story tropical building with a real roof, not like the thatched ones in CuChi. Next to the Service Club, was a series of block buildings that housed a laundry and barber shop. The sign above the doorway of the laundry read "Kansas Cleaners."

Above: Stateside Service Club in DiAn, VietNam, 1967.
Below: The Kansas Laundry

Our shopping center in DiAn, VietNam, 1967.

    On the other side of the club was a swimming pool protected by a ten foot concrete wall. It was there when they built the camp, like the laundry and barber shop buildings. The pool wasn't used that much; I don't remember that it was ever open, but I do remember the GIs who were in charge of pool maintenance sneaked four of us girls in one night so we could swim for a while. The pool was heavily chlorinated which bleached our swim suits two shades and lightened the color of our tanned skin at least one shade. Modesty, as well as the disapproval of our Special Services supervisors, dictated that we not be seen in our swim suits, so we never used it during the day. It wasn't much fun swimming in the dark, so we never went back again at night.

The swimming pool at DiAn, VietNam, 1967.

    All of the camp buildings were surrounded with sandbags and concertina wire. Our hootch was a long, large tropical building with the extra protection of a moat-like ditch surrounding it with a little bridge. There were three buildings in our area, the hootch itself, the latrine, and the shower building. Inside the hootch was a living room with a round table, some wood frame chairs with ersatz leather cushions and a small bar that was probably made for us at the Crafts Shop. The windows were covered with dark colored curtains and a grass-weave rug covered part of the dusty vinyl floor. In the bar we kept C-rations, booze, and soft drinks. The rest of the building was divided into ten cubicles, with six-foot plywood partitions instead of walls. Each of our cubicles was about eight by ten feet, furnished with a bunk, a dresser, and a rack for hanging our uniforms. The hootch was about a city block from the Service Club, and only a couple of blocks from the mess hall, the Chapel, and the Officers' Club.
    The most attractive thing about DiAn was that it hadn't been mortared in human memory, which was the length of a year's tour of

duty. That was thrilling. The second most attractive thing was that our quarters were shared with the Red Cross girls, so there were ten girls under our roof and I would never be left alone. A third most attractive thing about DiAn was that a guard was on duty every night. The newest soldier in country pulled guard duty at our hootch, because he was more concerned about the possibility of the camp being overrun by Viet Cong, and mortar attacks, than he was interested in us girls.

The path to our hootch in DiAn.

Above: Our bunker and clothesline. Corner of our hootch on right side.
Below: Our shower and latrine.

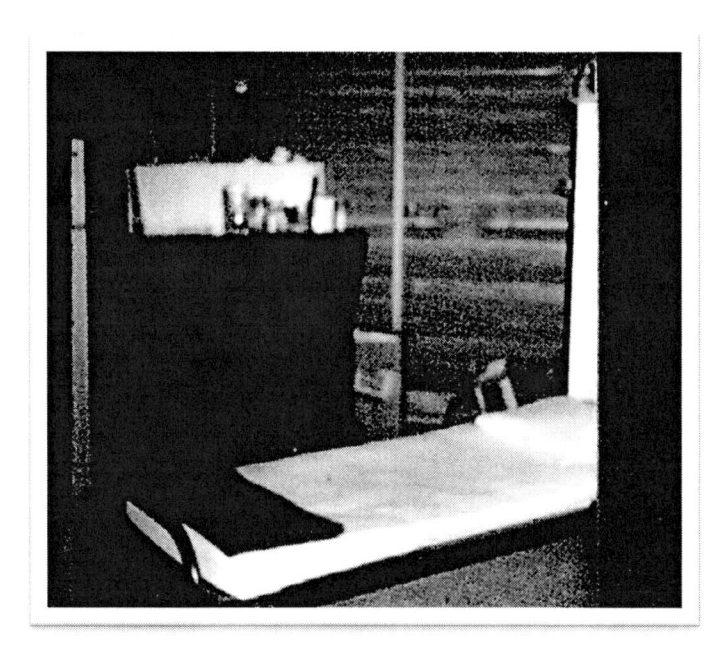

My bedroom area in the hootch in DiAn.

    Other than these wonderful attractions, the Service Club was well furnished and well-staffed. The furniture was the same Army issue, but Joyce and Nancy had been thoughtful enough to cover the bare vinyl floors with grass-weave rugs and the small windows with curtains to make the place look homey. There was even a real water fountain against the back wall next to the kitchen. It looked great but never worked. Whoever ordered it didn't remember that we didn't have running water.

Inside the DiAn Stateside Service Club, 1967.
The water fountain in the back next to the kitchen serving window never worked because we never had running water.

Above: I'm taking names for the next pool tournament at the DiAn Stateside Service Club.
Below: The Service Club pool room is visible in the background.

The Checkout Desk was in front of the door to our offices at the DiAn Stateside Service Club. The kitchen door and serving window are on the left and the pool room door is in the center.

A young sergeant by the name of Dixon, a hardcore infantry man, was one of our staff members. He had been wounded in the leg and had a distinct limp. The wound was so severe he couldn't be sent back into combat so he was assigned to the Service Club to work for three months until his DEROS (Date of Estimated Return from Overseas). Happiness to him was working in the Service Club, because it meant he didn't have to go back into the jungle. I remember Dixon telling me about his wife, Anka. They met and fell in love in Germany during his last tour of duty. His version of the story was that they had not talked about getting married, when his orders transferring him back to the States came earlier than expected. According to him, it was a sad but bearable goodbye. A short time after he arrived at his new duty station in the States, Anka unexpectedly appeared. He was so impressed that she loved him enough to follow him all the way back to the United States that he proposed immediately. They had only been married a year when his orders came for VietNam. When he spoke of Anka, he tried to sound gruff and masculine, but it was with a camouflaged tenderness. He couldn't mention her name without smiling.

Sgt. Dixon was a quiet and formal man. He never called me by my first name and I never knew his. He never spoke about his wound or the time he spent in combat. He just smiled and hummed while he mopped and waxed the floors, made coffee, and any other chores we needed done.

The GIs had different names for being in combat: "in the bush," "in the boonies," or "in the jungle" were the most common ones used in polite company. The soldier who talked about going on patrols or living in the jungle had probably never seen a day of combat. The ones who didn't talk about it were the ones who had been there. They had survived the almost intolerable living conditions: living in the swamp, being wet all the time, fearing a sniper behind every bush or a booby trap with each step, battling insects, avoiding snakes, seeing friends wounded and killed. Sgt. Dixon was one of them and I respected him.

Every morning that I was scheduled to open the Club, I arrived at 8:00 a.m. Before I reached the front door, I could hear the strains of the Mamas and the Papas singing "Monday, Monday" or "California Dreaming." They were Dixon's favorite group and he played their tapes over and over all day long. When I opened the door, I could smell the familiar floor wax and brewing coffee, smells that always remind me of a Service Club.

We knew the men on the base camp who were not combat troops. The combat troops only came in from the jungle for very short breaks. They usually had little time and spent it getting a shower, sleeping and eating a hot meal. Since they didn't stay long at the base camp, we never got to know them. The ones we did talk to, often thanked us for being there. They would tell us that they were thrilled to sit in a dry, cool place. It was no small pleasure for them to read a book, a magazine, or just sit and listen to music. The club was a safe haven for them and they were wonderful, respectful, and appreciative.

Like the other clubs, we offered a program every day and sometimes more than one a day on the weekends and holidays. Even though the weekends and holidays were regular workdays, we tried to make them special in some way. One of the special events I planned at DiAn was a Fourth of July Festival and Parade.

I invited as many American girls as I could, civilians who worked in Saigon, Red Cross girls from different camps, and a couple of new Special Services girls who were not yet assigned to Clubs. I planned as many active events as would fit in a twelve-hour day. We featured a pie eating contest, a cookout, athletic competitions for prizes, and a parade around the base camp with decorated Army jeeps and trucks. The men were great, and happy to participate in all our silly games and to meet the girls. They were stunned to see so many round eyes in one place.

One of our decorated parade floats with my Irish friend, Claire, and our clown.

The girls served the refreshments, presented the awards and prizes and just generally were there for the soldiers. During the parade, they sat on top of the vehicles waving like celebrities as the men lined up along the road and leaned out of windows to wave and cheer. One of our guys agreed to dress up in a clown outfit. He looked and acted like Clarabelle from the Howdy Doody T.V. show and made everyone laugh.

Awards for tournaments and contests were presented by our visiting "round eyes."
Above: Joyce, my Club Director and my friend, Claire Hoban.

Barbara Jay has some fond memories of her tour in VietNam partly because she met her husband, Roger Laderoute when at Long Binh, but also because she was pleased to do her part to support our soldiers. She remembers programming an American fashion show and parade at the Tiki Hut Service Club in Can Tho.

> Six other Service Club 'round-eyes' flew by choppers to CanTho to help us make the fashion show a success. We had a crazy Special Forces unit near our camp who attended the Service Club sometimes. The fashion show interested them so they decided to participate in the fun. They made me a Vietnamese camouflage shirt and a very-very mini skirt to model in the show, and to match my outfit they gave me an

M-16 as an accessory. Of course, they didn't teach me how to shoot it. The Club was packed for the show, standing room only. It was a smashing success, the guys loved it.

Another of my favorite programs was a Thanksgiving Day parade with a contest for the best parade float. The units at Can Tho tried to outdo each other in creating the most unique and elaborate float by decorating Army vehicles with anything they could find. I invited my area supervisor, Ann Campbell, to come from Saigon to judge the floats. Six floats made up the parade that drove throughout the base camp ending at the mess hall for a big Thanksgiving dinner. I forgot what first prize was, but I remember the first place winner was a jeep decorated with a turkey made of toilet paper rolls! The only downside was that the GIs used all their existing and future toilet paper supplies to create the float! Sacrifices for fun and entertainment were small stuff and nobody sweated the small stuff.[10]

Barbara Jay in the costume the Special Forces unit made for her.

Judy Jenkins Gaudino was the Program Director for the club in DiAn after I left. She has some fond memories of DiAn. She placed a sign over the library books to attract guys' attention: Take a book to bed instead. "It never failed to make them smile," she said.

At Christmas she had only been in country for a short time and everything was still new. She decided on her own to take some "Christmas spirit" to the men who had guard duty on the perimeter on Christmas Eve. She made up some gift baskets with candy, cigarettes, cards, soap, shaving lotion, razors, and other small gifts, donned a Santa suit, commandeered a jeep and went to every guard post. The posts were built on stilts and were accessible only by ladder. In the dark wearing a bright red and white Santa suit, Judy climbed to the top of each guard post and gave each soldier a Christmas basket. When she returned to the Club, her worried Director explained to her calmly and quietly that she was a big red and white target for the Viet Cong snipers and sappers. Judy was stunned, but learned a lesson she never forgot: never make trips at night without permission and proper protection again.[11]

Judy Jenkins Gaudino in VietNam, ca. 1967-68.

I had been in country for almost six months and by then the heat, humidity, long hours, and interrupted sleep had taken their toll on me. We didn't have the constant mortar attacks at night in DiAn like we did in CuChi, but I could never quite convince myself that it was all right to sleep through the night. At times it felt like I would never get home, that I would live my life in this world of stress, mortars, and fear of dying, or worse. Sometimes it felt like the world was in constant motion. Other times it felt like time stood still. The GIs joked that if you slept eight hours a night, your one-year tour of duty would seem to be only eight months. The crazy calculation was something like eight hours was one-third of a twenty-four hour day which would reduce the number of days by one-third of the year leaving eight months. The only problem was that no one ever got to sleep eight hours a night.

    The officers at the Division headquarters did not seem to have the esprit de corps that existed at other base camps where I'd been. While they were polite, they seemed distant. I rarely visited the Officers' Club although some of the Red Cross girls had friends among the officers and I was often invited to join them. Whether I brought some of the fearful feelings with me from CuChi, or was too tired to make an effort, I didn't try to make friends among the officers. I felt isolated and on my own. The Club Director, Joyce Blevins, was a wonderful woman who was calm and reasonable. Her Midwestern roots showed in her common sense, her stamina, and her gentle understanding attitude. All of my hootch mates, the Donut Dollies (Red Cross girls) were pleasant, fun-loving, and easy going. Even in our pleasant environment, I couldn't shake the feeling of being betrayed by the Army in the way they had handled the incident at CuChi.

    One evening after work when I was tired and looking forward to a quiet night to read and get to bed early, Gay Nall, my Red Cross friend, asked me to go with her and several of the other girls to the Officers' Club to meet some of their friends who had just come from a combat area. They were only going to be in camp for that night, and then they would go back to into the bush. I tried making excuses not to go, but finally agreed. The officers were in fatigues and still wore the dust from the road and the sweat from the jungle, but they were so happy to be in camp and out of the field. They were drinking beer, laughing and having a good time when we arrived. We joined in. The group was loud and boisterous, but not disruptive. As they finished their beers, they stacked the cans in a pyramid on one of the tables. I was standing in front of the can pyramid when suddenly a can came sailing through the air just missing me, crashing into the stack of cans. I felt instant fear, then anger. I whirled around to see a major in dress uniform leaning against the bar for balance, with a pleased smirk on his face, glaring at me. He out- ranked all of our visiting friends, so no one moved. Instead of ignoring him as I should have, I marched up to him and demanded to know who he was and why he'd thrown the can at me.

He swayed a little because he was drunk and said in a loud voice, "Well, we don't have to ask who you are. Everyone knows you're just another camp follower!"

Stunned and shaking with anger, I left the club in tears. Growing up as a military brat, I was well aware of what the term "camp follower" meant. It was devastating to be called a whore. The best thing I could have done was ignore him. The second best thing I could have done was to punch him in the mouth, but I've never been a physical person and violence was not my first response, so I didn't do either.

Capt. Ted Sales, the Special Services Officer, happened to be in the club office and heard everything. He and my friend Gay caught up with me and walked me back to the hootch trying to console me. Ted said things like, "That guy is just a ring knocker (West Point graduate) who doesn't know squat about anything." I appreciated his efforts but it didn't help me. I can only think that it was an accumulation of things that made me overreact. That's what stress does to you, makes you do stupid things.

I was called into the base commander's office the next day. Colonel Nougat, the commander, was a small, nervous man who wore thick black rimmed glasses. His nickname among the troops was "Goober." He seemed uncomfortable and not pleased with the task of talking to me. He asked me to describe the episode. When I finished he said, "I'm sorry this happened. We don't tolerate bad behavior, and I'll have the Major make an apology in person." I thanked him for his time and left, thinking it would make a difference if the Major apologized.

Several days passed and finally on a Friday afternoon, Colonel Nougat came to the Service Club office where Joyce and I were working. His adjutant accompanied him. It was as though he needed protection or he was afraid to appear alone. "I came to apologize for the Major. He left on a plane for the States today and was unable to come himself."

I laughed to myself and thought the "good old boy" system is alive and well. I should have expected it. Then, without thinking, I blurted out, "Thank you, Colonel Nougat. But since the Major couldn't come to apologize for himself, I'm happy the rumor is circulating that he will not be promoted because of this incident and his behavior."

The colonel's eyes widened and his face went blood red. I thought he would explode when he whirled and stomped out of the office with his adjutant trailing behind him. Joyce said quietly, "I wish you hadn't said that."

When I returned to the club after dinner, Joyce told me that as soon as the colonel returned to his office he called our Special Services Headquarters shouting, "I want that woman out of my command immediately!"

Joyce helped me pack my bags. My orders were to report to Special Services Headquarters in Saigon immediately. A chopper was made available that evening and I was in the Director's office at 8:00 a.m. the next morning. I knew I was in big trouble but I couldn't quite care.

Instead of meeting in her office, the Director invited me to sit in the office lounge, have a cup of coffee and chat. I was emotionally drained, exhausted from lack of sleep. I was numb. When she asked if I'd like to go home, I broke down and cried. I didn't want to give up, I wanted to finish my tour. It was the honorable thing. I'd come to do my part for the war effort and I could not leave before the end of my tour. She handed me a box of Kleenex, and gave me time to recover.

"Why don't you take the weekend off, visit VungTau, rest, and then make your decision Monday. I'll make all the arrangements." It would have been exciting, but I was too distraught to care. I'd never been to VungTau but had heard that it was a charming French built town on the coast with the most beautiful white sand beaches.

It was even nicer than I'd been told but at that time any place would have seemed like heaven. After a couple of days of sleeping late, lying on the beach, dining at the hotel instead of a mess hall, I felt almost normal. I returned to the Headquarters in Saigon rested and with renewed determination to complete my tour of duty.

The weekend gave me time to get a better perspective of the situation. It was a stupid incident to which I overreacted and handled poorly. It was a revelation to realize how much I was suffering from the stress, the wear and tear of the war. My self-image suffered a major blow because I didn't know I could be vindictive. It was hard to admit to myself that I was not the person I thought I was.

Postscript:

I was transferred from DiAn to LongBinh in September, 1967, and TayNinh in November. Five months later, February, 1968, before the end of my tour, I received a formal letter from the Special Services Officer, 1st Infantry Division Headquarters, aka The Big Red One, offering me the position of Program Director for the Stateside Service Club in DiAn, VietNam. It was vindication for me. I was surprised and pleased that the command had invited me to return. My DEROS was March so I didn't have time to accept the invitation. Even if I had more time, I don't think I would have accepted the offer. I was too tired and the bad memories were still with me. In spite of all that, it was a nice gesture, and I appreciated it.

12

MEMORIES OF LONG BINH

"I Heard it Through the Grapevine" by Marvin Gaye played over and over in the Service Club and in my head while I was in Long Binh. I still remember the words.

VietNam, 1967

After DiAn, my new assignment was 90th Replacement Battalion at Long Binh, to help build the new Service Club. I suppose the assignment was to give me a breather by putting me in a place where the tensions weren't so high and combat was not so visible, if that were possible. The Long Binh base camp was one of the largest in country, home to two hospitals, 24th Evacuation Hospital, 93rd Evacuation Hospital, Long Binh Jail, aka LBJ Ranch, a huge ammunition dump, and a number of other Army units. The base camp was dusty and without foliage although I remember a couple of scrawny trees next to our hootch. I had a separate room which was furnished exactly like my rooms in CuChi and DiAn. The Service Club was down a dirt road about three city blocks away. It was a nice walk except during the Monsoon season, when it seemed like you could swim or slide to work.

The 90th was a transient place, where the new soldiers came into country, stayed for a couple of days, and then were assigned to their units elsewhere in VietNam. It was also the last stop for the soldiers who had finished their one-year tour of duty before getting on that "Freedom Bird to go back to the World." Freedom Bird and the World were terms that the men used to describe boarding a plane for home to the "good old U. S. of A." Our clientele were those who were just arriving and fearful of what it was like to be in a war and those who were tired, relieved that they made it through their tour alive, and were on their way home. It was a combination of joyful and very solemn young men. For us it was easy to tell which was which just by looking at them. Those returning home were tanned, lean, and tired. Some of them who had spent too much time in combat in the boonies had eyes that looked vacant and distracted. It was called the thousand yard stare. The men who were new in country were usually pale faced, well-fed and nervous looking.

My assignment in LongBinh was only three months. Even though the ammunition dump was a regular target for the night attacks and the hospitals were often hit, the 90th was far enough away that I don't recall running for a bunker while I was there. My three months were uneventful, which was a good thing; but it was not without its issues. I joined June, the Club Director who had been in Long Binh for a few weeks, working with the Army Engineers to redesign a two-story barracks building to accommodate all the functions of a Service Club. June was a quiet young woman who had a strong background of managing recreational facilities much larger than most of our Service Clubs. There was an attractive air of confidence and self- assurance about her. She knew exactly how she wanted the Service Club to look, and exactly what the floor plan had to include. I learned a lot listening to her explain what equipment or furniture would be used in what part of the building, so that the floors would be reinforced, and where we needed open space for programming and card tables. She was diplomatic and patient with the Army Engineers and the carpenters who built barracks buildings only one way and did not allow for use as anything else. It was my first experience participating in the planning phase of a Service Club building. We had to think through all of the programs and services we had in the Club and what areas we needed, size, shape, and access. June did a masterful job. She had to be creative to deal with the lack of space, and one of her original designs solved the problem of the recording rooms. Usually in a Service Club, music and recording rooms provided space for the men to listen to taped music, or to record a tape, privately, to send home. But this barracks building was too small to accommodate more than one private room and that had to be a music room for our musical instruments. The men played the electric guitars at max volume and drummers played as loud as they could. One sound-insulated room was an absolute must.

Since we couldn't have separate rooms for the tape decks, she designed a configuration of four carrels for the carpenters to build. A carrel is a table with a sideboard on three sides to block the view in front and two sides of the occupant. In this case four carrels were set up in a square with electrical outlets in each, so that four people could sit in one area each with a tape deck and ear phones and not see or hear each other. It was minimum space for maximum usage. I thought it was ingenious.

The pool tables had to be located on the ground floor because of weight. Everything else had to be located based on the building size and shape, and not the way we would normally arrange things for programming and supervision purposes. It was a challenge, but she did a great job.

Because of the importance of the project, the Base Commander required that she work closely with him. When I arrived, she told me she had just about exhausted her diplomatic resistance to the Commander's advances. She was delighted to see me and from then on, I was the liaison between her and the Commander. She stayed at Long Binh only until the construction was completed and we had our grand opening. Then, either she or the Commander "arranged" for her transfer, which left me as Acting Club Director. Fortunately the Commander left me alone. Sometimes too alone, since I suspected that our supply requests were "delayed" and sometimes "lost," accidentally or on purpose. I guess it was his way of expressing his disapproval or revenge for the rebuff.

My most vivid memory from my LongBinh assignment was a visit to the 24th Evac Hospital. I knew that a number of the Special

Services girls and many of the Donut Dollies visited the hospitals to cheer up the wounded soldiers. It was one of the things I couldn't bring myself to do, but when tragedy struck, I could no longer avoid it.

The Black Horse Battalion of the 1st Infantry Division was a favorite of my Irish friend Claire Hoban who fell in love with the American soldiers and the American cause in VietNam while she and her friend Karen were on their 'round-the-world tour.

Gay Nall and some of our Black Horse friends at Lai Khe

Claire and Karen got jobs working for Ford Motor Company in the PX, selling brand new Fords to GIs who were finishing their tours of duty and returning home. The servicemen could pick and choose the features they wanted on any Ford, buy it at a huge discount and it would be delivered to them at home. It was a great program for all the military men. Claire and Karen worked separately and were limited to working at base camps with PXs and female quarters.

I met Claire when she worked at the P X at CuChi. She stayed with me and Riki. Claire was the most independent and self-reliant person I had ever met. If I were to choose my most unforgettable character it would be Claire. She was Irish; she was beautiful, untiring in her efforts to help the troops, and devoted to the U. S. Army soldiers. Among her regular routes was Lai Khe, home of "The Black Lions." I think she knew all of the GIs and officers by their first names. On one occasion, she had invited me, my Red Cross friend Gay and a number of other American girls to Lai Khe for a party. The base camp was an old French plantation. The main house was a beautiful French villa that served as the Officers' quarters, mess hall and club. It even included a sauna and massage room in the back of the villa. Before the party, we girls were given exclusive access to the sauna and the masseurs. I'd never had a massage before or visited a sauna, so it was quite a treat. I decided that the sauna was nice, but I could do without the massage. We were treated to an elegant steak dinner and dance with a live band. It was a wonderful party.

I had been in Long Binh only a few weeks when Claire called to give me the bad news. I could barely understand her on the phone because she was crying so hard. One of the units of the 1st Infantry, 28th Infantry Regiment, 2nd Battalion, known as The Black Lions, had been ambushed while on a search and destroy mission. The unit was almost wiped out. Those who survived were in the 24th Evac Hospital. Claire needed someone to go with her to see her friends. I couldn't refuse.

We took a taxi to the hospital. I had never seen her so upset. She'd been drinking the night before and had a raging hangover. She was so distraught that we had to stop the taxi at least once so she could get out to vomit. I didn't know if she'd make it, and I could do nothing to help her. It was early afternoon when we arrived at the hospital. We were directed to the ward where most of the men from the unit were. I was so concerned about Claire on the way, that I had no time to think of how I would control my own reactions when we finally saw our wounded friends. We were taken to the bed of the ranking officer, a young lieutenant named Jeff. His head was bandaged and the part of his face that showed was a purple color I'd never seen before or since. He was unrecognizable.

As soon as he saw us he stood up to greet us. Claire hugged him and began asking who was there and where each one was. Jeff was excited and grateful to see us. "Claire, how great to see you. The guys are a little down, but seeing you will perk 'em up." He spoke animatedly and seemed oblivious to his own wounds.
"Jeff, this is Sandra Lockney. She came to that party at Lai Khe we had a few months back. Did you two meet then?"
"Yes," and he added, "What a great party it was." I smiled and agreed. Jeff led us from bed to bed, greeting each man by name

and with some enthusiastic or positive comment, like, "Sam here had his feeding tube pulled yesterday and ate his first meal last night," or "Joe here is going home next week." I went on automatic pilot. So many of them had such severe wounds I wanted to cry. I knew that they would be sensitive to my reaction and think whatever they saw in my face would be the reaction they would see on the faces of their mothers, their sweethearts or their wives. With all the strength I could muster, I smiled, made small talk, and tried to act as if nothing bad had happened to them. Some of the men had head wounds with bandages covering their faces so they couldn't talk. We stopped by each bed, held a hand or patted an arm gently and said we came by to say hello and ask if we could do anything for them. When Claire paused to talk to someone, I stopped at a nearby bed.

A young redheaded, freckle-faced soldier was sitting up in bed watching us as we walked down the aisle. His leg was in bandages and he had bandages on his chest and head, but he had a big smile and blue eyes that hadn't lost their twinkle. "Hi, my name is Sandra. What's your name?"

"Red."

"Where are you from, Red?"

"Georgia." He just stared at me like I was a mirage.

"Really? I used to live in Albany. I went to Albany High School for two years. Where in Georgia?"

"Atlanta." He continued to stare with a look of wonder on his face.

"The big city, huh. I visited there once and saw Roger Williams play at the Henry Grady Hotel. It was grand. Can I do anything for you? Write a letter or get you something to read?" I finally broke the ice and he smiled and began to talk.

"Thanks, but I can't think of anything. The nurses take pretty good care of us," he said softly. "You could talk to my buddy over there. He can't talk now, but the nurses say he'll be able to when they take out the tubes and take off all the bandages on his face. Him and me have been together since I came in country. He was supposed to go home a month before me, but now we'll get to go home together."

"Sure, I'll go over and say hello. What's his name?" I asked.

"Jackson, Tony. He's from Alabama, Dothan, I think."

"O.K., Red. You concentrate on getting well and hope you get home soon. If you go home through Long Binh, come to the Service Club. That's where I work."

I found a chair and sat next to Tony Jackson. His eyes were glued to my face so I smiled and said. "Tony, I just talked to Red over there and he tells me that you two will probably be going home together soon." He could move his head a little, and he nodded yes. I said, "I just came by to visit with you a while. Can you write while you're in that position?" He nodded yes.

"Would you like writing paper?" He moved his head slightly sideways, no. "Can I get you something to read?" Again his movement said no, but his eyes squinted like he was smiling. I was at a loss for something to say that didn't require an answer and didn't sound stupid. "Red tells me that you're from Alabama. Is that right?" He nodded yes. "I've driven through Alabama but never lived there. I know it's hot and humid there in the summer, kinda like Georgia. I know you'll be happy to get home." His eyes squinted a smile again.

"Well, I guess I'd better say hello to some of your buddies before we leave. You take care of yourself Tony. Hope you get home soon." I left his bedside and walked to the next bed to say hello to a young black soldier who was lying flat because he had one leg in a cast suspended in air and one arm in a sling. He smiled and I said, "Hi. Where are you from?"

"Sopchoppy, ma'am." We talked for a few minutes and he told me about his small hometown in Florida. He eyes sparkled and he became animated telling me about the fishing in Sopchoppy. I asked if he knew when he would be going home and with a broad grin he said, "Soon, maybe."

We were probably only there a short time, but it seemed like forever. When it was time to go, we said goodbye and waved as we walked toward the door. Those who could, waved, smiled, or said "bye" and thanks for coming. Claire and I said, "Say 'Hi' to the World for us when you get home."

We rode in silence for a long time. Both of us were completely drained and numb from all the emotion. There is no way to describe the sadness and the overwhelming emotion that I felt. It was one of the most difficult and emotional experiences of my life. A lesson in humility made me realize I was not as strong as I thought. From then on, I knew exactly why I admired the nurses and doctors who treated the wounded day after day. They deserved the greatest respect and admiration for their dedication and devotion to the wounded. The Red Cross girls and the Special Services girls who visited the hospitals regularly had my respect and admiration too, because I couldn't do what they did. I never visited a hospital in VietNam again.

Life at Long Binh was pleasant in spite of the attitude of the base commander. While I was acting Club Director, Special Services Headquarters assigned a Recreation Specialist, Lynn Brooks, a new girl in country, to help me with the programming of the Club. It was fun to have a new girl bring new ideas and new energy to the Club, and Lynn had plenty of both. We worked together well and I was thrilled that she wanted to do something different and something that we knew the men would enjoy. She planned a Fashion Show. We invited as many round eyes as we could to be our models and all of them that could get away from their own Club for a day came. The fashions were parts of the combat uniform that we decorated as outlandishly as we could. We used colorful scarves, handkerchiefs, crepe paper, and paint. We did throw in some civilian dresses that we really wore, so the men wouldn't feel cheated. We made crepe paper flowers for the helmets. We pinned colorful handkerchiefs to the flack jackets. The poncho became a formal. All the girls contributed their own ideas. The show was named, "Fashions from the House of Flowers." Each of the models made up a silly sign and carried it around the stage. Some of the signs were: "Down with Guard Duty," "Long Binh Losers," "Saigon Warriors." The show was a great success and the men loved the fact that there were so many round eyes to talk to.

Above: I'm dressed in the latest high fashion helmet and flack jacket.
Below: Terry Condon wears the latest style poncho.

Above: Lynn Brooks designed a formal uniform of fatigues, black tape, crepe paper, and Filipino hat.
Below: Our Grand Finale with MP helmets and some real girl dresses to remind the guys of home.
L to R: Claire, Sandra, Riki, Lynn and Terry.

Above: Our own GIs made music for the Fashion Show entertainment.
Below: Our "MC" ad-libbed describing our outfits because we made them up as we went along. His descriptions and narrative each time one of us appeared on stage were amazing. The audience was in stitches for the entire show.

No matter how good a job we did, we couldn't please the commander. There was one incident I remember well. I was just finishing the evening program, a quiz game, and it was about 9:00 p.m. The program had gone well and the club was still crowded. Major Vaughn, the base commander's adjutant, and his clerk walked into the club. I had never seen him come into the club even in the daytime, much less at night. I supposed that he was the duty officer which was a rotating job among the officers and he was bored with nothing to do. He stopped to study one of our window air conditioners. I finished the program and approached him. "Hi, Major Vaughn, how are you this evening?"

He answered, "Fine."

"May I give you a tour of the club?"

"Thank you, but we've just walked through, and we're on our way out."

I was curious about the purpose of his visit, but didn't ask, and continued my usual routine, made the closing announcements and started putting away the program materials.

The next day, I received an official report indicating that there was an infraction of the rules that covered building maintenance. It took a while to get through the jargon, i.e. the citing of Regulation numbers, the military descriptions, etc., but I finally figured out that the report said that the air conditioner filters in the Service Club were dirty. It reminded me of the IG incident about dirty dishwater in the sink at Camp Howard in Korea. Remembering how my friend and Club Director, Kay had handled the incident, I dutifully completed the attached form with all the multiple copies and in the space to write the corrective action, I typed:

"Changed the filters."

Some people in the war didn't have enough to do.

There were other irritations when a command was not totally supportive of the Special Services Program. I learned early how to scrounge, barter, trade, and sometimes make midnight requisitions for the supplies we needed, when we couldn't get them through the normal channels. When a commanding officer considered us more a liability than an asset, sometimes paperwork got lost or filed in error and we didn't get what we needed. If my request for supplies wasn't filled or work orders for repairs to maintain the building were

An explanation of barter, comshaw, midnight requisition, our resourcefulness.
Courtesy of Terri Zuber

delayed or lost, I went to the source. The supply clerks, company clerks, plumbers, electricians, motor pool mechanics and everyone else who did the work, frequented the Service Club and I knew them. All I had to do was phone or visit the company area, exchange something we had that they needed, or explain my dilemma and the problem would be solved. In a way, it made me feel capable and resourceful. It taught me self-reliance, independence and it was fun. Like I said, the GIs were wonderful; the officers, sometimes, could be a pain in the butt.

THE CLUB LEAKS A BIT SINCE THE LAST ROCKET ATTACK BUT IT ISN'T MUCH OF A PROBLEM CLEANING IT WHEN THE LOCAL NATIONALS RETURN FROM THEIR HOLIDAYS ... AND THE GENERATOR SHOULD BE REPAIRED WITHIN TEN DAYS ...

When we didn't have Command support we developed a positive attitude.
Courtesy of Terri Zuber

13

TAY NINH AND TET

Herman's Hermits singing "There's a Kind of Hush All Over the World Tonight" reminds me of Tay Ninh and the night of Tet.

Tay Ninh, VietNam, 1967

    A bedroom in a bunker and a bathroom with running water just outside the entrance was a dream come true! This wonderful place was Tay Ninh, Headquarters of the 1st PHILCAGV, the Filipino Command and my fourth assignment. It was one of the safest places in VietNam because the Filipino Army was in country for civic action, not as combatants. The local community was so grateful to the Filipinos for their assistance that Tay Ninh was never attacked, at least while I was there.
    I reveled in my good fortune to be there. For the first time in VietNam, I could sleep all night long without fear of being

awakened to run to a bunker; I slept in one! The Filipino Army Nurses shared their multi-bedroom bunker with the Service Club Director Carrie and me. We each had our own bedroom underground. The hospital building was next to the bunker, and the women's latrine was located just outside the entrance. I thought I had died and gone to heaven.

    The base camp of Tay Ninh was established in 1966, when the Filipino President, Ferdinand Marcos, agreed to send troops to VietNam for Civic Action. Their focus was economic and technical assistance. Civic Action Teams (CATs) provided food, soaps, and medicines to the 143 villages in Tay Ninh province. They taught the Vietnamese how to grow "miracle rice" which had four growing seasons. They built a resettlement village so that families displaced by the Viet Cong could return home. Filipino medical and dental teams visited the villages on a rotating basis to provide basic services and to educate the people about personal hygiene and health care. The Filipino engineers built bridges, schools, and roads. The Vietnamese were grateful and welcomed the Filipinos in Tay Ninh City as heroes.[12]

    Ironically, almost all of the officers and men of 1st PHILCAGV were combat experienced, professional soldiers. They had volunteered to go to VietNam to fight the Viet Cong and North Vietnamese Army. Talking with some of the officers and men, I learned they were disappointed that their mission was civic action. Their orders explicitly stated that they could only fire their weapons when fired upon.

    The Philippine base camp in Tay Ninh was the show place of the Allied Forces in VietNam and General Gaudencio V. Tobias, the Commanding General, welcomed every dignitary, American, European, Filipino, or Asian who came to VietNam, with a VIP tour of the model village and the miracle rice fields.

    He wanted a Special Services facility to add to his showplace and for his men. His government was willing to provide all the money and material support required by the U. S Army, and since the 25th Infantry Division shared the base camp, it was appropriate for the Special Services to locate in the Filipino Command. He chose the name, The Free World Service Club, as soon as his request was approved.

The Free World Service Club in Tay Ninh, VietNam, 1967. General Tobias, center and his American civilian and Filipino Army staffs

General Tobias was excessively generous with materials, supplies and labor. He placed few restrictions on the size and design of the Club, which was remarkable. At CuChi, the Club was a thatched-roof hut; at DiAn, it was a single-story frame tropical building. At Long Binh, the Club was a two-story barracks building. This facility was to become the largest U. S. Army Service Club in VietNam and, without question, the most beautiful in VietNam in 1967. Upon completion of the Club, General Tobias added The Free World Service Club in the VIP tour of the model village and the miracle rice fields. Shortly after the Grand Opening, Carrie, the Club Director rotated back to the States and I became the Acting Club Director and the tour guide. Marilyn Ramge was sent to be the Program Director and became a friend and partner sharing all the duties and work at the Service Club.

The Club had mahogany paneled walls and highly polished bamboo floors. Beautiful Rattan furniture was flown directly from Manila.

Visitors to the Free World Service Club
Above left: An Army four star General Dwight Beach
Above: An Air Force two star General
Below: General of the Army Creighton Abrams Commander of Armed Forces VietNam

Marilyn Ramge and I are pictured above with a Filipino Senator (center) and unidentified officers.

The Sergeant in charge of the Filipino and Vietnamese staff assigned to the Service Club to maintain the building was the "Soldier of the Year" recipient. He was the most outstanding soldier in the entire Filipino Army and he was assigned to us. We rarely saw him, but his staff kept the facility spotlessly clean and well organized which was an amazing feat. We were as proud as General Tobias and his command of the Free World Service Club

The Club included the library, a crafts shop, a woodworking shop and a large auditorium with a stage where we conducted programs and hosted local and USO shows. Music rooms and game rooms were sound-proofed and located so that our soldier musicians could play during our programs and not hear us or be heard. A director of each of the Special Services programs came to Tay Ninh to help with the design. The District Librarian, Rozanne Berry, drew the plans for the library; the District Crafts Director, Susan Esslinger Selig, drew the plans for both the Crafts Shop and a Woodworking

Shop. A shortage of personnel in country prevented us from having a permanent librarian or crafts professional at TayNinh; however, both directors visited us to check on their areas at least once a month, which meant there were more round eyes on our base camp than Carrie and me most of the time. Almost every day was a special occasion.

Only the flight line separated the Filipino Command from the 25th Infantry Division which I knew from CuChi, so we had Americans and Filipinos at the club. Our programming for the club was the same as all others. The Filipinos spoke English as their second language and were pretty much Americanized, so they enjoyed the same games and activities. Like the American GIs they loved Bingo, pool, ping pong, and any kind of friendly competition.

The American and the Filipino soldiers participated in our programs with the same enthusiasm.

Cathleen Cordova was assigned to the Free World Service Club after I left. She wrote a Christmas in Tay Ninh memory called, "Cookies" for the Special Services Reunion Committee Newsletter in October, 1999.

Christmas Eve 1968, at the Free World Service Club in Tay Ninh, Viet Nam...an encounter between a young American Christian woman and an elderly Vietnamese Buddhist man named Thi...also known to the GIs as the Service Club 'Grill Sergeant.'

Thi was assigned to our Service Club as a cook, and it was well-known the Service Club kitchen was his domain. The kitchen was fully equipped to military standards, but rarely used. Nevertheless Thi kept it spotless and shiny. No one really knew how Thi got his job at the Club since he could only cook two items: steaks on the outdoor, home-made, BBQ grill and cinnamon rolls for Sunday morning Coffee Call. But, I being the 'newbie' at the Club didn't know this yet.

On this particular Christmas Eve Day, I was feeling homesick so I purposely set out to keep very busy with preparations for the Club's big Christmas Party. I began by daring to enter Thi's kitchen to inquire about the cookies I'd asked him to bake, and to offer my suggestions and assistance.

'Good morning, Thi. How are you?' I asked, as I smiled brightly for all I was worth, and bravely set foot on Thi's turf. 'What kind of cookies will you make today, and are you OK with the spaghetti lunch?'

Thi glanced up from his baking at my inquisitive intrusion to reply, 'Cinnamon rolls. No cookie. Thi make cinnamon rolls.'

'No Thi, today is special holiday for G.I.'s. Must have cookies, Thi, We need cookies.'

'No cookie. Thi make cinnamon rolls!'

Well, it was obvious Thi had no intentions of making cookies. If we were to have any at all, I could see I'd have to make them myself. So I got busy. I gathered the ingredients, made the dough from memory and hoped it would be OK. I rolled out the dough under Thi's curious side-long glances. When he was finished with his cinnamon rolls and had them in the oven, I showed Thi how to cut out cookies using a small empty C-ration can. We then baked and decorated the round little Christmas cookies with kool-aid tinted frosting.

Without saying so Thi made it clear he resented my presence in his kitchen, but he learned to make Christmas Cookies under duress. Worse yet, I had the audacity to ask, "Thi, are you going to be able to cook the spaghetti OK without my help?' His reply, 'Thi know!' left me with considerable doubt. So, much to Thi's distress, I went over the menu and cooking directions, and ended with 'Spaghetti with mushrooms, jello with marshmallows, garlic bread, cookies and coffee, OK?'

'Yes, yes, Thi know. Spaghetti/mushrooms, jello/marshmallow, special cookie! Yes, yes!' he shouted as he impatiently waved his hands in the air at this meddlesome woman who not only invaded his space, changed his plans, but left his kitchen a cookie-encrusted mess!

As I walked out of the kitchen brushing the flour and cookie dough from my face and blue uniform, I heard Thi mutter, "G. I. Mamasan beaucoup dinky dau!'

Hours later as I watched the guys line up for our Christmas spaghetti lunch, I was pleased to see Thi grinning from ear to ear as he served up his new culinary creations to complimentary remarks from surprised and hungry G. I.s.

'Thi, everything looks beautiful,' I said.

'Thank you." Thi beamed and replied, 'Spaghetti/mushroom, jello/marshmallow, special cookie.'

I thought, 'Great! It's all turned out so well, and Thi's no longer upset with me.'

It wasn't until several minutes later that I noticed the odd white blotches (marshmallows!) in the spaghetti, and the suspicious dark particles (mushrooms) in the green jello.

I looked at Thi. He grinned and said, 'Spaghetti/mushroom, jello/marshmallow, special cookie!'

Perhaps it was all a cultural misunderstanding, but thanks to Thi we had a very memorable Christmas lunch. And, as it turned out the spaghetti and jello didn't taste any worse than the mess hall's, and were a sight more colorful. But in truth, it was the 'special cookie' that saved the day. Everyone was so delighted with the prospect of enjoying home- made, sugar cookies for dessert, that our less than perfect spaghetti and jello were graciously consumed in anticipation of our Christmas treat.[13]

Above left: Cathleen Cordova in VietNam in 1969
Above right: Cathleen Cordova in ca. 2010.

It was interesting to observe the Filipino culture up close. We ate at the Filipino Officers' mess hall which was like a resort restaurant in Manila. The food was a delicious combination of Asian and Mediterranean cuisine. We ate vegetables, rice, and sometimes, noodles or pasta. The meat was often pork, sometimes chicken, rarely beef. Soy sauce was the seasoning of choice. After about a month, I craved a hamburger with ketchup, and French fries. The Filipinos didn't use ketchup so there was none on the camp. If there had been, I couldn't have used it in the mess hall anyway for fear of offending the chefs and my gracious Filipino hosts. Before I had time to figure out a way to solve my craving, our club was visited by an American Army captain with a truck load of his men from across the flight line.

"We were told there were round eyes here on base and we didn't believe it. I had to check the place out before I could allow my men to come over." Of course it wasn't true, but it was flattering that he came to visit. I gave him the grand tour of the facility and described some of our programs.

"Your men will be safe with us, Captain. You can take this month's calendar back to your company area so they won't miss any of our programs."

He was properly impressed and before he left he said, "The mess hall gave us some steaks and we're having a cookout on Saturday evening. Would you and your Club Director like to join us for dinner?"

"If you can get me a hamburger with ketchup and some French fries I'll be there," I blurted out. His smile turned into a loud burst of laughter. "You mean you want a hamburger instead of steak?"

"Absolutely, with lotsa ketchup." I couldn't help smiling and I couldn't wait till Saturday night. From then on, at least once a month, the captain's jeep would pick us up and take us across the flight line to the company area for a cookout. And, I always got my hamburger, ketchup, and French fries. Sometimes, I was hungry enough to eat the steak, too.

The Filipino officers and men were charming and gracious. Their heritage, I was told, was Asian and Spanish, a very attractive combination, the romantic Spanish and the inscrutable Asian. The men were all chivalrous and gallant, gentlemen to the core. They held our chairs to seat us at the dining table, and opened the doors for us whenever we appeared. The enlisted men were respectful, equally gracious and called us "Ma'am." The nurses were all petite, lovely and friendly. They shared their quarters with us and treated us like close friends from the moment we arrived. Hospitality is a large part of the Filipino culture and whenever any visitors came to TayNinh, the Command would host a reception, cocktail party, and elaborate dinner. We Special Services ladies were always included in the invitations and were always treated like special guests.

General Tobias, the Commanding General, was a tall slight-built man with an enigmatic, inscrutable expression. I rarely saw him smile. He seldom came to the Service Club and we saw him at the Officers' mess only on special occasions. However, his presence and demand for perfection were felt throughout his command, from the highest ranking officer to the lowest PFC.

Col. Raphael Zagala, Commanding Officer of the Security Battalion was a true friend and an example of the gracious hospitality and generosity of the Filipino Officers. His wife, Cynthia met me in Manila to show me the city. When he visited his sister in New York City he came to Washington, DC to meet my father and mother and spend time with my family.

Col. Raphael Zagala, CO, Security Battalion

Above: Riki Coll (left), me, and Susan Esslinger Selig (right) were invited to a reception and dinner party for Mr Salientes a Filipino Senator.

Below: Another welcome honoring another Filipino Senator. I'm sitting next to General Tobias on the left and Marilyn Ramge is sitting to the right next to Col. Zagala.

207

General Tobias (right) cut and served his Birthday cake as everyone sang "Happy Birthday to him. I'm on the left and Susan Esslinger Selig is in the center.

    The Officers and men of his command were considered the most outstanding in the entire Filipino Army. His Chief of Staff was Lt. Col. Fidel V. Ramos, a West Point Graduate, who spoke English like an American. He had a square full face, an engaging smile and wore thick black rimmed glasses. Sometimes he ate in the mess hall at the same time Carrie and I did, and he always attended the special receptions, parties, and dinners. He was a reserved and private man; however, during special celebrations when he joined the festivities, he was a charming and good-natured participant. I remember one occasion when Col. Ramos thoroughly enjoyed one of the parties we attended. Susan, Carrie, and I were asked to demonstrate some of our recreational skills for Filipino Officers and their guests. We selected two mind reading games we thought would entertain them.

    For the first demonstration, I wrote a different word on each of three slips of paper and gave them to Capt. Allende to guard, but not read. Then I asked for a volunteer and a dozen raised their hands.

I chose one of the young officers, Lt. Galvez, who was a good-natured, happy fellow. Everyone gathered around as we placed a chair in the middle of the room and asked Lt. Galvez to sit facing me. As soon as he was seated I gave him instructions. "I'm going to ask you three questions. Say the first thing that enters your mind. Don't try to think of an answer, just answer the first thing that comes to mind. Are you ready?

"Yes."

"What is your favorite flower?" I asked.

He quickly answered, "Rose."

"Good. Now, what is your favorite color?"

Again he immediately answered, "Red."

"Okay. Name a piece of furniture," I said.

"Uh, a chair."

I then asked Capt. Allende to read the words I had written on the pieces of paper.

"Rose, red, chair," he called out. Everyone gasped then laughed and clapped their hands, astonished at my psychic powers. They pressed me politely to explain how I could read Lt. Galvez' mind and I told them it was Service Club magic. They were delighted.

I began the game by asking, "What's your favorite flower?"

Then Carrie initiated another game called "Under the Cover." She asked for two volunteers this time and selected Lt. Garcia and Capt. Suarez who were both enthusiastic and eager to be part of the entertainment. She explained the game.

"Both of you lie on the rug side by side. I'll cover you with a tablecloth so you can't see me. I will think of something you have on that I want you to remove and you will read my thoughts and remove it."

The two volunteers laid down and we covered them with the tablecloth. Everyone circled the two, straining to see the two participants and hear what Carrie said. "I'm thinking of something you have on that I want you to remove." Laughter and giggles came from under the tablecloth and from the crowd. The tablecloth moved nervously and finally a shoe came out from either side of the tablecloth. "No," said Carrie, "that's not it. Try harder. What am I thinking of that you have on that I want you to remove?" This time two belts came out.

Finally Capt. Suarez burst out laughing, jumped up and threw off the tablecloth and said, "It's the tablecloth!" Everyone clapped and cheered that the two had figured it out, because some of them had not. I knew Colonel Ramos enjoyed the game because he laughed and cheered loudly.

Col. Ramos was an appreciative observer of our party games.

Above: Capt. Suarez popped up when he realized it was the tablecloth he was supposed to take off. Susan Esslinger Selig and Marilyn Ramge watch.
Below: Susan and I appreciate Col. Ramos' funny story.

In 1992, Colonel Ramos became the President of the Philippines. He chose another officer who served with him at TayNinh, Capt. Renato S. DeVilla, a company commander, as his Secretary of Defense. Another officer from TayNinh destined for success was Lt. Alfredo Filler who became a Major General in the Philippine Army before he retired.[14]

I was due for a week-long R&R (Rest & Recreation leave) beginning January, 31, 1968. Gay, my Red Cross friend from DiAn, and I planned to catch the first R & R flight to Australia. The U. S. and the Australian Governments had negotiated an agreement to include Sydney as a leave site for American service personnel and civilians stationed in VietNam. The Australians were preparing an elaborate ceremony and celebration to welcome the first plane load of us "Yanks" down under, and we were excited to be part of the historic event. Gay decided to fly down to Saigon the night before we were to leave, and I was to join her the next morning in time to catch the flight. I had arranged for the chopper to Tan Son Nhut AFB and a jeep to take me to the plane. That night the Tet offensive began.

One of the most important Vietnamese holidays, Tet, is the first day of the Lunar New Year. In 1968, the holiday began on the 31st day of January. Both North and South Vietnamese governments announced on national radio that there would be a two-day cease-fire during the holiday. Instead, the North Vietnamese Army and the Viet Cong violated the truce and launched a massive campaign attacking thirty U. S. targets and dozens of cities in South VietNam at the same time. Many of the American base camps were overrun and Saigon was attacked from multiple directions.[15] We were on high alert and the Filipino Command prepared for an attack.

As with many of my experiences in VietNam I can't remember much about that night. It's not unusual for traumatic memories to be blocked. Forgetting is how the mind protects itself from harmful memories.

I remember the waiting, anticipating and dreading the worst. We held our collective breath and walked around intensely scrutinizing our surroundings waiting for the attack. Everyone moved in slow motion, as if in a weird dream. My most vivid memory, which makes no sense, is standing outside of our bunker during the blackout seeing bright stars in the dark sky and hearing music. Someone was playing a tape or a record of the song, "There's a kind of hush all over the world tonight" and it played over and over.

Someone said, "Saigon's been overrun. All our base camps are under attack."

I thought, "Is this the end? Funny, I don't feel anything." It was a sleepless night.

The next day was spent trying to concentrate on the routine things, but without much success. Every conversation began with "What have you heard? What's happening now?" I can't remember how long it took, but I think only a couple of days to find out that the death toll and wounded count was devastating. How had we been so vulnerable? We were the most powerful country and the most effective military force in the world. So much damage and chaos had been inflicted on us by this small, primitive country with its ragtag guerillas, the Viet Cong, and much smaller army. It was hard to believe, much less understand.

While the Tet offensive was a tactical win for the Americans because they had pushed the enemy back, the media portrayed it as an American loss. It was a severe psychological blow to the morale of the troops and the American civilian population back home. [16]

The following week the situation became the "new" normal. The High Alert was still in effect when I flew to Saigon to board my R&R flight to Australia. I had missed meeting Gay and the first R & R flight to Australia. She caught our original flight the day after Tet, so I went alone. Alone, that is, with two hundred GIs who were on R & R, too.

Nothing exciting happened on that flight. Everyone slept. We were all exhausted and very happy to be out of country.

After my R&R to Sydney I returned to work in TayNinh.

Above: Our office in the Free World Service Club.

Below: My Farewell Party at the end of my tour in March, 1967.

General Tobias presented me with a plaque of appreciation and two photo albums.

14

R & R, REST AND RECREATION

"Candida" by Dawn and "Knock Three Times" by Tony Orlando and Dawn remind me of a Disco Club with a glass dancing floor in Tokyo.

Every overseas assignment included a mid-tour leave called R & R, rest and recreation. The military provided free flights to several vacation locations for the servicemen and women and civilians while they were serving in Korea and Vietnam. During my overseas tours I took advantage of every leave opportunity and traveled to exotic places that I only dreamed I would visit. Hong Kong, China--Tokyo, Mt. Fuji, and Kyoto, Japan--Penang, Malaysia--Bangkok, Thailand--Sydney, Australia--and Hawaii.

Camp Howard, Korea, 1964
    I was eligible for leave at the same time my friends, Kay Strasburg (Bardsley) and Frankie Milligan, were going back to the States. Kay was my first Club Director in Korea and Frankie was the

Service Club Director at a small U. S. Air Force Base at a remote site in Kunsan, Korea. Kay and Frankie worked together at Ft. Lewis, Washington, and volunteered for a tour of duty in Korea at the same time. On their way home, they planned a world tour, stopping in Hong Kong where we planned to meet and spend a few days sightseeing. I wanted to go because it would be fun sightseeing with the two of them and I wanted to have some clothes made by the famous Hong Kong tailors.

When I arrived in Hong Kong, I walked up the ramp to the terminal to find my luggage, wondering where to go for a taxi, how to get to the hotel, if I had enough change to tip the baggage handlers, the taxi, or if anyone spoke English. I heard my name called. "Miss Lockney?" It was a very distinguished Chinese man dressed in a black chauffeur's uniform. He smiled and said, "We've been expecting you." He was from the President Hotel in downtown

Left:

Kay and I in front of our hotel.

Right:

Kay and Frankie shopping in Hong Kong.

Hong Kong where I had made reservations. The personal greeting made me feel like a celebrity.

View of the Hong Kong Harbor from the top of the President Hotel.

Kay and Frankie had arrived at the President Hotel the day before, explored the area close to the hotel, and made a list of places of interest. Together we took day trips to the Tiger Balm Gardens, the Snake Temple, and beach front hotels on the other side of the island.

We dined at the best restaurants but my favorite was at the top of our hotel overlooking the harbor. The view from the bar was so spectacular that we sat silently for a long time, sipping our drinks, enjoying the panoramic view of the harbor and the city. An older lady who wore a fur wrap and walked with a cane sat next to us. After a while she leaned over and said, "My name is Elizabeth Rothman.

"I couldn't help overhearing you. Are you Americans?"

"Yes," we said almost in unison.

"Are you here for business or pleasure?"

Kay answered for the three of us, "We're civilians working for the U. S. Army in Korea. Frankie and I are on our way home after a year's tour, Sandra has been in Korea just a few months and she's going back at the end of the week. Are you American?"

"Yes, but I don't spend much time there anymore. I own an import/export business and travel quite a bit. I make this trip to Hong Kong about twice a year."

Fascinated we listened to her talk about her initial experiences in the Chinese city. She described some of the cultural pitfalls to avoid and explained some of the common courtesies we should practice. We were most attentive when she suggested interesting sites to visit. From where we sat, she pointed out places as she described them. One of the vessels in the harbor was a floating restaurant.

"If you have time, I recommend that you dine there for the experience. You might find it interesting to taste the local cuisine and amusing to observe the Chinese relaxing in their element."

We finished our drinks, thanked her for her advice, said goodbye, and went into the restaurant for dinner. I ordered grilled frog legs for the first time. They were delicately seasoned and delicious. I expected the flavor to be exotic and was disappointed that it tasted a lot like chicken.

The next night, we hired a water taxi to take us to the floating restaurant, a replica of an old Chinese junk, for dinner. I had just purchased an 8mm movie camera for the trip and was madly filming everywhere we went. The girls were getting exasperated with me since I made them back up and re-do everything, so I could record it. Chinese boys swam alongside the small water taxi, laughing and pointing at my camera, making signs to communicate with us. The harbor was cluttered with junks, the ancient Chinese sailing vessels, where families lived, and children played in the water. Unusual subjects for my movies were everywhere, and I tried to record them all. At the height of the activity, when the boys were performing their antics, the film in my camera ran out. People on the junks had begun waving, smiling, and posing for my camera. I pressed the button to open the case and before I could do anything the film flew off the spool and out of the camera up into the air. The wind caught it blowing it curling and twisting across the top of water with the children laughing as they swam to catch it! I was stunned. Kay and Frankie burst out laughing. Overcoming my disappointment, I realized what a hilarious scene it was and joined them. Kay and Frankie said I had been giving them such a hard time that it was a relief to have me join them without the camera running.

We boarded the floating restaurant to the sound of wood knocking against wood. On the deck of the ship were tables of Chinese men playing mahjong. The atmosphere was intense. They didn't say much but the slapping of the mahjong blocks was almost deafening. The sound was a different sound, but the atmosphere was the same as Las Vegas casino. We watched for a time and then went into the restaurant where we didn't notice the gaming sounds as we became engrossed observing our fellow diners. The only Westerners in the place, we were as interesting to them as they were to us. The waiters spoke a little English, and the menu had amusing Chinese-English explanations of each meal. Someone armed with a Chinese/English dictionary wrote phrases using word-for-word translations which didn't mean anything in English. We giggled, but realized what a disaster it would be if we tried to translate an English menu into Chinese. Whatever it was that we ordered there was plenty of it. The table was covered with large and small dishes of multi-colored treats, mostly fish, rice, vegetables, and a variety of sauces. Everything was delicious and we enjoyed a quiet, pleasant, albeit unique dinner.

Unfortunately I lost all of the footage of the harbor trip, the Tiger Balm Gardens, the Snake Temple and other places I have forgotten we visited. Fortunately, I had some of the film I took of us on the streets of Hong Kong.

I wish I had taken pictures at the tailor's shop. Hong Kong tailor-made clothes represented wealth and high fashion. There was a tailor's shop on every street corner, but we chose the posh looking tailor shop in the lobby of our hotel. Every time we went to the shop for a fitting, which was at least once a day, we were greeted at the door by a polite young Chinese man who offered us a comfortable place to sit and a cocktail while we waited. We thought it was a hoot! Even when the fitting was in the morning, the same young man would greet us with his usual offer of a cocktail. The cocktails were always the best quality booze money could buy: Chivas Regal scotch, Tanqueray gin, and Old Grand Dad whiskey or any kind of Kentucky bourbon. It made sense that they had the best British liquor but we marveled at the variety of high quality American liquor.

I bought five outfits of the most beautiful British lamb's wool and silk in five different designs I selected from the pictures in British and American fashion magazines. The tailors brought me gorgeous bolts of fabric to choose from, took my measurements, and, as if by magic in a couple of days, I had a custom-made suit. Each piece of clothing had exquisite stitching and a label with my name and the tailor's name sewn into the lining. I selected three colors of lamb's wool and had a suit made in each color: muted red, a rich blue and mossy green. The black suit I chose was made from a velvet material the tailors described as "vicuna." The fifth ensemble was an Indian silk sari in a deep rose color with gold trim. The total cost was less than $200.00. It was a shopper's dream come true. Later, I had them altered when miniskirts became the vogue, and even though I didn't wear them after the 1970s, I kept the suits in my closet until 1997, when I finally gave them to Goodwill. I kept the labels.

DiAn, VietNam, 1967

When my Red Cross friend Gay and I went on R & R to Malaysia and Thailand, we caught the flight at Tan Son Nhut AFB in Saigon to Georgetown in Penang, Malaysia. We chose to stay at the Eastern & Oriental Hotel in the center of downtown Georgetown over the hotels on the beach, because we got enough sun in VietNam. We were on vacation to stay cool, dry and clean, and to sightsee. We could step out the front door of the E & O, a landmark in the city, and walk to shops and restaurants. Famous author, Somerset Maugham, allegedly wrote one of his books while staying in the hotel, but I never found out which one.

Gay and I shared a lovely room with cool white sheets, our own bathroom with bathtub, a telephone, and connection to room service. It was heaven. The hotel was like an old Humphrey Bogart,

The Eastern & Oriental Hotel or the E&O in downtown Penang, Malaysia.

WW II movie set. The lobby was a cavernous room with fifteen-foot ceilings. The slowly revolving fans hung over tall rattan, high-backed chairs. Gay and I were sure at any minute, the actor Sidney Greenstreet would saunter into the bar wearing his signature white suit and Panama hat.

The wall clock on the way to our room was stopped at 5:00 p.m. so every time we walked by one of us would say, "It's cocktail time!" Then we'd go to the bar and have a drink. Feeling very extravagant one afternoon, we called room service and ordered drinks delivered to our room. A little balcony on the front of our room was a perfect place to relax with a cocktail. We ordered the house specialty without a clue what it was. It turned out to be something with fruit juice and a tiny umbrella. It tasted too sweet and didn't have enough ice. After that we ordered our usual scotch and water or martinis at the bar.

We toured Georgetown in a taxi with a driver who was a terrific tour guide and con artist. He bargained with us about his fee as taxi driver and tour guide. It was the custom to haggle over the price, but we weren't much good at it. We managed to save face by not paying him his full price. He took us to the beach to see some of the other resort hotels which were large typical beachfront hotels, and we were glad we didn't stay there because we couldn't walk to any shops or markets or interesting sites.

We visited botanical gardens, elephants, and temples of different religions. Georgetown was a city of almost every nationality and faith in the world: Christian, Jewish, Muslim, Buddhist, and Hindu. The unique thing about Malaysia in those days was that everyone apparently got along.

During the five days in Georgetown, we spent a couple of afternoons lounging at poolside where we met Mrs. Rose and her daughter, Karen, who were vacationing in Penang. They lived in Bangkok while her husband, Mr. Rose, taught at a university in South VietNam.

It was thrilling for us to be tourists and pretend we didn't have to go back to our base camps.

Above: It was unusual to see a sign in English especially on a Buddhist Temple

Below: Allegedly, this was the world's largest Reclining Buddha. Note: The Buddhist Monk standing below the Buddha gives an idea of how large the Buddha was.

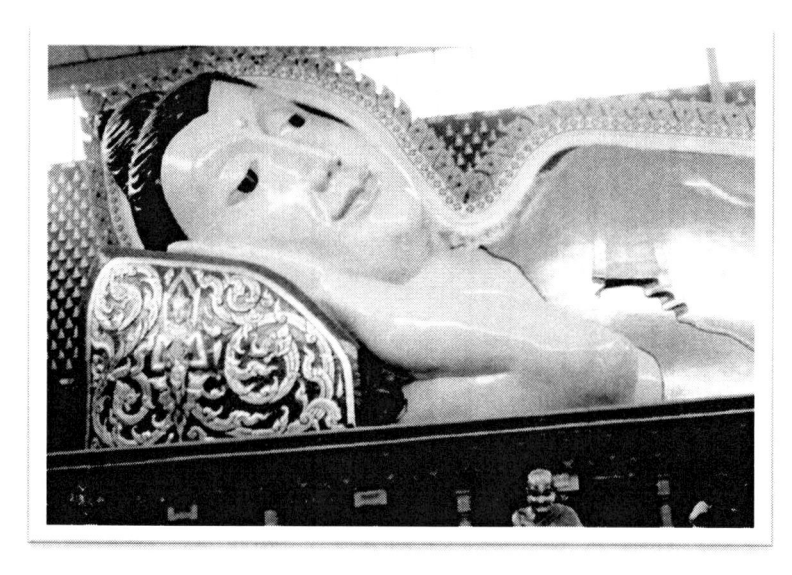

Left:

I found it amusing to see American films everywhere we went and couldn't resist taking pictures of some of the billboards. It was weird seeing a film hearing familiar actors speak a foreign language.

Below:

It was also amusing that Coca Cola existed in every country I visited.

Mrs. Rose was a small matronly woman with fair hair, fair complexion, and striking blue eyes. Her daughter, Karen, was a pretty, petite blond who looked only twelve or thirteen years old, but she had just celebrated her eighteenth birthday and high school graduation. She was preparing to return to the states to attend college and the trip to Georgetown was a graduation present from her parents. After exchanging pleasantries and why we were all in Penang, I discovered that the Rose family was from Parkersburg, West Virginia, where I was born. Both my parents grew up and went to school in Parkersburg, and if that wasn't coincidence enough, we determined that Mr. Rose taught math at Parkersburg High School the same time my father attended PHS. It was the most remarkable "small world" incident I've ever experienced. I couldn't wait to write my dad about it and Mrs. Rose was as excited as I was to tell her husband.

When she found out Gay and I planned to catch a plane for Bangkok before we returned to VietNam, she insisted we stay in her guest room and she show us Bangkok. We tried to decline politely, not wanting to intrude, but she was adamant and we finally accepted.

We would never have seen the places she took us to see in Bangkok. She introduced us to Thai food at her neighborhood restaurant. We saw a Thai play complete with beautifully colorful and elegant Thai costumes. Every time I see the movie, "The King and I," it reminds me of Bangkok. She took us shopping at the floating market and drove us around the city to see how the Thai people lived.

Mrs. Rose took us to see the Siamese Temples.

When it was time to leave, she drove us to the airport and we parted, promising to keep in touch and try to see each other in the States though we never did.

Gay and I had not scheduled our return flight because we hadn't decided all the places we might visit before we returned to work, so we didn't have airline tickets. Because we were young and fearless, we felt secure having military orders which authorized us to travel on U. S. Government transportation. We caught the Embassy flight that flies regularly from capital city to capital city around the world. From Bangkok, the next stop was Saigon. It wasn't a plush flight; we sat facing the rear of the plane and the attendant had only coffee to serve us. It was like sitting in a cargo plane but for us, it was another adventure. What we hadn't anticipated was our arrival time in Saigon and the curfew.

The Embassy flight landed about thirty minutes before curfew and we were the only people leaving the plane in Saigon. We were left stranded on an empty flight line, no vehicles, and no people. Alone, we stood with all of our luggage, which we couldn't carry by ourselves, with curfew imminent, on a regularly mortared flight line, with no transportation, no hotel reservations, no phone, and no one to call for help. It seemed forever until we spotted a jeep across the runway in the distance. We jumped up and down, waved our raincoats and yelled until we were hoarse. The two airmen in the jeep finally noticed us and came to our rescue. They worked on the flight line and were on duty all night, so they couldn't go very far from the flight line. There were no hotels nearby, so they drove us to

We visited the floating market which gave grocery shopping a whole new meaning.

the Officers' BOQ across the street from the flight line. We thanked them over and over again, and said to come see us if they were ever at DiAn. They laughed and said, "No thanks, they shoot at people up there."

The BOQ was permanent quarters for the Officers stationed at Tan Son Nhut AFB. When we asked for a room, the Vietnamese clerk at the desk said he had no rooms and could not help us. By then, the curfew was in effect, so we begged him to let us sleep in the lobby which had a couch and a chair, but he kept saying it was against regulation and he could not help us. Exhausted, frustrated and feeling a little panicky, we were about to give up, when three officers came into the lobby. An Army colonel called the clerk by name and asked what the problem was. Gay and I and the clerk started talking at once. We all laughed which was a much needed tension reliever.

When the colonel heard our desperate story, he turned to the clerk and said that a major, who lived in the BOQ, was on TDY for a month and no one was using his room. "Give it to the ladies for one night."

Words can't describe how relieved we were. The officers helped us with our luggage and bought us dinner in the snack bar located in the same building. It was our good fortune that the colonel's command happened to include a unit of choppers. He graciously offered one of them to fly us back to our camp, DiAn, the next morning. It was like we'd hit the jackpot. We could get a good night's sleep without worrying about how we were going to get back to camp the next morning.

As a footnote, five years later, 1972, I was invited to play golf at the Ft. Benning, Georgia, Golf Club. I was surprised and pleased when one of our foursome turned out to be the same colonel. We laughed, exchanged "war stories," and enjoyed telling our golf mates about our previous encounter. I was pleased to have the opportunity to tell him again what a hero he was to us.

TayNinh, VietNam, 1967

    I missed the first R & R flight out of VietNam to Sydney, Australia because of Tet. As soon as they could schedule a second flight, I was on it. I can't remember whether it was day or night when we landed in Sydney. All I wanted to do was get to the hotel, take a hot shower and sleep in a clean bed in an air-conditioned room. And that's what I did. The next day, at breakfast, I met three of the men who had been on the same flight. We exchanged ideas about what to see and do in Sydney and decided to do the tour thing as a group. During the next three days, we visited the opera shell in the harbor, took the boat tour of the harbor and a bus tour of the city. In the evenings when I didn't want to stay in my room and read or watch TV, I met my fellow R & R travelers at the bar on top of the hotel to exchange stories of our day's adventures. Since I was the only female in the group, they asked my advice about what to send home to their wives or girlfriends. Shopping was the same experience we encountered at the bars and restaurants; we were treated like visiting royalty. Everyone wanted to buy us Yanks a drink, and all the shopkeepers gave us samples and deep discounts on merchandise. Everyone acted genuinely glad to see us no matter where we went.

    Les Brown and his Band of Renown were performing at one of the big hotels near ours. A group of us went to see him, but it was so crowded that we couldn't get any closer than the lobby and couldn't see anything. We left and went to a local bar for a drink where we ran into some other members of our flight. They had befriended some local young ladies who were showing them the city and not just the tourist spots. The girls were all fascinated I was in VietNam with the guys. They couldn't get over a woman in the war zone. We spent the evening drinking, getting acquainted, and learning a lot of Australian drinking songs. By the end of the evening we were all best friends. One of the Australian girls, Maureen, who was concerned for our safety back in the war and particularly for my safety, gave me her necklace, a silver chain with a delicate oval charm of tiny milk Opal nuggets embedded in a black background. I kept giving it back to her assuring her I would be perfectly safe, that all our handsome young soldier friends were there to protect me. She refused to take it back and insisted I wear it all the time I was in VietNam. She said it was her lucky charm and it would protect me. I still have her lucky charm.

Taegu, Korea, 1969

I was stationed in Korea for two tours. One of the perks was that my orders authorized me to catch a ride with the courier flight from Seoul to Tokyo whenever there was space and I had leave. Tokyo became a frequent vacation spot for me since it was so accessible.

Tokyo was like visiting New York City.

In Tokyo, I usually stayed downtown at the Sanno Hotel, managed by the U. S. Military. It was more like transient quarters on any U. S. Military installation, sparsely furnished with no frills but all the conveniences: a snack bar, and dining room, small PX and U.S. Post Office. It was an adventure just to walk outside the hotel onto the streets of the city. Tokyo was and is a metropolitan city of bright lights, lots of people, shops, restaurants and bars. I found a favorite place across the street, down one of the alleys near the hotel called Tommy's. It was a small short order café. The counter with stools took up most of the space but there were a couple of small tables. Tommy with his full body apron stood behind the counter and cooked your order to suit you. He grilled everything on a stick and served beer and Saki. Tommy was a character, who could talk to anyone about anything in several languages. And he knew a little about everything. He was a wonderful host and in his establishment you felt like you were his guest. Every time I visited Tokyo I had to go to Tommy's and everyone I met in Tokyo I took to Tommy's. The only thing I remember ordering there, other than Kirin Beer, was grilled chicken on a stick. At least it tasted like chicken.

Camp Howard, Korea, 1964

On another occasion, I visited Japan to tour the country. My traveling partner was another Special Services girl, Nancy Grove, whom I'd never met before our trip. Our Club Directors, Kay and Frankie, were friends and introduced us by phone suggesting that, since we were both eligible for an R & R, we share expenses and travel together. Since we were at different Army Posts in Korea, we spent hours on the military phone lines, getting acquainted, planning our trip, dividing the responsibilities of making hotel reservations and booking train trips. That may sound simple, but the military phone lines were an adventure in themselves. First of all the operators were GIs who were always surprised to hear an American female voice. Each time either of us called the other, we had long conversations with the operators: "Hey, where you from in the States?" And "What's a nice girl like you doing in a place like Korea?" After we finally got connected to each other, our new friends, the operators, joined in our conversations from time to time to recommend a place to see or visit when we finally got there. In later years, every time I saw Radar make a phone call in the T.V. show M*A*S*H, I was reminded of my time in Korea. The only difference was we didn't have to crank the phone.

Nancy and I discovered we had much in common and we both had the same idea about sightseeing. We researched what we wanted to see, compared notes, and selected the sites to visit well in

ght I was
lap of
staying
Frank
Wright
al Palace
n Tokyo
964.

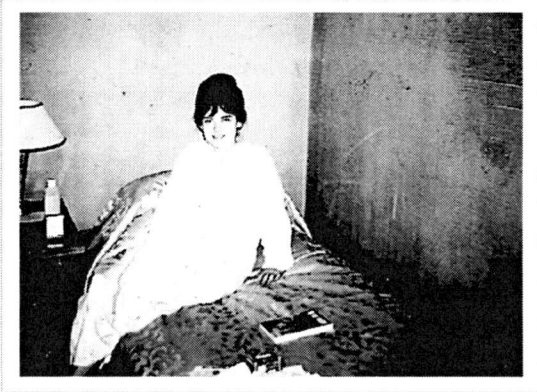

advance of our trip. We met in Seoul in time to board our flight and got acquainted during the flight.

One of the most exciting parts of our trip was our hotel in Tokyo, It was the Imperial Hotel across the street from the Imperial Palace, where Japan's Emperor lived. I was reading the book, <u>The Wise Bamboo</u> by J. Malcolm Morris, when we stayed there. The book relates the very funny stories about differences in the Japanese and American cultures and the author's attempts to convert the Imperial Hotel to a BOQ for the high ranking Allied Officers, during the Occupation immediately after World War II. Mr. Morris described the hotel with accuracy and humor.

> The Imperial Hotel was built for the Japanese by Frank Lloyd Wright, the American architectural genius. The Grand Opening was held at noon on September first, 1923 and five minutes later Japan was struck by the worst earthquake...." The hotel survived that quake and many more.
>
> The shape of the hotel is roughly that of a capital letter 'H' with a capital letter 'I' as the crossbar. From the front of the building it looks like a giant crab eating a stick of chewing gum with the tinfoil still on it...It (the building) splatters out from the focal point of the lobby in all directions. The corridor system is so long and winding and complicated that when you try to retrace a path you have just followed, the pattern seems to have changed while your back was turned.[17]

It was the strangest floor plan I've ever seen before or since. The building didn't look as large as it was. The floors were designed so you could walk from floor to floor, without using stairs, never aware that you were walking on an incline. Nancy and I could never find our room without getting lost at least once. We threatened to tie a string around the door knob when we left in the morning and tie it to something in the lobby so that we could find our way back. We even considered a popcorn trail but they didn't have popcorn in Japan in those days.

From Tokyo, we took the electric train to Kyoto the ancient capital of Japan. The electric train was a marvel. It was almost completely silent and traveled so fast that the landscape was blurred for some distance from the track. Visible from the train in the distance, at one part of the trip, was Mt. Fuji, majestic and regal. It was snow-capped just like in all the pictures I had ever seen of it.

In Kyoto, we visited the former Emperor's Palace. It was another strange design. The royal family's living quarters were located in the center of the palace, surrounded by a wide hallway of wooden floors. As you walked on the floor, the boards moved slightly making the twittering sound of a thousand birds. The floors, called "Nightingale floors," were an ancient alarm system. No one could approach the royal family without alerting them.

My friend, Nancy Grove

JAPAN GRAY LINE
"MEET JAPAN TOUR"

ISETAN DEPARTMENT STORE
TOKYO JAPAN

Above: Our tour group posed before the Japanese Emperor's Imperial Palace. I'm fifth from the right and Nancy is behind the seventh person from the right.

On the return train ride to Tokyo, Nancy and I sat next to a charming and gracious Japanese gentleman in a western business suit. He had spent time in the States and his English was perfect. He was as interested in talking to us as we were to talk to him and by the end of the train ride we were all old friends. He insisted he treat us to dinner at his private club when we reached Tokyo. This was the first time I had ever heard of the "private clubs" that were popular in Japan. It reminded me of the old speakeasy in America during Prohibition. Our friend knocked on the door and the doorman looked at him through a small opening to make sure he was a member before he let us in. Inside was an elegant bar and restaurant with lots of soft velvet chairs and low tables. The lights were dimmed so it was hard to see. It was filled with mostly men and only a few women. Our friend introduced us as his new friends, and I think we must have met everyone in the bar. He ordered us a meal he said would not offend our American palates. We drank Saki, rice wine, laughed, and exchanged funny stories about our experiences as

Americans in Japan and his experiences as Japanese in America, just like old friends. His English was so good, we felt comfortable asking him questions we were unable to ask others whose English was not as good. We thought, since he had spent time in the States he wouldn't misunderstand or take offense. Our most pressing question was, "How can you tell if someone is from Japan, not Korea or China?" He shook his head slightly, chuckling to himself, and then launched into an elaborate explanation.

"If one has the typical characteristics of their race I can tell. For example, the Chinese are smaller than the Japanese. The facial features of the Koreans are blunt and their body shape is broader than either the Chinese or Japanese. The Japanese facial features are more delicate than the Korean, but not as delicate as the smaller Chinese. It's like you Westerners say, the typical German is blond and blue-eyed, the typical Italian has black hair and brown eyes, and so on." But then, he paused, and added, "Otherwise, they all look alike to me." The three of us laughed till tears ran down our cheeks.

After a wonderful meal and delightful conversation, we had to leave to get back to the Imperial to check in. We shook hands and thanked our host for a lovely evening. He hailed us a taxi and loaded our luggage.

In the taxi, I said, "Who would believe we've been wined and dined by a stranger we met on the train, a gallant gentleman, who treated us like royalty?"

"No one," Nancy answered. Both of us, giddy from the Sake and high on the excitement of our adventure, giggled all the way back to the hotel.

15

MY KNIGHTS IN SHINING ARMOR

Listening to Judy Collins sing "Both Sides, Now" or Petula Clarke sing "Downtown" or the Ramsey Lewis Trio play "The In Crowd" makes me nostalgic remembering the Romeos of my youth.

      Romance in Korea and VietNam was difficult but not impossible. Fear, stress, isolation, short assignments, long working hours, and other obstacles were factors that defined relationships. In Korea my one-year tour was divided into three assignments, four months at each post. In VietNam, I was assigned to four different base camps, three months at each. It was difficult to find time to spend with one person to develop a lasting relationship. We worked ten to twelve hours a day seven days a week, the same as the men. When I was assigned to a large base camp, it was common to work twelve hours, rush from work to happy hour at different officers' clubs or company parties, back to our hootch for a couple hours of sleep, to work another twelve hour day, and after work rush to another happy hour or party in a merry-go-round existence. On smaller camps, only one club and one mess hall existed and few parties. In Korea it was fun, in VietNam I was more concerned with surviving and escaping reality than looking for a lifetime partner.

    I was amused and sometimes bewildered by the layers of complexities and the obstacles to surviving in the world of military men. The married men always outnumbered the single men and most of them were "straight arrows," i.e., those who were dedicated to their wives and families and while they enjoyed the company of women, would never get involved romantically with any of us. They were often our friends. Most of the men were very protective of us, but they also competed for our attention, so it was nice to have married friends who protected us and were just good company. First, among the many obstacles was a Special Services rule: no fraternizing with enlisted men after duty hours. Enlisted men were the majority of the men in the Army and it was our job to socialize with them at the Service Club, but never outside the club. A second obstacle was rank among the officers; higher ranking officers often monopolized our time preventing us from getting acquainted with eligible young officers. A third obstacle was identifying the real bachelors from the geographical bachelors, i.e., those who were married but didn't admit it. Still another obstacle was the living conditions. For dining there was the mess hall where we all ate together. For drinking or partying, there was the Officers' Club where we all met when we weren't in our quarters, which were usually dorm-style cubicles with no room for entertaining. In spite of all the obstacles and circumstances, some of my Special Services friends did find their soul mates and I met wonderful men and consider myself fortunate to have known them.

    Living on Army base camps in Korea and in VietNam was like living in a fish bowl. Rumors were a form of pastime and ran rampant. Idiosyncrasies and eccentricities were laid bare and were magnified by living in close quarters. Fear and fatigue added to the equation, made the experience intense, interesting, sometimes exciting, oftentimes humorous, but never lonely. The television show "Northern Exposure," with its quirky characters who were isolated from the rest of the world during the long winter months, reminded me of living on a base camp.

    Strong bonds and caring relationships were formed just because we were a long way from home and family. Isolated together we had only each other to rely on for support, camaraderie,

and affection. My friendships and romances in both Korea and VietNam are sweet memories and remembering them will continue to entertain me in my old age. I can still see the faces of my close friends, my protectors, and my gallant young suitors. In case their memories are not as fondly remembered, I have used fictitious names to protect the innocent and the guilty in my recollections.
Camp Nabors, Korea, 1965

The first time I saw Lt. Derek Smoot, I thought of Jean Paul Belmondo, the French heartthrob. He wasn't handsome, but had a rugged outdoorsman macho appeal. When he smiled his eyes squinted giving him a slightly roguish expression. His admission that he liked classical music and his favorite instrument was the violin showed his gentler side. The first day I went to dinner at the mess hall, he appeared out of nowhere, sat next to me, introduced himself, and for the next three months we spent as much time together as we could. He coached his troops' football team and they challenged the other units' teams to games both at our camp and the nearby camps. They were so good that the camp had a pool betting on them to win the championship. When he wasn't coaching or playing football, he was on the volleyball courts. After work at the Service Club I joined him to watch his games, cheer him on, and take pictures to send home. He helped me write questions and answers about sports, hunting, and fishing for my Service Club program quiz games.

"Here's one for you," he would say. "Who won the 1960 and 1964 Olympic Marathon Gold Medal, running both races barefooted?"

Never knowing any of the answers I'd say, "Okay, I give up. Who?"

"Abebe Bikila from Ethiopia."

"What's a baby bekila?" I asked. He hollered, hooted, and hugged me, laughing and saying how much my education lacked.

Always sweet and attentive, his charm was irresistible. Our DEROS for return to the States were about a week apart, mine November first and his, the fifteenth. As soon as he got home he sent me a ticket to fly to his home near Washington, D. C., to meet his parents. Although we had not promised each other anything, I thought the invitation meant he was thinking of a long-term commitment. I was thrilled.

Everything went as planned. His teenage twin sisters were adorable and we became friends. His mother was a warm, friendly lady who treated me as if I were already part of the family. Derek's father was an older version of the son, rugged and masculine with a gentleness I identified in Derek.

His sisters adored their older brother, even though he teased them unmercifully. They warned me, "You better know now, that Derek's spoiled because he has two sisters and a mother that wait on him hand and foot. And he's fussy, even about his peanut butter sandwiches. We have to make sure the bread slices match. He gets upset if the pieces are upside down or on crooked." We all laughed, including Derek.

He and his dad spent a lot of time together hunting, fishing, and rock climbing. I was impressed with the closeness of their relationship and flattered when they invited me to see their favorite climbing cliff. They were like two buddies enjoying each other's company.

At Christmas, Derek visited me and my family in Ft. Walton Beach, Florida, where my dad was stationed at Eglin AFB. Dad got him a room at the BOQ at the base and Mom loaned him her sports car. Dad was reserved in his judgment, but I could tell he liked Derek. Mom was quite taken with him. She liked to tease and exchange verbal barbs, and that was Derek's strong suit. As soon as she learned he was a serious beer drinker, she brought him a huge beer mug that held over a quart of beer and ceremoniously presented it to him filled to the brim with his favorite brew. He loved it and felt right at home after that. We took long walks on the beach, visited the local shops and sites. Dad arranged for us to go to the Christmas party at the Officers' Club where we danced, drank champagne cocktails, and dined by candlelight. Everything was perfect.

Two days before he was to leave to report to his next assignment in Colorado, as we were driving home from a movie, he said, "I guess it's time we got married." I was stunned speechless but managed to say, "I guess so."

Before we told my parents or his, we shopped for a ring. I chose a beautiful solitaire diamond, but instead of the yellow gold setting I liked, we chose white gold because Derek preferred it. When we got home, I flashed my ring until my mom finally saw it, squealed with joy, and rushed to hug us both. My dad shook Derek's hand, gave me his famous bear hug, and said he was happy for us. My feet didn't touch the ground. We decided on an April wedding date.

I took Derek to the airport, we kissed goodbye and lingered as long as we could. He said he'd write me every day and call me every week and I promised to answer every day and be waiting for his calls. It was an exciting time. Mom helped me with the invitations, the arrangement with the Base Chapel for the ceremony and the reception at the Officers' Club. It was the way I always thought it would be and I was happy.

Derek did call every two or three days for the first month. The letters came irregularly and then stopped. Three weeks went by; I didn't hear from him and I began to worry that something was wrong. Finally his letter arrived. Among other things, he said, "We haven't really spent enough time together. I think you should come to Denver, get an apartment, so we can get to know each other better before we get married." It was a crushing blow. My first thought was that he had found someone else and this "getting to know each other better" really meant, "I've changed my mind."

As soon as I stopped crying and feeling sorry for myself, Dad, trying to console me said, "There are lots of women who have successful careers instead of getting married." I know he meant well, but that translated in my mind as "You'll never get married." I packed my bags, asked Mom to return our wedding gifts, gave her my engagement ring and left with my bruised ego to visit my friend Kay, who was working at the Service Club at Ft. Eustis, Virginia. Kay, who had been my mentor in Korea, was a wise and wonderful listener. Her common sense and levelheadedness were exactly what I needed. She said, "Here's the test. Do you love him and want to marry him enough to fly to Denver and fight for him?"

"No," I said without hesitation. It was a relief and I realized that Derek had been right. I should have called him to tell him but I didn't.

The Ft. Eustis Service Club was advertising for a Recreation Specialist and I qualified, so I took the job. Kay and I rented a little house near the post. My experience with Derek freed me from the obligation of settling down and my parents never mentioned marriage to me again.

I didn't realize it at the time, but Kay and I were quite the celebrities. We were featured in several articles in the local newspapers.

RECREATIONAL SPECIALI

Kay, Sandy Travel Servic

By HARRIET NACHMAN
Daily Press Women's Writer

When the two women said goodbye in the Land of the Morning Calm they had little hope of ever meeting again much less landing twin assignments in the states.

But the improbable became reality and in March of 1966 there they were, recreational specialists in the largest Army service club in the world at Fort Eustis.

The world of dark eyed olive-brown skinned women with high cheekbones and flat noses seemed a million miles away. Days of jogging down dirt roads to get supplies, of stopping half way to Seoul to warm frozen knees and feet, of rationing spray net and nylon hose, were only memories. What was important now was to build an entertainment program to meet the needs of the men at Eustis.

The task was monumental but not insurmountable for the women who had learned a valuable lesson early in their membership in the uniformed civilian corps, Department of Army Civilians. Keep your programs simple and flexible.

Of course a birthday party for the soldiers in a Quonset but in Korea would be less elaborate than the monthly cake and ice cream fests for 200 at the Virginia post. But a service club was a service club anywhere in the world. Loneliness was not confined to the isolated regions of the earth.

Kay Strasburg and Sandy Lockney, four-month veterans at the neighboring fort, have planned a balanced program of activity with appeal for everyone. If the soldier is not a bridge, table tennis or pool enthusiast, he can go on a group tour, attend a coat and tie mixer or enjoy the solitude of a quiet corner and a guitar.

"We check out the guitars, but don't give any instructions," Kay assured me. "We do give advice," Sandy interrupted, "like play softly."

Kay Strasburg and Sandy check out guitar and instruction manual to service club visitor.

241

Club Circuit

The bulk of the visitors to the special services club are in the 17 to 25 age bracket. "Some come to play poker, some only for the dances, some live here from 3 to 10," advise the women.

The recreation directors estimate club weekend attendance at somewhere around 1,000. Good pickin's for any single girl, but the odds were better in Korea, laugh Kay and Sandy.

At the Asian Peninsula post, the ratio of men to American women was 500 to two—Kay and Sandy were the sole representatives of the fairer sex from the U.S.

But everything wasn't coming up roses even with such favorable odds. "Our main problem was getting supplies," says Kay. "Once a month we could look forward to bumping down a dirt road for four hours to Seoul. In the winter we could count on stopping at least four times to warm up even though we had sweaters under our uniforms and blankets over our legs."

At Eustis the women have no shortage of supplies, only an occasional shortage of energy. On the hour, every hour, for nine hours, the specialists have to check the rooms in the expansive club building—the card room, the patio, the two television rooms, the two music rooms.

"I don't know how many rooms there are—I do know how many miles I walk a week," said Kay as she relaxed a moment in the modern gold, green and blue club lounge.

The women, working a five day week, try to arrange their schedules to get a weekend off once a month though they don't always manage it.

"Weekends are our busiest time—that's when we have the floor shows and parties and the bus loads of girls come in."

Bright and early Sunday morning Kay and Sandy brew up enough coffee for the 200 to 400 morning guests who come for their weekend pickup. Yummy glazed doughnuts share top billing with the warm, refreshing liquid.

"Sandy and I wash dishes interchangably," says tall, slim, dark-haired Kay. "Dish washing is a big part of our job."

Despite the routine that surrounds the recreational specialist's job, Sandy and Kay wouldn't trade their posts for any job in the world.

To be eligible for their position, a woman must have a college degree in liberal arts, six months working experience and be single.

"It's a perfect job for a single girl," avows Kay, six years a uniformed civilian. "You can see the world—I had never been to the East coast before my Eustis assignment—you get good pay plus good vacation benefits."

Then too, there's the satisfaction that comes with seeing the men enjoy the programs "you've worked so hard planning."

"Oh they don't admit they're having a good time, but after the dance they edge up to you and ask, 'When are we going to have another party?'"

Sandy, carrying out her second tour of duty for the DAC, has learned there is no such thing as an average day at a service club.

One day it's an egg dyeing contest in a Quonset hut in Korea, another day a little fellow comes up to you three times to say goodbye before leaving for a far away port. Another day you're off to the Orient or Kansas or Tim-

Sandy Lockney, recreational specialist at Fort Eustis service club, explains popular television "money game" to soldiers.

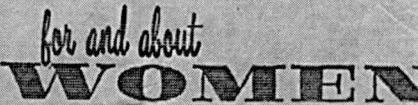

for and about WOMEN

DAILY PRESS, NEWPORT NEWS, VA., SUNDAY, JULY 17, 1966   SEC. B

NEW SERVICE CLUB PERSONNEL—Sandra Lockney (left) and Katherine Strasburg (center), newly assigned to the Ft. Eustis Service Club, loan records to Pvt. Robert Schorsch. (US ARMY PHOTO BY David W. Byrd)

Two Young World Travelers Join Fort Eustis' Service Club Staff

FT. EUSTIS, Ca.—The old recruiting slogans about joining the military to see the world might well apply to recreation personnel if the two new employees at the Ft. Eustis Service Club are typical examples of Army-employed civilians.

The pair, Katherine (Kay) Strasburg and Sandra (Sandy) Lockney, have covered most of the world in some service-connected capacity before arriving recently at the world's largest service club.

Miss Strasburg, a native of Central City, Nebr., is now in her sixth year of service club work. Miss Lockney has been working service club assignments for about a year herself and has already spent a tour in Korea.

"We are both recreation specialists," Kay says. "That means we help plan the dances, games, parties, bingo nights and other recreational activities at the club in coordination with the club director."

Born and raised in Central City, Kay didn't stay in the area long after she graduated from high school. "I went to Kearney, Nebr., and majored in physical education at Nebraska State, taking out my Bachelor of Arts degree in 1957. I went into the public school system in Portland, Ore., where I taught physical education at the elementary level for three years.

"It was after the third year with the Portland school system that Kay decided to enter the recreation field.

"My first assignment with the Army service organization was at Ft. Lewis, Wash., where I stayed for three years. In April, 1963, I was transferred to Eighth Army in Korea and stayed there until Nov. 1965."

During her tour in Korea, Kay was assigned to several camps within the command, including a few pretty far out of the sphere of influence which radiates from western-oriented Seoul. Among her posts were Camp Long, _____ and _____'s Command, "places where there are a number of service clubs," she says. "Each one is unique, some type of _____. Mine were so far out that we were lucky to get more than a quonset hut number on them."

Sandy has done even more _____ across the globe, but right in the capital. Among her assignments were Mayor Club, Continental Club and Camp Nators.

Sandy began her travels long before she got involved with the Army, however. In fact, by the time she was a sophomore in high school she had attended 22 different schools.

Among her stops were Parkersburg, W. Va.; Louisville, _____; Lowrey Air Force Base, Albany, Ga.; Silburg, Germany; Yorico, Ariz.; Munich, Germany; Ft. Walton Beach, Fla.; and Washington, D. C.

Finally graduating from high school in Germany, Sandy began college at the University of Maryland extension in Munich in September, 1959.

After completing her freshman year there, she transferred to Arizona State U. at Tempe. Meanwhile, her father was assigned to the same school under an Air Force program to complete his studies.

"Oddly, we both graduated together. We got a lot of publicity from that, with pictures in the Air Force publications and in most of the local papers in our various hometowns," she said.

Following her graduation, Sandy worked for some commercial organizations and then moved to Washington, for a position in the Library of Congress.

APRIL 1, 1966

"After I graduated, I worked for a finance company for a few months and then in January, 1964, I went into a clerical job in the legislative reference service at the Library of Congress. From there, I went into the service club system and my tour in Korea. Both girls joined the staff at Ft. Eustis in March, Sandy beginning work March 6 and Kay starting eight days later.

"We both work 40-hour weeks," Kay says, "With five eight-hour days each. Every week we get two days off, but quite often the days off are different each week."

"There's no way of telling how long either Kay or Sandy will remain at Ft. Eustis, but the odds are good that one of these days, they'll both peek off for an assignment in London, Longview or Lima.

243

BIRTHDAY PARTY—Festivities participated in by, left to right, PFC Bruce Mitchell of the 38th Army Band, Pvt. Bill Morrisey of the 551st Trans. Co., and Sandy Lockney of the Service Club Staff. (US ARMY PHOTO by David W. Byrd)

CuChi, VietNam. 1967

Lieutenant Tim Thompson, whom I described in "Almost my Worst Nightmare," was a special person and good friend. He had a strong protective instinct and felt responsible for me. Tim was one of the infantry lieutenants who allegedly had the shortest life span in VietNam. He led troops into combat, the most dangerous job in VietNam, yet he worried about me. Before he left on one of his combat missions, he offered to leave me a .45mm revolver, but I couldn't take it. When I was transferred from CuChi, I didn't hear from him.

Two years after I returned to the States, I was attending graduate school in Washington, D. C., when he telephoned me to ask if he could come to visit. While some of our shared memories of CuChi were not pleasant, I was happy to hear from a dear friend from VietNam and delighted that he wanted to see me.

It was spring, the cherry blossoms were blooming and the weather was spectacular. Tim was still the caring and gallant young man I remembered. His warm brown eyes, deep voice and strong Bostonian accent were familiar to me, yet he was different. My folks insisted that he stay at our house in Virginia, close to the city. Every day we drove into Washington to see the sights. We spent time walking through parts of the Smithsonian and along Constitution Avenue, the National Mall, visiting the National Monuments. We worked at getting accustomed to who we were away from the war. It was strange, like getting acquainted for the first time.

    I noticed that he had a pronounced limp. When I asked about it, he laughed and called it his old war wound. It was the reason we lost touch. He was wounded shortly after I left CuChi and his wound was so severe he was sent home.

    "I wrote to you when I got home," he told me.

    "That's funny, I never received it," I said.

    "The letter was returned marked, 'Deceased.' I thought you had been killed. My mother cried, when I told her about you."

    "Tim, I'm so sorry, what a shock, but how did you find me?"

    "It finally occurred to me to contact Special Services in D.C. to find out if it was true and they told me where you were. What a relief it was to find you, and it made my mom happy, too." His mother's reaction was touching; Tim had inherited his mother's caring nature.

    We spent hours talking about what had happened since we left VietNam and about the future. He had adjusted to being back in the States somewhat, but still had some unresolved issues that he didn't want to talk about. He wanted a family and a stay-at-home wife, but I had things to do, places to go and people to meet. We continued to be good friends, corresponded for a while, and called each other from time to time until I graduated. Tim got a new job and moved west; I accepted another tour in Korea to help pay off my student loans, and we lost touch.

Long Binh, VietNam, 1967

    Larry Bailey was a lieutenant I met at Long Binh. He had the coloring and features of a handsome Arab prince, and the temperament of a saint. He was one of the few men who recognized my need for quiet time away from the crowds. Oftentimes, he picked me up in his jeep saying, "Let's ride around and talk." It was great for me because I didn't have to divide my attention among a dozen men and it was great for him because he had my undivided attention. I loved the fact that he understood how important it was for me not to be the center of attention sometimes. I was transferred to DiAn after three months and we lost track of each other.

About a year after I returned to the States, when I was working for the assistant district attorney in Plattsburgh, New York, Larry found out where I was and called me. We laughed and talked for an hour. He insisted we get together to reminisce and invited me to Montreal so he could show me the city. We agreed on a time and place to meet.

It was strange being together not in the war, riding in a car, not a jeep, and feeling free to go where we wanted when we wanted. Larry was easy to talk to and while it was awkward at first, we soon felt like old friends again. In Montreal, we spent a day visiting the old city and the second day before I had to leave, walking through the remaining exhibits from the 1967 World's Fair. He was just as considerate, gallant, and chivalrous as he always was. One of my memories of that weekend was our first evening. Late in the afternoon, he asked, "How do you feel about lamb curry? I saw an authentic Indian restaurant near your hotel." I didn't want to tell him that in college I tried to eat lamb stew and thought it was the worst thing I'd ever put in my mouth; so bad I couldn't eat it.

"I've never had lamb curry, but I like chicken curry." So we walked a block to the restaurant where we ordered a lamb and a chicken curry dinner. When our orders arrived, he insisted that I taste his lamb curry. I resisted as long as possible, then braced myself and took a bite. It was the most delicious thing I'd ever eaten. He smiled and pushed his dish in front of me and said, "I thought you'd like it." He ate my chicken curry.

We talked until dawn, each of us describing our adjustment to life in the States. There was too much affluence, too much of everything and too much waste. Our "plastic, throwaway society" was powerfully obvious and it made me feel uncomfortable after experiencing the poverty and scarcity in the war. He felt the same, and like me, found that no one else understood. At the mention of VietNam, people acted like we were somehow uncivilized or less than human. For him, an Army veteran, it was worse than it was for me, a civilian. His family, like mine, didn't ask about our experiences. I couldn't tell whether it was because they thought I'd be uncomfortable talking about VietNam or they would. It was hard not to be able to share even the fun and funny times with anyone. By the end of the weekend, Larry and I realized that we would always be just friends. During our time in the war, we needed each other, but in the real world we had little in common. We wished each other well and hugged goodbye.

DiAn & TayNinh, VietNam, 1968

Dan Rider was a senior warrant officer who had worked his way through the enlisted ranks to become a chopper pilot. His salt and pepper hair against his tanned skin distinguished him among his fellow pilots. He had steel blue eyes, a deep velvet voice, and a smile that reassured you everything was going to be all right. He never had much time off because the pilots were in demand both in the bush picking up wounded and transporting the able-bodied to battle as well as transporting supplies. Dan was always there when I or any of my friends needed transportation or needed supplies delivered. His favorite phrase was, "No problem," and I never knew him to say no to anyone. He made everything seem easy, which was remarkable in VietNam where everything was difficult.

Typical of Dan's generosity was to call me when he could, and say, "Hey Little Lady, you and your friends need a day off and a steak dinner on Wednesday?"

We were always grateful for a ride or transportation for supplies.

"Dan, how do you always call at the right time?" I always said. "It's been an awful week and we're all ready to run away. Claire, Gay, and I'll be ready when you get here. What time will you land and when can we get a ride back?"

"You girls be on the pad at 1630 hours Wednesday and I'll get you back by 1000 hours Thursday."

Often we couldn't get away, but when we could, we were thrilled for a short trip with no worries about finding transportation back to work. It meant I could order a dinner in Saigon instead of mess hall food, sleep on clean sheets without sand in an air-conditioned room and take a hot shower. But as hard as we tried, we couldn't escape the war even in Saigon. From the rooftop lounge of the Rex Hotel we could see the tracers and the explosions of the war outside the city. When we had dinner on the floating restaurants, we could see the visible signs of mortar and grenade damage created by some Viet Cong who tried to blow up the place to kill Americans.

Sometimes Dan would fly us to Vung Tau, known as the Riviera of VietNam. He would drop us off and come back to pick us up even if he couldn't join us. Vung Tau was the in-country resort area for the Americans and I learned while visiting there, that the Viet Cong used the adjoining beach for their vacations. Even the bars were segregated; one end of the bar was for the Americans and the Aussies, the other for the Viet Cong. It was surrealistic and bizarre, but that was a common thread living in the war zone.

The Vung Tau Hotel, which was approved for U. S. personnel, was like a lovely old French villa. It was white stucco, with wrought iron trimmed balconies. The ceilings were ten feet high with windows that reached from ceiling to floor covered with thin, vaporous drapes that moved delicately when the air from the ceiling fans blew them. I always liked to stay on the side of the hotel with the view of the beach across the street. Vung Tau beaches were some of the most beautiful white sand beaches in the world. The only drawback was the number of street vendors hawking their wares along the beach. One could buy anything there, American cigarettes, liquor, or parts of Army uniforms. The Black Market was alive and well in Vung Tau and more visible than in other cities I'd visited.

The center of the city and the upper class neighborhoods were all built in the French architecture. The houses were beautiful, stately, white, and cool looking. Huge old trees formed a canopy over the streets. I could make believe I was somewhere away from the war.

Dan often helped me with supply problems that I couldn't solve myself through normal channels or through the Army's chain of command. One such occasion was when I was transferred to Tay Ninh from DiAn to help with the building of the Free World Service Club. It was to be a show place for the 1st PHILCAGV (Philippine Civic Action Group VietNam). The Filipino President Ferdinand Marcos had an agreement with the U. S. and South VietNam that their armed forces would provide economic and civic assistance to the South Vietnamese but not engage in combat except to defend themselves. Ironically, the civic action part of the agreement was not understood by the troops because all of those who volunteered were the country's best, most seasoned combat soldiers. There were some disappointed troops when they found out they were in VietNam to show the locals how to grow "miracle rice" to harvest four times a year, to build a model village, and to provide medical and dental care for the rural areas. The Vietnamese loved them for their accomplishments.

General Tobias, the Filipino Commanding General, wanted U. S. Army Special Services to to establish a Service Club with a library and crafts shops on his base camp for the benefit of his troops and he wanted it to be a showplace. All of the dignitaries, regardless of nationality, who visited VietNam, were flown to Tay Ninh to show off their wonderful "People to People Outreach Program," to demonstrate their success making friends with the Vietnamese. The usual VIP tour went through the model village, the miracle rice fields and later, when the Free World Service Club was built, it was added to the tour.

When I arrived, the construction engineers and carpenters were adding the final touches to the building. The mahogany paneling and tile floors had been installed. The exquisite Filipino rattan furniture was in crates, waiting to be unpacked. There was one problem. The building was designed with a large, specially-cut, Plexiglas window on each side of the double front doors. The day before the Grand Opening, the windows had not arrived, because they were delayed in Saigon. We could hide a lot of flaws and unfinished things, but not these windows because the ribbon cutting ceremony was to be held directly in front of them. Without the glass there were two gaping holes in front of this impressive structure. No one knew how to get them in time for the extravaganza. American and Philippine generals, foreign and domestic diplomats would be attending. People were flying in from the Philippines for the occasion. It would be a dramatic loss of face for the Filipino Commanding General if the ceremonies were flawed in any way. It was up to us to make this event perfect for our wonderful Filipino hosts who generously supplied us with all the materials and support we asked for and then some. The intensity of concern for such a small detail, in the middle of the war, was another example of bizarre behavior in the stress of the situation.

These were desperate circumstances, and it appeared there was no other way to get those windows to Tay Ninh by the next day. I thought of Dan and tried to think how to justify our dilemma, to make it important enough to merit a special trip for one of Dan's choppers. Knowing that choppers were on call 24/7 to pick up wounded and deliver troops to the field, I knew what I was asking was illegal, maybe even immoral. I was not authorized to make such a request. Rationalizing that maybe one of his pilots would just happen to have a mission nearby, I called. "Dan, we've got a problem," I said when I reached him on the phone. "The Ribbon Cutting Ceremony is tomorrow and the windows for the front of the club are still in Saigon. I hate to ask, but can you help us?"

"No problem," he said with his velvet voice. I loved that favorite phrase of his. "If they are in Saigon, I'll get 'em to Tay Ninh by 0700 hours tomorrow. Have someone meet me to unload on the flight line."

"What a relief! You are really a life saver and I can't thank you enough. Be safe. See you at seven in the morning." I don't know how he managed it, but he was at the helipad at 7:00 a.m. unloading the windows. I met him with a truck and some of our staff members to make sure the windows were transported safely to the club and installed properly and quickly. From that point I didn't have to worry, because our staff was supervised by a senior master sergeant who had been awarded the Philippine Army's "Sergeant of the Year" and who out-ranked any other sergeant at Tay Ninh. He was a most impressive man, very quiet, but effective. I rarely saw him because he supervised the staff so well; I rarely requested anything of him or gave him instructions because he knew what to do instinctively. It was hard to believe that such a high ranking outstanding NCO was assigned to us, but it was evidence of how much respect we were shown and how important the Philippine Command considered our Service Club. The Grand Opening was a tremendous success and we gave Dan all the credit. He was truly our "go to" man and a dear, dear friend.

In 1969, while I was attending graduate school in D. C., I answered my phone and heard, "Hey Little Lady, have you had any good steak dinners lately?" He had contacted the Special Services Office in D. C. to find me. We talked for hours reminiscing about the good times. We agreed to get together, but we never did. It was all right, because we were both alive and well in the world. Surviving the war made everything after that easy.

Camp Henry, Taegu, Korea, 1970.

My second tour was a pleasant experience seeing what great progress had been made since I was there in 1964. The Seoul to Pusan highway was completed making driving a pleasure and reducing the travel time dramatically. My position as headquarters librarian supervising three libraries with a very capable Korean staff was challenging, but rewarding. I was enjoying the community of Taegu and planned programs with the University of Taegu and our local dependent school.

Unlike my earlier tour in a primitive Korea and the intensity of my VietNam tour, work and life were stimulating but in a manageable way. My secretary, Mr. Ham, a clever and likeable man of great influence among his peers, suggested that we buy books in the Korean language for the Korean Army troops (KATUSAs) assigned to our command. The Special Services Officer and the Command liked the idea and allowed me a small budget for the books. Mr. Ham, wheeler and dealer that he was, let the local Taegu newspapers know about the project and they requested an interview.

I have no idea what the article said, because Mr. Ham was my interpreter, but the Colonel and I were recognizable in the picture so the Command was happy to get credit for the good will the project generated.

My father was serving his tour in VietNam and when he could get leave he hopped a military flight and met me in Seoul. He spent a week with me sight-seeing in a country where twenty years earlier he had flown one hundred combat missions. When I brought him to Taegu, the only place he wanted to see was the Taegu K-2 Air Base on the opposite side of the city from Camp Henry. I borrowed a car and we drove to see the base where he had been stationed during the Korean War. After seeing the base, I asked if he had recognized anything. He smiled and said, "The only change I saw, is they've built a new Officers' Club." We both laughed.

Dad visited me in Taegu from his tour of duty in VietNam, 1970. He met the officers in the Command, my Special Services supervisors and my library staff.

Mr. Ham, my secretary, and one of our library clerks, Mr. Yi.

One of my favorite romantic encounters occurred unexpectedly one weekend in late October during my second tour of Korea when I wasn't thinking about romance. I decided to go to Seoul to shop for Christmas presents. In those days overseas you had to mail your packages six to eight weeks early to get them to the United States in time for Christmas. I was feeling a little overloaded at work and needed some quiet time to myself, so only my supervisor knew where I was going. I caught a hop to Seoul and took a taxi to the transient BOQ on a Friday afternoon. It was a pleasure to take a hot shower, lounge around, and read in my room for a whole evening. The next morning I went to breakfast early, then took a cab downtown and spent the morning in the "shopping stalls" of Seoul looking for interesting gifts to send home to family and friends.

    For my mom, I found a gorgeous bright pink silk quilt. It was embroidered with Buddhist symbols, and Korean words that meant, "health, wealth, and happiness." For my sisters I found a couple of small, very ornate, lacquered jewelry boxes with inlaid mother-of-pearl on the top. For my brother, I chose one of the enigmatic oriental wood puzzles. I went to the 8th U. S. Army PX to find a present for my dad who had spent a year flying one hundred combat missions during the Korean War, so he was not much interested in memorabilia. I bought him something he could use, a Swiss Army knife.

    It was dark by 4:00 p.m., and not being a dedicated shopper, I was happy to finish my gift list. I caught a cab back to the transient quarters to drop off my packages, then walked down the hill to the Eighth Army Officers' Club. It was "happy hour" and crowded with officers, secretaries, and teachers from the dependent school on a nearby post. I took a seat at a small table against the window and treated myself to a glass of wine. From the window I could see the lights of the compound and in the distance the twinkling lights of the city. It was a lovely scene, because I couldn't see the huts, or dirt floors, or unpaved roads, or smell the particular aroma that was Korea. It was a pleasure to sit alone, enjoy the view, and I was happy that no one knew me. People were so busy talking to each other that no one paid any attention to me in the dimly lit bar. I enjoyed my wine and then went into the dining room for a dinner I could order, as opposed to eating whatever the mess hall was serving. That was a treat in itself. Another quiet evening, a good night's sleep and I was ready to go back to work. The next morning I caught a hop back to Camp Henry in Taegu.

    The work week was uneventful until Thursday morning. I arrived at the library at my usual 8:00 a.m. and began working on book orders. The library was two Quonset huts end to end and a third, connecting the two forming a T shape. My office was located behind the circulation desk facing the front door which I could see through a large glass window. From my desk also, I could see most of the library. There was always a clerk on duty at the circulation desk, so anyone who wanted to see me had to come to the desk first. It was a very convenient arrangement.

The phone rang and I answered, as usual, in the military fashion, "Camp Henry Library, Sandra Lockney."

"This is Major Jim Victor. I was wondering if this is the same Sandra Lockney that was at Eighth Army in Yongsan last Saturday."

I had to think a minute, since when I answered the phone at work it was usually a reference inquiry or a library business question.

"Well, yes."

"I thought I saw you there. Will you be at the library tomorrow?"

"Yes, I'm on duty."

"I'm stationed at Osan AFB, but I'm flying in to Taegu tomorrow and I'd like to know if it would be all right if I stopped by the library."

It was a little confusing, but I managed to say, "Yes that would be fine."

I was busy all day, but I did have time to wonder why this mysterious Major had made an appointment to see me. I wracked my brain trying to remember where he might have seen me, but I couldn't figure it out. The telephone conversation caught me off guard and I couldn't think quickly enough to ask such things as what he wanted to meet about, and where he saw me. I just had to wait until the next day to find out.

The next day was Friday and I arrived at work as usual in my uniform. I was sure he'd have trouble recognizing me since I was off duty and wore civilian clothes to Seoul where he'd seen me. On duty in my uniform I wore my hair pulled up in a twist so that I could wear my hat and because the uniform regulation was that your hair must be worn above the collar. When off duty, however, I wore it long and very unmilitary-like.

At about 11:00 a. m., I heard the front door open. When I looked up, there stood a dashing young Air Force officer in flight suit and leather jacket, wearing Air Force issued pilot sunglasses. He looked like Colonel Steve Canyon, of comic strip fame, complete with long white silk scarf casually draped around his neck. He was tall, tanned, with the build of an athlete and the features of a Greek God. He walked in confidently, like he owned the place.

I thought, "Anyone with such movie star good looks and so full of himself has got to be a real bore."

He walked up to the circulation desk and formally asked to see Miss Lockney. I went out to the desk and invited him into my office.

"When I saw you last weekend, I wanted to meet you then, but I'm sure you are always overwhelmed with men introducing themselves," he said. "You looked like you wanted to be alone, so I thought I'd call you later to introduce myself."

It was impressive that he recognized that I wanted to be alone. He was perceptive, and it was certainly a "line" I hadn't heard before. We visited for a while until he said he had to fly back to Osan.

"Could I come back to visit next weekend?"

"Yes, I'd like that."

What a long week it was, but Friday finally arrived and so did he. We took long walks and talked for hours. Jim brought a picnic basket filled with fruit, cheese, and wine. I had no idea where he'd found it. We had our picnic on a hill overlooking the camp. I couldn't imagine anything more romantic. It was like the meeting place of Jennifer Jones and William Holden in "Love is a Many Splendored Thing," one of my all-time favorite movies. We discussed books, philosophy, and our world views. Jim's favorite book was <u>Atlas Shrugged</u>, by Ayn Rand, his favorite author. We both admired her philosophy of self-reliance and demand for perfection.

After getting acquainted that weekend, we saw each other often. Either he came to Camp Henry or he flew down to pick me up for a weekend in either Osan or Seoul. We planned our annual leave time together. He made all the arrangements for us to fly to Tokyo to spend a couple of days in the big city and meet another couple who were friends of his. In Tokyo we found a disco across from our hotel and spent our evenings drinking champagne and dancing on a glass floor below a glittering disco ball to the music of Tony Orlando and Dawn singing "Knock Three Times."

From Tokyo we flew to Sapporo, on one of the northern islands of Japan, to see the Ice Festival and ski. It was two years before the 1972 Winter Olympics were to be held in Sapporo, but we were able to visit the ski slopes and see all the Olympic preparation.

Jim was an accomplished skier and spent most of the time teaching me how to stay on my feet. I had taken some

Sapporo was a modern city and getting ready for the winter Olympics.

basic skiing lessons when I was younger, but never got past the beginner's slope. With his instruction, I was skiing down everything but the expert slopes.

Since he was also an outstanding dancer, we found every club and restaurant in Sapporo with a dance floor. One of the restaurants I remember fondly was the Crab Palace. The restaurant was world famous for its crab dishes. The menu listed crab in every dish. We had a seven course

One of the exhibits at the Sapporo, Japan Ice Festival, 1971

meal with crab meat in every dish including a crab pudding for dessert. Days on the slopes and evenings of fine dining and dancing for a whole week. It was like a dream, more romantic than any romance novel ever written.

As with all things, there was an end. Jim was sent TDY to another base for a couple of weeks and I was transferred. It was difficult to meet, we made new friends, and we gradually grew apart. When it was time for me to rotate home, I boarded the plane at Kimpo International Airport and there was Jim! It was one of those lovely coincidences. We sat together, reminisced for the twenty-two hour flight back to the States and when we landed at SeaTac, the Seattle-Tacoma Airport, to transfer to our separate flights, we wished each other luck and parted.

It is hard to explain how these friendships and relationships were so different from those we make in the real world. There was an intensity of life imposed on us by the war. The isolation and living close together in a small area, reducing life to basics made us know each other intimately in a shorter time than under normal circumstances. Everyone needed to feel close to other human beings because of the fear or boredom and stress of the situation. The strengths that were absolutely necessary to survive in the war zone were not necessarily the most attractive characteristics in our civilized and affluent society. Pretty, handsome, or availability were not the primary attractors. We didn't have time for the frivolous. Humor and fun ranked right up there with strength, stamina and courage.

Maybe it was because of the atmosphere in VietNam. Regardless of how you felt about the war, we were all in this together; everyone focused on getting the job done and going home, "back to the World." We all worked for the same boss, the U.S. Army, and everyone worked 12- to 18-hour days. Any time off was spent frantically trying to have fun, to forget where we were, and how long we had to be there. No one talked about not making it home everyone just lived as though we might not. I didn't want to get too attached to anyone because one of us might not be there the next day and others felt the same way.

Even though I haven't seen or heard from any of my Knights for forty-plus years, if we met today, we would feel the same affection and kinship. I understand the bond "old Army buddies" have, because when I meet men and women who served in Korea, I feel a similar bond that's hard to describe; and for anyone who served in VietNam, whether I knew them or not, I feel a special affinity. In Korea, I shared a year of hardship living, but with those who served in VietNam, I am forever connected because we shared the most intense, raw, emotional, and demanding experience of our lives, living through a war.

16

EPILOGUE: LIFE IN THE REAL WORLD

Memorial Day Weekend
Pensacola, Florida, 1981

    Lying in the sun at poolside with a glass of white wine, I was about to fall asleep, when I heard Edna say, "Sandra, let me introduce you to Charlie Davis." I opened my eyes to see a tall, handsome man with salt-and-pepper hair and mustache, sky blue eyes, dressed in a Hart, Schaeffner, Marx suit. I nodded, he smiled and said, "Nice to meet you." Edna continued chatting with him, while I listened to their conversation and his charming Southern accent.

    "You're so dressed up. Are you on your way somewhere?" Edna asked.

    "I just got back from an appointment and on my way home to get comfortable," he explained. "Ladies, you're almost out of wine; may I get you a refill?"

    "You don't have to do that, but why don't you join us?" Edna said.

"Well, why don't I do both?" he said with a boyish grin and turned to walk back to his apartment.

"Edna, what a charming man," I said. "Are you interested in him?"

She hesitated and said, "I might be if he were interested in me, but he's not. I can tell." Edna Sanders was my friend since I moved into the apartment across the street from the college where I worked in Pensacola, Florida. She was a beautiful redhead with sparkling blue eyes and a soft Southern drawl that made you feel warm and welcome. As the Assistant Manager of the Royal Arms Apartments, Edna was the first person I met when I moved into the apartments. We became instant friends and she took me under her wing to help me find my way around my new hometown. She introduced me to her friend, Ann Ribar, a tall, striking blonde, and we became the three musketeers. We spent the weekends at poolside, on the beach or strolling through one of the local festivals. With Ann and Edna there was always something to do. Edna met the new tenants and let us know when a single man moved into the complex.

Edna Sanders and Ann Ribar, my two dear friends.

She was discreet and professional, never disclosing any personal information, but she introduced us to newcomers when the opportunity presented itself. Ann had a steady beau so she wasn't interested in meeting anyone, but ever the matchmaker, she was always looking for someone for either Edna or me.

A short time later, Charlie returned to the pool wearing white Bermudas and a pale blue shirt, balancing two giant plastic, convenience store cups filled to the brim with white wine. I smiled to myself thinking this man is no drinker; no one would serve wine in a big "go cup." He sat down on the end of a lounge chair and said, "If you all are free this evening, I'd like to invite you to dinner at my place. I have some steaks to grill."

"Charlie, what a sweet thought," Edna said, "I'd love to, but I have other plans, maybe Sandra can join you and I'll take a rain check."

Not wanting to be too eager I said, "I'd love to come, but maybe you'd like to reschedule when we can both join you."

"I've thawed the steaks for tonight so I have to cook them. Why don't you and I have them tonight and we'll plan a second dinner when Edna can join us?" Suddenly he looked at his watch, stood up, and said, "Sorry, I have to leave, I put some bread pudding in the oven and it's time to take it out. I'll come by your apartment to pick you up. Will 6:00 p.m. be too early?"

"No, that would be perfect. See you then." When he was out of ear shot, I turned to Edna and said, "He's beautiful, he's sweet, and he cooks! I think I'm in love." We both laughed.

Charlie and I dine in Ft. Walton Beach.

That evening Charlie and I talked for hours over a wonderful steak dinner with bread pudding for dessert. We made plans for the next evening, and from that day forward, every evening after work he came by for a drink, we went out to eat, or one of us cooked.

It was the custom in the Davis Clan to stop by Ms. Flossie's house at lunch or anytime to catch up on the family news. Ms. Flossie, Charlie's mother, prepared lunch every day from Monday through Friday never knowing how many people would show up. He took me to meet his mother shortly after we met and we stopped by for lunch as often as I could get away from work. I asked her how she planned her meals since she never knew who might come to lunch.

Charlie and I visited my mom at Lake Holley.

She said, "Oh I'm used to cooking for a big family. We had six boys and a girl and they often brought friends home, so it's not much different from when they were all at home except now I only cook one meal a day." According to Charlie, his dad, who was an elected county official for thirty-two years, was known to bring home entire families to eat and sometimes stay overnight if they needed a place to stay.

"But what if more people show up than you cooked for?" I asked.

"I just add another bean to the pot," she said and we both laughed. In her eighties, she seemed youthful, curious about everything that was going on in the world, willing to learn something new or try something different, always with a positive attitude. I was awed by her common sense, her wisdom, graciousness, and generosity. She often said, "You can do anything, if you want to do it bad enough," and that was a philosophy she passed on to her children. She became my role model.

Not long after we met, Charlie invited me to her birthday party when all the family gathered to have cake and coffee. I arrived a little late to find the house totally dark, but there were a number of cars parked in the driveway. I was a little nervous arriving by myself, but walked up to the front door and rang the bell. Suddenly

Above: Mother Davis, center, and Charlie's siblings.
Left to Right: Tom (kneeling) Charlie, Emma Jean (seated), Bob, Bill, Ben, and Jack (seated), each of whom had a large family of their own.

all the lights came on and the door opened. Charlie greeted me and led me into the foyer. I turned to see a living room filled with people all staring at me. I must have looked like a deer caught in headlights, because everyone laughed. Marilyn, Brother Bob's wife, called out, "Come on in and join us, Sandra, we're just looking at pictures of ex-wives." That brought another round of laughter. I loved them all immediately. Like Charlie's mother, his brothers, his sister, and their spouses accepted me as if I'd been a friend for years. Gradually, I got to know his sister, all the brothers and their spouses: Ben and Jean, Bill and Carol, Emma Jean and Norman, Bob and Marilyn, Jack and Rosemarie, and Tom and Sue. Getting acquainted with the nieces, nephews, cousins, aunts and uncles took a much longer time. There were so many of them.

Charlie was candid about his two marriages and his four children. His oldest, a son, Chuck married to Laura, had one daughter, Julie, and lived in central Florida. Oldest daughter Lolly was ready to graduate from Florida State University and move to St.

Augustine where she would make her home. His two younger children lived in Pensacola. Son Frank was seventeen, a senior in high school already working to support his active social life. Genie, the youngest, was a beautiful blond, blue-eyed twelve year old going on thirty.

He introduced me to Frank and Genie very soon after we met, when they visited him at his apartment. I was sitting at poolside when they came to meet me. After 30 years, Genie still insists that she remembers my pink bikini. Actually it was a rose colored, modest, two-piece swim suit. To introduce me to Chuck, his family, and Lolly, Charlie planned a trip to Tallahassee where we would all meet. Our day's outing included a visit to Wakulla Springs, where we took a boat ride, watched "Henry," the trained fish, jump on the command of the tour guide, and had a picnic. On the way back to Pensacola we stopped for dinner in Tallahassee at a pub across the street from the University where Lolly worked so she could introduce her dad and me to some of her friends. The younger family members, just like the older ones, made me feel like I belonged. I think they recognized that I loved their father and wanted only to make him happy which gave us all something in common.

I was fascinated by his large, loving, extended family, their incredible affection and respect for each other. It was a novelty to me, that they all lived in the same place all their lives, enjoyed each other as friends, and showed their affection openly. All my aunts, uncles, and cousins lived in Parkersburg, West Virginia, and I only saw them every few years for a couple of days. My childhood had been so different. We were a small close-knit loving family, my parents and the four of us children. As a military family we travelled and moved often so we were a self-sufficient unit. By the time I graduated from high school I had attended twenty-four different schools. I attended university in two countries and three states.

We were a small, tight knit family who traveled well together and supported each other. Left to right: Sandra, Kelly our collie, Pandora, Candace, Dad, Randolph and Mom.

Having grown up in one town, Charlie could remember all of his teachers from grammar school through high school. Until age nineteen, I thought my first grade teacher's name was Ms. Wheelbarrow. Then I met a young soldier in Germany who had coincidently attended the same grammar school. After laughing hysterically, he told me her name was Ms. Wagonheimer. It was hard to imagine what it was like to grow up and live in the same place.

Charlie was curious about me, my travels, why I'd never married, and how I came to Pensacola. Since he was a good listener, he heard my life saga. When my father died on active duty at Eglin AFB in 1974, I returned from Germany where I worked as a secretary for ACS, GmbH, an air charter company in Stuttgart, to help my mother and younger brother, Bill. My sister Pandora moved back to the Ft. Walton Beach area to help mom, too, so I decided to settle down near family. After six years in real estate I accepted a reference librarian position with Pensacola Junior College, where I worked for twenty-eight years, retiring in 2008 as a District Department Head of Libraries. My brother Bill worked for the government and built a log house in the woods on Lake Holley permanently making his home in Defuniak Springs, Florida. Pandora's career in condo management, maintenance, and interior decorating in Destin, Florida, ended when she met Chris Beal of Beal's Nursery and Landscaping. She joined him in the business; they married in 1999 and built their lakeside home on Lake Juniper in Defuniak Springs, Florida.

I was a Realtor for six years.

I retired in 2008, as a District Department Head from Pensacola Junior College.

My brother, Bill.

My sister Pandora and her husband Chris Beal own and operate Beal's Landscaping and Nursery in Winn Haven Beach, Florida but take time each year for a vacation. They fish in Alaska and bow hunt in Africa.

Charlie listened to my stories, never tiring of hearing about my escapades and close calls, always insisting that I should "write about it and write it like you tell it." From my high school sweetheart, to Korea and my engagement, to my tour in VietNam, my heroes, my knights, to my five years in Germany, my six years as a real estate Broker/Salesman and finally my librarian job at the local college, he heard about them all. He was patient and sympathetic when I described the feelings of abandonment I felt in VietNam and the disorientation I experienced when I returned to the States, feeling out of place, not belonging overseas or at home. Nothing felt right or comfortable. With no one to talk to about my experiences and feelings, I kept them inside which sometimes manifested as anger at the excesses in America, the protests and treatment of our military, and the waste produced by our throw-away society. It felt good to let it all out.

Originally, I thought Charlie and I were opposites and that the old adage "opposites attract" applied to us. But as we got to know each other, I discovered we had much in common. Our temperaments were similar in that we avoided conflict, preferred to go with the flow, enjoyed working on solitary projects, loved history, reading, and travel. Most importantly we enjoyed each other's company.

During his hitch in the navy, Charlie trained as a medic and became a dental technician attached to the Marines. He is a natural first responder and gentle care-giver. After his obligation to the navy, he had successful careers in insurance, real estate, and construction. As a Realtor in North Carolina, he owned his own brokerage firm. We shared stories about our adventures and misadventures in the real estate business, showing people property, listing property, our successful and disastrous sales, and closings. We had a lot to laugh about.

His approach to life was to enjoy the present while I was always thinking about the consequences and the effect on the future. He enjoyed working on a project, or as I call it, the journey. On the other hand, I focused on the destination, the completion of a project, finishing the job, and going on to the next project. With projects we worked together, we always had the same goal, but we started from different ends of the spectrum. We shared the same sense of humor and irony, but not exactly the same sense of timing. Perspectives notwithstanding, we made a great team. Instead of rushing to the finish line, he taught me to "enjoy the journey," and added twenty years to my life, while I concentrated on our getting things done.

I have never met a more talented, creative, resourceful man than Charlie. He can repair anything, design and build anything, write an entertaining story in perfect form and grammar, or speak amusingly to an audience of hundreds. To me, he's a combination of Mark Twain and Will Rogers, able to converse with anyone, rich, poor, young, old, foreign or domestic, and enjoy it. Strangers don't exist as far as Charlie is concerned. He continues to amaze me.

It took six years for us to make the decision to marry, or maybe it took that long to tell him my life story. My version of our courtship is that I waited him out. His story is that he let me chase him until he caught me. Whatever the case, I recognized him as the love of my life. We married Memorial Day weekend, May 24, 1986.

Over the years, we have enjoyed each other's successes. When I had the opportunity to enter the doctoral program, he said, "You study and I'll take care of everything else," and he did. When he decided to write his memoir, Growing Up in Pensacola, I made sure he had time to write while I learned the software to help him prepare and submit the

My favorite wedding picture.

manuscript. When I finally decided to write this book he said, "You write, and I'll take care of everything else," and he did.

Charlie helped me see my life through his eyes with a perspective I would never have discovered by myself. He allowed me to vent my anger and frustration in the loving non-judgmental, nurturing environment he created for me. He has gently encouraged me to examine my life and taught me it's okay to appreciate my accomplishments and not exaggerate my failures. He is my love, my best friend, my mentor, and my partner.

While I was living my adventures, I didn't think I was doing anything worthy or extraordinary. I have come to realize my career with U. S. Army Special Services was service to my country, it was important, and it's very special to me, now.

Charlie's housewarming gift to me when we moved into our dream house that he designed and built was a wall plaque with a quote from one of my favorite books, Out of Africa, by Isak Dinesen. He remembered I told him years before that I was touched by the quote, wishing someday I could experience it. The quote was:

"Here I am where I ought to be."

Today, I have everything I could possibly want and all the things I never thought I would have: a loving husband, four wonderful adult step-children, nine grandchildren, a great-grandchild, a large, loving extended family, an active, service-committed church family, and a beautiful home on the bay in the most wonderful, if imperfect, country in the world.

I am happy to be home...and so far, so good.

My Davis Family celebrating Brother Ben's 90th birthday, August 2011.
Left to Right: Rosemarie, Sandra, Charlie, Marilyn, Fannie, Bob, Jean, Ben, Emma Jean, Tom and Sue.

Part of my Lockney family in West Virginia gathered for a mini reunion in 2010
Left to right: Sandra, Cousins Gary, Sharon, Uncle Roscoe, Aunt Sybil, Cousins Mike and Cindy.

Our family

Above: Oldest son, Chuck's family: Chuck (center and on left) wife Laura and daughters, Julie, and son David. Oldest daughter, Lolly (far right) and her daughters, Kelsea and Lorelei (far left)

Below: Chuck's daughter, Ashley, her daughter, his granddaughter, Kailana, our great granddaughter.

Above: Son, Frank's family: Hunter, Meredith, Hayden and Frank

Below: Daughter, Genie's family: Genie, Samantha, Eric and Davis

Above: Celebrating Bill's birthday party on the Fourth of July at his house in DeFuniak Springs. L to R: Charlie, Sandra, Bill, Pandora and Chris.

Below: Celebrating Christmas with family and friends. L to R standing: Craig, Charlie, Chris, and Bill. Seated: Sandra, Cere, and Pandora.

Excerpted from **<u>Growing Up In Pensacola</u>**
**By
Charlie Davis**

54

"What did you do in the war, Grandma?"

I'm not disappointed that my grandchildren haven't inquired about my military experience during the Korean War. If my memory serves me correctly, I didn't earn any medals or citations as a dental technician attached to the Marine Corps at Parris Island. However, if they should ask my wife, Sandra, "What did you do in the war, Grandma?" she would have some great stories to tell about her experiences in Vietnam.

I used to kid her by saying such stupid things like the army must have sent her to Vietnam to teach our soldiers to fight dirty. That wasn't true or funny. The truth is she wanted to go, because going off to war was a family tradition, as her father, LTC William J. Lockney, was a fighter pilot in World War II, Korea and Vietnam. She really didn't go to Vietnam to fight. She was a member of Army Special Services, and had already served a tour in Korea, and subsequently served in Vietnam from March, 1967 to April, 1968. There was a big difference, since the Korean War had ended several years before she got there, but the Vietnam War was in full bloom when she

Sandra in the U. S. Army Special Services uniform in 1967

arrived. Her tour of duty just happened to be during the time of the Tet Offensive by the North Vietnamese and the Viet Cong.

LTC William J. Lockney, USAF

As a civilian employee of the U. S. Army, Sandra along with other women of Special Services staffed craft shops, libraries and service clubs, and coordinated an array of entertainment programs. They also coordinated USO tours of entertainers and celebrities, and produced, directed and acted in little theater productions. That was the kind of duty she was promised, but as a bonus she endured rocket attacks, mortar barrages and

Sandra at the firing range with rifle at 65thMedical Group Headquarters, South Korea in 1965

Sandra engaging some of the field troops in conversation at Stateside Service Club, DiAn, South Vietnam, 1967

commando raids mounted against her base camps. She had her "hootch" to live in, but often had to spend nights in rat infested bunkers. She traveled throughout South Vietnam by jeep and helicopters, and lived in such places as Tay Ninh, Cu Chi, Di'-An and Long Binh. It wasn't the lifestyle that you would imagine of a "Marian The Librarian" type, but Sandra endured because, as she says "I'm from good ole tough, West Virginia mountain stock." Today, the former U.S. Army Special Services employee is Dr. Sandra Lockney-Davis, a retired District Department Head from Pensacola Junior College.

Sandra's "hootch" in DiAn, South Vietnam, 1967

Sandra watching a Christmas parade with the troops at the Free World Service Club, Tay Ninh, South Vietnam, December 1967

Over 265,000 military and civilian women volunteered to serve in Vietnam, risking their lives to serve their country in whatever capacity they were needed. Most of them were in their early twenties. More than fifty civilian women died in Vietnam. On November 11, 1993 Sandra was invited to attend the dedication of the Vietnam Women's Memorial at the site of the Vietnam Veteran's Memorial in Washington, D. C. At the dedication ceremony, Admiral William Crowe, former Chairman, Joint Chiefs of Staff, made the following remarks:

> "This moving piece we dedicate today stands not only as a reminder of a painful era, but more importantly, as a tribute to an exceptional group of American women who answered their country's call at an extraordinary time in our history and did so at great personal sacrifice."

It is, or course, with a great deal of pride that I show friends and family her pictures in the publication, <u>Vietnam Women's Memorial: A Commemorative,</u> and the personal Certificate of Appreciation signed by the U. S. Secretary of Defense, Les Aspin.

The presence of women in harm's way existed in all of our wars. Vietnam was a new kind of war for our country, and once again, our leaders are adjusting to another "new kind of war" in Iraq and Afghanistan. Many of our young men and women are once again in harm's way. Let us pray that our country, along with our Allies, will find a way to end the threat of terrorist attacks without a prolonged war. If not, there will be another group of young ladies, just like "Grandma Sandra," who will be ready, willing and able to serve their country.

Top: Sandra gives a tour of the Free World Serivce Club in Tay Ninh, RVN to General Creighton Abrams, Commanding General of the American forces, with General Tobias Commanding General 1st PHILCAGV ca. 1968

Bottom: Sandra gives a tour of the Free World Service Club to General Dwight Beach with General Tobias, and one of Sandra's colleagues, Marilyn Ramge.

Grandma Sandra and her Grandchildren

Julie

Ashley

David

Kelsea

Grandma Sandra

Lorelei

Hayden

Hunter

Samantha

Davis

THE STORY OF A SERVICE CLUB GIRL IN VIETNAM

By TERRI ZUBER

Here are more of Terri Zuber's illustrations that depict other actual events and situations with her special wit and humor.

Usually we knew all the top secrets before any announcements were made.

Sometimes decisions that affected our Service Clubs were made so quickly that even we didn't know about them.

We had a lot a lot to keep track of and a lot on our minds.

Take headcount, no matter what!

Since the operators were GIs and they liked to talk to us round eyes, we could get telephone calls through to almost anywhere. It was like telephone power.

SAT AT THE HELIPORT FOR THREE HOURS FOR A RIDE TO TAN SON NHUT ... HITCH HIKED THROUGH HEAVY TRAFFIC TO 1ST LOG ... DROPPED OFF THE TIME AND ATTENDANCE REPORT ... CAUGHT A TAXI BACK TO THE CHOPPER PAD AND CAUGHT A COURIER FLIGHT THAT MADE 12 STOPS BEFORE WE GOT HERE ... WHAT A DAY OFF IT'S BEEN.

Many days off were spent trying to get paperwork to Headquarters by a deadline.

A great tragedy: missing your R & R flight and your precious vacation time.

FOUR MALARIA TABLETS TO GO... SHORT!

We had to take malaria pills daily. As we neared the end of our tour we could count the number of days until we went home by the number of pills left to take. "Short" and "Short timer" meant only a short time (days or weeks) until it was time to go home, to rotate back to the States.

ENDNOTES

[1] Fraser, Dr. Gael, AssociateVice President, Pensacola State College. Chair of National Women's Month Celebration, who thought of the title when she created a Women's History program to honor and recognize the achievements of female employees at Pensacola Junior College (now Pensacola State College) and the achievements of female community leaders whose extraordinary efforts helped make a positive difference in our community. "Guts, Glory and Lipstick." March, 2003. Dr. Sandra Lockney Davis, Honoree.

[2] VietNam. Vietnamese spelling of the name of their country in English. The spelling of the word I saw during my tour of duty.

[3] About.com. Rosenberg, Jennifer. 20th Century History. Vietnam War. http://history1900s.abou.com/od/vietnamwar.htm?p=1

[4] Ebert, James R., A Life in a Year, The American Infantryman in Vietnam, 1965-72. 1993. New York: Ballantine Books. Page xiii.

[5] Purcell, Judi. Letter to Sisters describing Seoul. 1964.

[6] Capouya, Renee Colter. The Monkey Caper. VietNam ca. 1967.

[7] Baker, Ruth and Cathleen Cordova. "The Service Club and the Minefield." Special Services Reunion Committee Newsletter. October, 1999.

[8] Jensen, Mary K. Letter home about CuChi, December, 1967. Courtesy of Rita I. Coll.

[9] Steinman, Ron. Women in Vietnam. New York: TV Books. 2000. Chapter: Elizabeth Allen, pg. 92.

[10] Jay, Barbara. "Barbara Jay Synopsis of a Wonderful Vietnam Experience – June 1969-1970." Essay Courtesy of Barbara Jay.

[11] Gaudino, Judy Jenkins. A memory of VietNam related to the author, November 11, 2011 at a mini reunion in Washington, D. C.

[12] Technical Committee, 1st PHILCAGV Tay Ninh, Republic of Vietnam. A Mission of Peace, The Officers and Men of the First Philippine Civic Action Group in South Vietnam—and Their Mission. 1967-1968. pg, 74.

[13] Cordova, Cathleen. "Cookies." Special Services Reunion Committee Newsletter. June, 1998.

[14] The 1st Philippine Civic Action Group, 'Philcagv', Tay Ninh 1966-1969. April 5, 2011. http://175thengineers.homestead.com/files/philcagv_ron_titus.htm>.

[15] Answers.com. Oxford companion to Military History. Tet offensive. Website. May 28, 2011. <http://www.answers.com/topic/tet-offensive>.

[16] Answers.com. Oxford companion to Military History. Tet offensive. Website. May 28, 2011. http://www.answers.com/topic/tet-offensive.

[17] Morris, J. Malcolm. The Wise Bamboo. Tokyo, Japan: Shinyodo Printing Company. 1954. pp. 13-20.

A Selected Bibliography

Butler, Robert Olen. A Good Scent from a Strange Mountain. New York: Grove Press, 1992

Cornett, Alan G. Gone Native: An NCO's Story. New York: Ballantine Books, 2000.

Davis, Charlie. Growing Up in Pensacola. Pensacola: East Bay Publishers/CreateSpace. 2011.

DeVanter Van, Lynda. Home Before Morning: The Story of an Army Nurse in Vietnam.
    New York: Warner Books, 1983.

Ebert, James R. A Life in a Year: The American Infantryman in Vietnam 1965-1972. New York: Presidio Press, Random House, 1993.

Fortin, Noonie. Women at Risk: We Also Served. Lincoln, Nebraska: Writers Club Press, iUniverse, Inc., 2002

Genz, Marilyn. 20,000 Men and Me. Carpenterville, Il.: Crossroads Communications, 1988.

Gruhzit-Hoyt, Olga. A Time Remembered: American Women in the Vietnam War. Novato, Calfornia: Presidio Press, 1999.

Hayes, Roger. On Point: A Rifleman's Year in the Boonies: 1967-1968. Novato, California: Presidio Press, 2000.

Hornung, Jan. Angels in Vietnam: Women who Served: Stories about Women Who Served in Vietnam. Lincoln, Nebraska: Writers Club Press, iUniverse, 2002.

Johnson, Tom. Betrayed. Denver, Colorado: Outskirts Press, 2008.

Jung, Sabastian. War. New York: Hatchette Book Group, 2010.

Lamensdorf, Jean Debelle. Write Home for Me: A Red Cross Woman in Vietnam. Random House, Australia, 2006.

Mangold, Thom and Penycate, John. The Tunnels of Cu Chi: A Harrowing Account of America's 'Tunnel Rats' in the Underground Battlefields of Vietnam. New York: Ballantine Books, 2005.

Marshall, Katherine. In the Combat Zone: Vivid Personal Recollections of the Vietnam War from the Women Who Served There. New York: Penquin Books, 1987.

O'Brien, Tim. If I Die in a Combat Zone, Box Me Up and Ship Me Home. New York: Broadway Books, 1975.

O'Brien, Tim. July, July: A Novel. New York: Houghton-Mifflin Co., 2002.

O'Brien, Tim. The Things They Carried: A Work of Fiction. Boston: Broadway Books, 1990.

O'Neill, Susan. Don't Mean Nothing: Short Stories of Vietnam. New York: Ballantine Books, 2001.

Steinman, Ron. Women in Vietnam. New York: T. V. Books, L.L.C., 2000.

Technical Committee, 1st PHILCAGV. A Mission of Peace: The Officers and Men of the First Phillipine Civic Action Group in South Vietnam—And Their Mission. Tay Ninh, Republic of Vietnam. Circa 1967-68.

Terry, Wallace. Bloods: An Oral History of the Vietnam War by Black Veterans. New York. Ballantine Books. 1984.

Turk, Michele. Blood, Sweat, and Tears: An Oral History of the American Red Cross. New Jersey: E Street Press, 2006

Vietnam Women's Memorial: A Commemorative. Paducah, Kentucky: Turner Publishing, 1993.

Walker, Keith. A Piece of My Heart: the Stories of 26 American Women Who Served In Vietnam. Novato, California: Presidio Press, 1997.

Zeinert, Karen. The Valiant Women of the Vietnam War. Brookfield, Connecticut: The Millbrook Press, 2000

GLOSSARY

A

AFN, AFTV, AFR -   Armed Forces Network (AFKN – Armed Forces Korea Network and AFVN – Armed Forces VietNam Network), Armed Forces Television, Armed Forces Radio.

B

BX -   Base Exchange (Air Force), Base Shopping Center.
Bally bally -   Slang in Korean meaning to hurry.
BOQ -   Bachelor Officers' Quarters. Permanent and temporary living quarters for officers and civilians.
Bulgogi -   Korean dish of beef, vegetables and rice.

C

C-rations -   Packaged food designed for troops to take into the field on maneuvers and into combat. Also known as K-rations in WWII and, currently, MREs or Meals Ready to Eat.
CID -   U. S. Army Criminal Investigations Division
Comshaw -   Military (Navy) slang for borrowing or taking without authorization or permission.

D

DEROS or DROS -   Date eligible for rotation from overseas
DMZ -   A Korean Demilitarized Zone is located in Panmunjom, Korea. Another Demilitarized Zone was located in VietNam.

E

EMAC -   Enlisted Men's Advisory Council. Enlisted men's group formed to advise and assist with programming of a Service Club.

F, G

GI - Government Issue. Slang for U. S. Army Soldier.

H

H & I - Harrassment and Interdiction. Artillery fire upon certain areas of suspected enemy travel or rally points, designed to prevent uncontested use and/or attacks on military compounds.
Hootch or Hooch - Slang for living quarters. A hutlike structure. Term from Japanese word for house.

I

IG - U. S. Army Inspector General.

J, K

KATUSA - Korean Auxiliary to U. S. Army. Korean army troops assigned to U. S. Army in Korea.
Kimchi - National Korean dish of fermented, highly spiced vegetables, usually served with rice.
Kimchi Kabana - Officers' dining room at Yongsan, Korea.

L

Latrine - Toilet, Bathroom, Loo

M

Medevac - Medical Evacuation, usually by air, either helicopter or plane
MACV - Military Assistance Command, VietNam

M16 -   The Standard-issue 5.56mm semiautomatic/automatic rifle that became the mainstay of the U. S. ground forces in 1967.
MP -   Military Police
Midnight requisition - Military (Army) slang for borrowing or taking without authorization.
MARS -   Military Auxiliary Radio Station. Amateur Radio
Moose -   GI slang in Korea for girlfriend
Mess -   Military (Army) eating facility, dining hall, or cafeteria. Separate facilties for Enlisted Men, Non-commissioned officers (NCO) and Officers.

N

NCO -   Non-commissioned officers (Army), i.e sergeants
NVA -   North Vietnamese Army

O

O Club -   Officers' Club
OCS -   Officers' Candidate School

P

Piasters -   Currency of VietNam.
Provost Marshall - Senior officer in military police
PX -   Post Exchange. Army shopping center

Q, R

Round eye -   Affectionate term for American and/or non-Asian women

R & R Rest & recreation -   Leave from duty for military and civilians on hardship tours of duty.

S

Slicky boy -   Slang term in Korea used to describe thieves.
Sapper -   VC/NVA soldiers trained to penetrate American and Allied defense perimeters of base camps and to kill and to destroy fighting positions, ammo dumps, and command and communication centers.

T

Tet -   Vietnamese New Year
Tet Offensive -   January, 1968 country-wide surprise attack of the North Vietnamese forces on the U. S. and Allied forces in VietNam.
TDY -   Temporary duty
Transient Quarters -   Temporary housing for officers and civilians in transient or between duty stations
Thousand-yard stare -   A strange look in the eyes of veterans who had experienced combat.

U, V

VC, Viet Cong -   Vietnamese guerilla forces fighting against the U. S. and Allied Forces in VietNam

W, X, Y, Z

Yobo -   GI slang in Korea for girlfriend.

INDEX

A
Abrams, Creighton. General – 199, 280
Allen, Elizabeth - 139-140
Aspen, Les, Secretary of Defense - 9

B
Baker, Ruth -   96-98, 130
Ballard, Cere – 275
Ballard, Craig - 275
Bardsley, Kay. see Strasburg, Kay
Baskin, George – 10
Beach, Dwight, General – 199, 280
Beal, Christopher – 267-268, 275
Beal, Pandora – 266-268, 275
Beall, Davis – 274, 281
Beall, Eric – 274
Beall, Genie – 265, 274
Beall, Samantha – 274, 281
Berry, Rozanne – 200
Beverly, Jack - 10
Blevins, Joyce – 178, 180
Brooks, Lynn – 189, 191

C
Campbell, Ann - 176
Capouya, Dave - 91
Capouya, Renee Coulter – 10-11, 90-91
Coll, Rita I. (Riki) – 6, 10-11, 121-163, 185, 191, 207
Condon, Terry – 190-191
Cordova, Cathleen – 10, 123-124, 201-204
Crowe, William, Admiral - 279

D
Daniels, Millie   - 26-31, 39-42
Davis, Ben – 264, 272
Davis, Bill – 264,
Davis, Bob, and wife Marilyn – 264, 272
Davis, Carol - 264
Davis, Charlie – 10, 260-275
Davis, Emma Jean, see Redding, Emma Jean
Davis, Fanny - 272
Davis, Flossie – 263-264
Davis, Frank – 265, 274

Davis, Genie, see Genie Beall
Davis, Hayden – 274, 281
Davis, Hunter – 274, 281
Davis, Jack – 264, 274
Davis, Jean – 264, 272
Davis, Meredith – 274
Davis, Rosemarie – 264, 274
Davis, Sue – 264, 272
Davis, Tom - 264, 274
DeVilla, Capt. Renato S. - 212

E
Esslinger, Susan, see Susan Selig

F
Fairchild, Effie - 121-124
Filler, Lt. Alfredo – 212
Freeman, Nita - 10

G
Goriesky, Gail – 10-11
Grove, Nancy - 10, 230-235
Guadino, Judy Jenkins. See Jenkins, Judy

H
Hage, Shirley – 10
Henderson, Joan – 10
Hoban, Claire – 174-175, 185-191

I
Jay, Barbara – 10-11, 175-176
Jenkins, Judy, aka Judy Jenkins Gaudino – 10-11, 177
Jensen, Mary K. -129-313

J
Johnson, Tom - 10

K
Kaiser, Rosemarie 264, 272
Kelsey, Ann. See also Appendix – 3-4, 10-11, 128

L
Laderoute, Roger – 175
Law, Carol - 10

Lockney, Bill – 266-268,
Lockney, Candace, aka Candace Bertelsen – 266
Lockney, Cindy - 272
Lockney, Gary - 272
Lockney, Grace – 17, 266-267
Lockney, Mike – 272
Lockney, Roscoe – 272
Lockney, Sharon - 272
Lockney, Sybil - 272
Lockney, Pandora, see Pandora Beal -
Lockney, Lt. Col. William J.- 15, 17, 18, 253, 266

M
Marcos, Ferdinand, Filipino President - 197
Milligan, Frankie – 10, 216-218
Moore, Harriet - 143-144

N
Nall, Gay – 178, 179. 185,-186, 222-228

O, P
Polk, Kelsea – 281, 273
Polk, Lorelei – 281, 273
Purcell, Judi - 10, 19, 29, 32-39, 45, 53, 58, 59
Purcell, Harry - 10, 19, 29, 32-39, 45, 53, 58, 59

Q, R
Ramge, Marilyn – 279, 199, 201, 208, 212
Ramos, Lt. Col. Fidel V. - 208, 210-212
Raye, Martha – 123
Redding, Emma Jean – 264, 274
Redding, Norman - 264
Reinauer, Linda - 10
Ribar, Ann – 261
Rogers, Ashley – 273, 281
Rogers, Chuck – 264, 273
Rogers, David – 273, 281
Rogers, Julie – 273, 281
Rogers, Laura - 264, 273
Rogers, Lolly - 264, 273

S
Sanders, Edna – 260-262

Selig, Susan. See Esslinger, Susan – 10, 200, 207, 208
Shannahan, Mary Carol – 10, 11
Stennes, Marcy – 10-11

Strasburg, Kay, aka Kay Bardsley - 10, 28, 41-44, 46-55, 65-84, 97, 105-107, 216-218

T
Tet – 212-213
Tew, Ron - 10
Tobias, General Gaudencio V. – 197-200, 206, 208, 215, 249, 279

U, V
Vincent, Vera - 27

W, X, Y,
Walker, Andrea – 10
Wills, Ora – 10

Z
Zagala, Raphael. Col. - 206
Zuber, Terri. See all illustrations – 10, 11, 122, 281-289

War Zone Diversions

An Overview of Women Volunteers in Civilian Staffed Recreation Programs in Vietnam

ANN L. KELSEY

© 2004 by Ann L. Kelsey. All rights reserved.

Background

In the Vietnam War, the support to combat personnel ratio was 1.8 to 1, as compared with a ratio of 1.5 to 1 in the Korean War and 1.4 to 1 in the first Persian Gulf War.[17] General William C. Westmoreland, in his book <u>A Soldier Reports</u>, commented that: "After the first influx of combat troops, priority did pass to support units as opposed to combat troops... Once the early crisis of supply had passed, creature comforts were ... a conscious part of the supply effort. Concerned about the effect of superimposing thousands of free-spending Americans on South Vietnam's tremulous economy, I tried to provide facilities that would keep American soldiers and their dollars on their bases and out of the towns and cities. A well-stocked PX, occasionally steak for dinner and ice cream for desert, volley ball courts, and a few swimming pools--those might make good copy for a newspaperman or a Congressman looking for something to criticize, but they served an important purpose."[17]

The discussion of the support to combat ratio and troop morale also surfaced in a study of medical support of the U.S. Army in Vietnam from 1965 to 1970: "Because of these distances [from logistical support bases and medical facilities], even with modern air transport, the need for self-sufficiency in the zone of operations is greater than that normally required within a combat zone. This fact is reflected by a higher ratio of combat, service support troops (including medical) to combat troops than is normally provided in more conventional situations. The distance of Vietnam from the logistical support base also has an adverse effect on the efficiency and morale of troops newly arrived in-country."[17]

Thus was the groundwork laid for the creation of a country within a country--Vietnam USA--in which the United States military developed an immense supply system, a logistical tail, if you will, that required large numbers of support personnel for it to function properly. Westmoreland's attention to "creature comforts" was a direct result of his desire to keep these Americans outside the Vietnamese economy. Although the success of his goal is open to debate, there is no question that one of the methods of achieving it was to place a high priority on boosting morale and providing wholesome recreation programs for the soldiers. Westmoreland stated: "While PXs, clubs and messes, and recreational facilities primarily helped keep troops out of the cities and reduced piaster[17] spending, they were also good for morale. These creature comforts...helped during the period 1964-69 to generate the highest morale I have seen among U.S. soldiers in three wars."[17]

Beginnings

Three groups, two non-governmental organizations, the Red Cross through its SRAO (Supplemental Recreational Activities Overseas) program and the USO (United Service Organizations), and one government agency in the Department of Defense, Army Special Services, were specifically charged with developing morale and recreation services in Vietnam. Their mission was to provide diversified and comprehensive recreation programs to enhance and support the morale and welfare of United States and Free World Military Forces.

The USO and Special Services began developing morale and recreation programs in Vietnam in the early 1960s at a time when dependents were still allowed to accompany military service members and civilian employees to duty stations in Vietnam. The first USO club opened in Saigon in April 1963, followed by the first Special Services library in February 1964. Other Special Services facilities, focusing on sports and athletics, soon appeared.

Military and other dependents were evacuated in January and February 1965, as the military and political situation worsened. In March, the first official American combat troops landed. In September, the first Red Cross recreation center began operating in Da Nang not far from the area where the Marines had landed six months earlier.

The Navy had had overall command responsibility for morale and recreation programs in the early 1960s. In July 1966, however, direct responsibility for the Special Services program transferred to the Army. The Army also assumed oversight responsibility for the programs administered by the two non-governmental organizations, the Red Cross and the USO. The Army assigned operational control over Special Services to the First Logistical Command, the unit in charge of the overall supply and logistics buildup in Vietnam.

In the months that followed the Special Services recreation centers, called Service Clubs, as well as the Arts and Crafts, and Entertainment branches of Special Services, began opening facilities. By 1967, all three agencies, Red Cross, Special Services, and USO, offered an array of recreational activities, including mobile programs for troops in the forward areas, in which Red Cross SRAO workers flew in helicopters to landing zones and fire support bases to serve coffee and Kool-Aid, play games, and chat with the soldiers. The "fly in-fly out" visits were the Vietnam equivalent of the World War Two club mobile runs, programs that helped the Red Cross achieve its twin goals of serving as many troops as possible in remote areas, and giving preference to combat troops.[17]

Both men and women were hired to staff these recreation programs and activities, but in Vietnam the number of women hired for these jobs significantly exceeded the number of men recruited for these positions. Men were often in management positions, such as the Executive Director of the USO, and the Special Services Command Entertainment Director. A small number of men worked along with women as librarians and as craft shop and entertainment directors. Only women, however, staffed the Red Cross recreation centers, the Special Services service clubs, and the USO clubs. Therefore, for the most part, those who worked directly with the soldiers, playing games, teaching photography in craft shops, and suggesting books to read in the libraries, were women. Some were career civil servants, but many were just out of college, in their early twenties, not very much older than the soldiers themselves.

The Game Players

Who were these women and why did they choose to volunteer to go to Vietnam? What were their backgrounds? Almost all had college degrees. A few were Hispanic, African American or Native American, but most were white, and regardless of racial or ethnic background, middle class. They went out of a sense of patriotism and idealism to do their part to support the soldiers. They went because it presented a challenge, both professional and personal. They went for adventure, in search of exciting and rewarding opportunities. Some supported the government's policies and some did not, but regardless of their political views, they wanted to see for themselves what the war was about and support the soldiers who had been sent there.[17]

The work they did emphasized the traditional women's roles of nurturing and care giving. Their job, as described by Sam Anderson, the USO Executive Director, was to be happy.[17] They did traditional women's work as recreation specialists, librarians, and entertainers. They played games.[17] They provided a place to relax in libraries, clubs, and craft shops. They combined caring and concern with all kinds of activities to remind soldiers of home and distract them, even for a moment, from the deadly business of war.

They were the surrogate girl next door, sister, wife, mom, and apple pie all rolled into one. A verse composed by Emily Strange (Red Cross SRAO, Vietnam, 1968-1969) for a donut dollie sweatshirt made especially for the dedication of the Vietnam Women's Memorial, underscores this philosophy.

> A touch of home in a combat zone
> A smiling face at a bleak firebase
> The illusion of calm in
> VIETNAM[17]

By playing games and being happy, these women shouldered the responsibility for becoming a symbol of support, caring, and home for every soldier with whom they came in contact. This responsibility may seem trivial compared to the life and death duties assumed by women working as medical personnel, and even those with assignments in areas such as military intelligence. It was, nevertheless, a responsibility taken very seriously, even, or perhaps especially, when their smiling faces masked deep emotional pain and physical misery.

Although the women who volunteered for the USO, Special Services, and Red Cross performed traditional women's jobs, which were often much the same as similar jobs in the States, the environment in which they performed these jobs was decidedly nontraditional. It was this dichotomy that made their roles so atypical.

These women, many in their early twenties, were thrust into hostile surroundings in terms of climate, living conditions, and physical danger. In order to do their jobs, they had to quickly acquire strong organizational, problem solving, and management skills. They assumed increasing levels of responsibility and leadership as they routinely worked independently of assistance from supervisors who were often hours away in Saigon or Long Binh. They developed the social and political expertise necessary to interact positively and professionally with large numbers of military men, both enlisted and officers, as well as Vietnamese local national employees.

The Challenges

Women in the morale and recreation programs, as well as most of the women, who served in Vietnam, regardless of employer or job, faced a similar set of challenges that included:

--The unbalanced ratio of men to women
--Never being able to be off-duty
--Required to suppress feelings of sadness, frustration, and anger
--Continually dealing with the presence of physical danger

No accurate statistics exist that reflect the total number of American women who served in Vietnam, since neither the military nor many civilian agencies, both governmental and non-governmental, kept statistical counts by gender.[17] The estimates, however, seldom exceed 12,000. According to the Red Cross, 627 women served with the SRAO program during the 11 years that the Red Cross operated in Vietnam.[17] It is estimated that between 300 and 600 civilians served with Army Special Services between 1966 and 1972. 75% were women.[17] The USO archives were destroyed in a fire at USO Headquarters in New York City in the 1970s, making it impossible to document the number of women who served with the USO in Vietnam.[17] Statistics on the total number of servicemen who served in Vietnam are also difficult to determine, but estimates range from 2 to 4 million.[17] Even without accurate figures, it is clear that the ratio of American men to American women was very high. This had several repercussions. The women lived a fish bowl existence, surrounded by thousands of men all day every day. Their workday was never done. They performed their jobs continuously. Even when they were off duty, they were expected to look and behave in a certain way, always happy, smiling, and pleasant.

For the women who worked in morale and recreation--because their job was to boost spirits, to bring a touch of home to the combat zone, to be perky and happy and smiling-- exhibiting stress, depression, sadness, or anger was not allowed. "Never let the men see you cry," said the Executive Director of the USO.[17] Negative emotions had to be suppressed. There were no outlets for fear and frustration. They were there to nurture and care for the men, but there was no one to take care of them. Judy Jenkins (Special Services Service Clubs, 1967-1970) underscores this: " So what do you do with all your fear and anger? You internalize it. You just absorb it. Because you have a job to do, and that job involves taking care of people. We couldn't let ourselves feel fear and anger. Just like we couldn't let ourselves feel hurt. For instance, once I got a letter from my great-aunt...telling me her parakeet had died... It made me cry. I was sitting there at my desk, crying. And I was supposed to be out calling Bingo for the guys. ...The woman I'm working with comes up to me. 'Look,' she says, 'I don't care what you just read in that letter, you go out there and you call Bingo. Those guys deserve a respite from the war. That's your job. That's your mission --- to make things better for them. Now get the hell out there!' And she grabbed me by the scruff of my neck and sort of scared me. So I went out and called Bingo. It was hard to let yourself cry."[17]

Under these conditions it would be natural to think that the women would be there for each other, especially the women who worked in the recreation programs and were often billeted in the same quarters. Generally, though, this wasn't the case. No one really knew or cared what the others were doing. Red Cross workers would use the Special Services libraries to research the programs they were creating to play with the troops. Librarians would answer reference questions from these women and have no idea what the Red Cross was doing that required answers to trivia questions. Moreover, it didn't occur to them to ask. Women were cordial and friendly to each other, but there was little bonding or confiding. There was no externalization of fear and anger even to each other.

This lack of bonding is puzzling and remains so to this day. One reason may be that each woman was so focused and intent on her own job that there was no time to wonder or communicate with others about what they were doing. Another reason for this isolation may be related to protective coping mechanisms. For women working directly with soldiers who might not come back from the next mission, it was devastating to bond with someone under these circumstances. Not getting too close to anyone, even co-workers and other women, might be a way of dealing with the constant presence of death and destruction. Women who were in Vietnam discuss this among themselves, but it is an aspect of the women's Vietnam experience that has not yet been addressed specifically as the subject of in-depth scholarly research.

The women had little control over their own safety and security. Although the USO and the Red Cross provided some orientation before sending women to Vietnam, the classes concentrated on programming, club operations, and instructions on what was considered proper and appropriate behavior. Special Services did not even provide that level of training. None of the organizations prepared the women for working in a war zone. Since women were non-combatants, the reasoning went, they were in no danger and the men would watch over them and protect them. It was, in fact, the responsibility of the military command hosting individual programs or facilities to provide security for the civilians assigned to them. This was explicitly stated in the case of the Red Cross in a memo sent on August 12, 1965.[17]

Vietnam, however, was not like World War II where there was a defined front. In Vietnam, there were no front lines. Non-combatant status did not automatically bestow a magic shield around each woman protecting her from rockets, mortars, shrapnel, airplane crashes, and all the other dangers inherent in a war zone. However, the military behaved as if that magic shield was firmly in place. Civilian women were not routinely issued protective gear of any kind, or given instructions as to what to do in the event of attack. Maureen Nerli (USO, 1969-1970) responded to an interview question regarding safety procedures and equipment with this statement: "helmets, are you kidding, helmets, are you kidding!

Never, boots, never, guns, never, vests, never, helmets, never. Nothing."[17]

Some units were more responsible than others in providing civilians with flak jackets and steel helmets and instructions in what to do in case of attack. For those assigned to facilities in units that were less responsible, these skills were learned "on the job" from those who had been there longer, and steel helmets and flak jackets had to be begged for or scrounged.

The face of danger was not always the enemy's. In some cases, it was the face of the soldier that the women had volunteered to travel to Vietnam to support. Although the majority of the men were respectful and grateful, most women encountered some forms of harassment. Sometimes the harassment was job related when military personnel, such as unit Special Services officers, attempted to undermine or subvert a civilian woman's role as manager of a program or facility. More often the harassment was sexual in nature. Some women were molested or attacked. American soldiers murdered two civilian women.[17]

Sexual and job related harassment are not peculiar to war zones. In fact these incidents reflect in microcosm negative behaviors that occurred in American society then and continue today. What made these negative experiences more intense in Vietnam was the fact that they were perpetrated on women who had voluntarily put themselves in harm's way by coming to a place that was by definition dangerous, and where they were clearly a minority. Perhaps they should have anticipated these behavior patterns, but most were hurt, disturbed, and angered by them.

Sexual harassment sometimes resulted from the assumption, held by some, that the only women who would volunteer to come to a combat zone were prostitutes. Women's responses to this stereotype varied. Some confronted it head on refusing to be intimidated. Some fought the image with humor. Judy Jenkins posted a sign on a shelf of books in her service club that said: "Take a book to bed instead."[17] Some women who were propositioned or molested rationalized the incidents, displaying potentially damaging self-conflict regarding the identity of the real victim. Cherie Rankin (Red Cross SRAO 1970-1971) accepted a ride from two soldiers who then molested her. They said: " Well, you do this all the time. You give it to the officers for free--what's the matter, you gonna charge us?" She was able to talk herself out of the situation, but then chose not to report the incident. "I felt I really did understand the men's perceptions of us. It's reasonable to think, 'What would healthy, intelligent American women want to be running around in a war zone for--unless they're making money out of it?' "[17]

The women learned to live with the stress and danger that became daily occurrences in their lives. The abnormal became normal. They did their jobs to the best of their ability, gaining satisfaction from what they were able to accomplish under difficult circumstances, and from the thanks and admiration they received from the majority of the service people with whom they played their "silly" games.

Was It Worth It?

Most of the women who worked in the morale and recreation programs feel that what they did was meaningful and worthwhile, that it made life a little better for the soldiers. Whether it was helping a convoy driver use the base library to complete an assignment for a college correspondence course, escorting professional football players on a handshake tour in a hospital, teaching a soldier how to develop photographs in a Craft Shop dark room, or creating programs and special events to entertain the troops in recreation centers, on club mobile runs to fire support bases, or in service and USO clubs, these women faced daily challenges that required creativity, professional knowledge, and organizational skills to do their jobs and accomplish their mission.

Some women, however, particularly those who were in the recreation programs, feel that their care-giving roles, their image as doughnut dollies, Kool-Aid kids, chopper chicks, or service club girls, undermined their professional personas. Some wonder if their presence was in fact more a negative than a positive, both for the soldiers and for themselves.[17]

Perhaps the final resolution to this question lies with the veterans themselves, the soldiers who played the games, read the books, watched the shows, and called home from the USO club. They write messages in guest books on Internet web sites dedicated to the Red Cross and other women who served telling how much these women's presence meant to them. One such message[17] says: "A belated thanks for your presence and a belated apology for being 'above' participating in your games and below knowing why…" [17]

Veterans come up to women at the Vietnam Veterans Memorial, at Moving Walls, and at other memorials and parades around the country where Vietnam veterans gather with 40 year old stories about the games at the fire base, the pick-up band at the service club, the USO recreation worker guest disk jockeying on USO Showtime on AFVN (Armed Forces Radio Vietnam). They say "Thank you." One of these veterans approached Maureen Nerli in 1987. "…After many years, [he] was finally able to thank her for the wonderful Christmas the USO volunteers gave him. The former soldier recalled feeling depressed because it was Christmas and he had not received any letters or cards from his family or friends. He said when he walked into the Saigon USO Club, the Christmas spirit was truly in the air. They had a tree, gifts, food, and singing. The USO volunteers were running around trying to make it a good Christmas for all the guys. He told the audience that was the best Christmas he ever had."[17]

Homecoming and Aftermath

In the years following the end of the Vietnam War, the civilian women who worked for Special Services, Red Cross SRAO, and USO disappeared into the woodwork of society, as did many Vietnam veterans. Some women remained employed by the organizations they had worked for in Vietnam. This was especially true of the librarians, who had to have master's degrees to be hired and were, until the very end of the war, Federal Civil Service career conditional employees. It was also true of the older women who were in career tracks. Most women, though, were let go, abandoned as it were, by Red Cross, Special Services, and USO. They were expected to move on with their lives, but this turned out to be not as easy as it sounded.

Vietnam was an unpopular war and those who chose to go to Vietnam faced personal derision and scorn on their return. Their war experience set them apart from their peers and their families. They were irrevocably changed and no longer fit seamlessly into their previous lives. As female civilians it was relatively easy to hide their Vietnam service, but its effects surfaced nevertheless in troubling emotional reactions, career dislocations, illnesses, miscarriages, and other health issues.

Even when Vietnam veterans began to surface after the dedication of the Vietnam Veterans Memorial in 1982, women who worked in morale and recreation were often overlooked. This began to change in 1993 when the Vietnam Women's Memorial was dedicated, but recreation specialists, librarians, and entertainment professionals are still very much an unknown element when the general population thinks of women who served in Vietnam.

These women, the game players, came of age at a time of major social upheaval when demands for racial and gender equality were among the forces shaking the fabric of society. They volunteered to go to Vietnam to support the troops, when their peers were marching in anti-war demonstrations or getting married and having babies. They were trained to do women's work, but in order to do that work in a war zone, they had to develop survival and coping skills, which included taking responsibility for acting independently, making decisions, and dealing with the consequences of those decisions, often on their own without the benefit of a support structure. They were confronted daily with the death and destruction of war, but continued to do their jobs, exhibiting stoicism, fatalism, and the inherent optimism and invincibility of the young.

They may not have thought of themselves then as leaders in the feminist movement. Indeed they may not have thought of themselves as feminists at all. The careers they had chosen steered them into the traditional path of women in American society, that of nurturer and caregiver. The way, however, that they chose to use those skills, when they volunteered to go to Vietnam, turned them down a very different and much more difficult path, where they became women in war, a place where women were not supposed to be and where their roles were ill defined and sometimes misunderstood and undervalued, even by themselves. Surviving and succeeding in this environment in and of itself was a challenge to stereotypes of what women are capable of doing and what their place in society really is.

Now, as these women begin to tell their stories, no longer as unknown and invisible as before, it may be that history will view them as women who practiced the principles of feminism while their contemporaries back in the world were only talking about them.

For history to recognize these women, and indeed all of the American women who served in Vietnam, it is important that the study of these women's service expand beyond oral history and personal narrative into published scholarly studies. However, except for Elizabeth Norman's fifteen year old study, *Women at War*,[17] developed as an outgrowth of her doctoral dissertation, "Nurses in War: A Study of Female Military Nurses Who Served in Vietnam During the War Years, 1965-1973"[17], no published books reflecting scholarly research on this topic currently exist.

Women in Vietnam: Orphans of Scholarship

The number of titles, both scholarly and popular, on the topic of the Vietnam War has grown exponentially in the last several years. Well and not so well researched books and anthologies examine the war or conflict, as it is officially known, from many different points of view. Scholarly titles reflect published research in different disciplines including history, American studies, literature, film, sociology, psychology, and health sciences.

The study of American and third country national women who served in Vietnam, however, remains virtually untouched by scholarly researchers. It is interesting to note that there are two published scholarly studies focusing on North Vietnamese and Viet Cong women.[17]

A literature search in two online databases, OCLC WorldCat[17] and Dissertation Abstracts Online[17] resulted in fifty-one listings for unpublished doctoral dissertations, bachelor's theses, master's theses, and undergraduate honors papers on the topic of American women in Vietnam.[17] Eighteen of these focused specifically on nurses, five on civilians (three on Red Cross), one on the Women's Army Corps (WACs), and twelve on post-traumatic stress disorder (PTSD). The two most popular subject areas of research were history and American studies with twenty-three dissertations and theses, and social sciences (psychology, sociology, and ethnology) with twenty-one dissertations and theses. Other subject areas included education (two), literature and film (three), and health sciences (two).

The earliest scholarship was a bachelor's thesis written in 1980, entitled "Women in War: Vietnam."[17] A master's thesis, "Women Vietnam Veterans and Mental Health Adjustment: A Study of Their Experiences and Post-Traumatic Stress" appeared in

1982.[17] The first doctoral dissertation, in 1983, also focused on PTSD and adjustment problems of women Vietnam veterans.[17] The most recent dissertation, published in 2002, uses oral history interviews to study the relationship between gender and what the author terms martial citizenship.[17] The majority of the remaining unpublished dissertations, theses, and papers were submitted in a time period ranging from the late 1980s through the mid-1990s.

Fifty-one scholarly studies in a time period covering almost a quarter of a century seems to indicate that the surface has barely been scratched in terms of research on the American women who served in Vietnam.[17] One reason for this may be that because these women are so invisible, scholars don't know to focus on them when selecting areas of research. The fact that many of the theses and dissertations that do exist were written in the mid-1990s may well be due to the dedication of the Vietnam Women's Memorial in 1993. This event raised the curtain of invisibility that covered these women and possibly opened the door to a flurry of scholarship centered on them.

Another reason why scholarship is lacking may be related to the relative paucity of primary source material on the American women who served that is available to researchers. Many official records were burned or otherwise destroyed in country and, as a result, were never returned to the States from Vietnam. For example, only records of the Special Services Entertainment branch are available to researchers in the National Archives. Records from the Library, Arts and Crafts, and Service Club branches were never sent back.[17] As mentioned earlier the USO headquarters in New York City burned in the 1970s destroying archival material related to the USO's presence in Vietnam. American Red Cross records are located at its Hazel Braugh Record Center & Archives in Falls Church, Virginia. However, the National Archives and Records Administration holds the organizational records of the American Red Cross from 1881 to recent decades. Information about the Red Cross' presence in Vietnam also often appears in military records. Since there is no way to search these different collections globally, significant sleuthing is often required to unearth records having to do with the Red Cross recreation program in Vietnam.[17] Individuals did bring back records and files on their own from Vietnam, but it is only recently that some of these, along with personal memorabilia, are finding their way into archives where they will be available for study and research.[17]

While these explanations may partially clarify why so little research has been done on this topic, they do not explain why the research that has been done has not been published. A brief questionnaire attempted to elicit from writers of some of the theses and dissertations reasons why they chose not to publish their works.[17] Questionnaires were sent to eight individuals and six responded.[17] Of the six, one had served in Vietnam and her master's thesis focused on the Red Cross, the organization for which she worked. One had lived in Vietnam during the war as the child of missionaries and his dissertation studied civilians, both male and female, in the broadest sense. A third worked for the Red Cross in a hospital in Japan and her study focused on Red Cross hospital workers there. Many had also served in Vietnam, as had most of the patients. The fourth, a master's thesis, concentrated on mental health adjustment and post-traumatic stress of returning women Vietnam veterans. The remaining two dissertations focused on literature (a comparison of war genre novels about women who served in the Crimea and Vietnam and their basis in fact), and a history of women who served in Vietnam. The latter was written in French for a doctorate at a French university and is not available in the United States.

All of the respondents felt that their subject would generate interest and all but one had considered publication. One said that he was continuing to research and hoped to publish all or part of his work some day. The author of the dissertation comparing genre literature about women of the Crimea and Vietnam also said she would like to expand her work and then try to publish it. One of the two women whose theses focused on the Red Cross said she decided not to move forward towards a Ph.D., and at that point decided she would not publish her work. She did write some magazine and newspaper articles based on her research. The other stated that she had never considered publishing her work, even though she had been told that it was a story that needed to be told. She didn't think she was a good enough writer to transform the thesis into a publishable book. The Frenchwoman is considering turning her research into a film documentary, but is encountering problems in finding funding for production. She is also concerned about retaining editorial control of content. The author of the thesis on mental health adjustment wrote chapters for two books on women Vietnam veterans and their adjustment problems based on her research, but did not know how to further disseminate her research. She did give talks based on her study and testified before a Congressional committee as well.

Job and personal commitments also took priority, with no time available to devote to transforming research from a thesis or dissertation into a book. Since only the two people who expressed active interest in pursuing publication are in an academic environment, this latter reason may be pivotal. Without the support of an academic institution to pursue research, independent researchers have more difficulty in finding the time and the funding to develop an unpublished dissertation or thesis into a published work. They are more likely to speak on their topics or to write articles, as some of the respondents have done.

It is important to note that, while it is beyond the scope of this discussion, a body of article literature exists, but most of these articles, except for health-related studies in the medical literature, appear in popular magazines rather than scholarly journals and only a few are related to previous scholarly research.

This informal survey can only suggest possibilities as to why research on American women who served in Vietnam has not been published. Because no one who responded to the survey had actually tried to publish anything other than articles or individual chapters, the question remains unanswered as to whether publishers would respond positively or negatively to submissions of a scholarly nature on this topic. Certainly, personal narratives, memoir, and fiction have enjoyed some success, but in this era of electronic publishing, many are self-published rather than being released by a mainstream trade publisher.

While the lack of published scholarship is disheartening, some resource materials, published and unpublished, do exist. The following brief bibliographic essay highlights some of these that deal specifically with civilian women who served in the morale and recreation program in Vietnam.

War Zone Diversions: Available Resources

Resources fall into four broad categories:
--Primary source material located in archives
--Published books and articles
--Films and plays
--Internet web sites

The National Archives Textual Records section in College Park, Maryland contains some files of the Army Special Services Entertainment Branch. While the records are not complete, they are the only official files from Army Special Services returned from Vietnam. Included in the files are some materials dealing with the libraries, craft shops, and service clubs. In addition, information regarding civilians processed in and out of Vietnam is contained in records of the Office of the Civilian Personnel Director. These, too, are incomplete.[17] As was mentioned previously, some Red Cross records are also housed at the National Archives.[17] Primary and secondary source materials on civilian women in general are also in a special collection at the Penrose Library, Denver University, "A Circle of Sisters/A Circle of Friends: American Civilian Women and the Vietnam Experience." The Archive of the Vietnam Conflict at Texas Tech University is expanding its collection related to women. Civilian women who worked in the morale and recreation programs are contributing to its Oral History Project and also donating personal memorabilia. The archives of the American Red Cross and the Women in Military Service for America Memorial Foundation also contain primary source material, objects, and memorabilia.

Theses and dissertations dealing specifically with civilian women include Carol A. Hunter's " 'A Touch of Home': Red Cross Recreation Workers in the Vietnam War" (1994)[17], Nanette J. Reckart's "What I Did in the War, Mother: A Study of the Women in the American Red Cross at the 249th General Hospital (1965-1971) during the Vietnam Conflict " (1990)[17], Maxine B. Salvatore's "Women After War: Vietnam Experiences and Post-Traumatic Stress: Contributions to Social Adjustment Problems of Red Cross Workers and Military Nurses" (1992),[17] and Maryann L. Weber's "Forgotten Sacrifices: American Civilian Women in the Vietnam War" (1996).[17]

Broader studies of women in Vietnam that include material on civilian women include Lenna H. Allred's "Women in a Man's

World: American Women in the War in Vietnam" (1995),[17] Angela M. Kearney's "The In-Country Experience: American Women Who Served in the Vietnam War" (1997),[17] Ronald J. Rexilius' "Americans Without Dog Tags: U.S. Civilians in the Vietnam War, 1950-1975" (2000)[17], Julia A. Sexton's "Women Warriors of the Crimea and Vietnam: A Comparison of Fact and Fiction" (2000),[17] and Isabelle Vigla's "Les Femmes Americaines, Veterans de la Guerre du Vietnam--Leur Role, Leur Vie de 1965 a Nos Jours" (1999).[17]

While women who served in Vietnam in both the military and in civilian capacities have published memoirs and personal narratives, the women in the morale and recreation programs generally have not. Their interviews do appear, however, in oral history anthologies, including Christian G. Appy's *Patriots: The Vietnam War Remembered From All Sides* (New York, 2003),[17] Olga Gruhzit-Hoyt's *A Time Remembered: American Women in the Vietnam War* (Novato, 1999)[17], Kathryn Marshall's *In the Combat Zone: An Oral History of American Women in Vietnam* (Boston, 1987),[17] Ron Steinman's *Women in Vietnam* (New York, 2000),[17] and Keith Walker's *A Piece of My Heart: The Stories of Twenty Six American Women Who Served in Vietnam* (New York, 1987).[17]

Frank Coffey's *Always Home: 50 Years of the USO: The Official Photographic History* (1991),[17] and Katherine J. Harig's *Libraries, the Military & Civilian Life* (Hamden, Conn., 1989)[17] discuss the role of the USO in morale building in Vietnam and the history of the library service program in Vietnam respectively.

Published articles, written by the civilian recreation workers themselves, include Jeanne Marie Christie's "The Basic Premise of the 'Donut Dolly' Program was Simple: A Soldier Couldn't Laugh and Cry at the Same Time" (1998),[17] Carol A. Hunter's "At Least 58 American Civilian Women-Government Employees as well as Others--Died in Vietnam" (1998),[17] and Sharon Lewis-Dickerson's and Ann Kelsey's "For the Troops: Civilian Women in Vietnam" (1993).[17]

Other articles and books discuss women's Vietnam service more broadly, but devote some attention to the women in morale and recreation. *Vietnam Women's Memorial: A Commemorative* (Paducah, 1996)[17] includes much of the text from the dedication program of the Vietnam Women's Memorial. Joe P. Dunn's "Women and the Vietnam War: A Bibliographic Review" (1989)[17] is one of the earliest bibliographic essays on women in Vietnam. Karen Zienert's *The Valiant Women of the Vietnam War* (Brookfield, Conn., 2000) is an overview written for upper elementary and middle school students.[17]

Some women who served in Vietnam choose fiction as the vehicle for telling their stories, including two women who served in Vietnam with the USO and the Red Cross. Diana Dell's *A Saigon Party (And Other Vietnam War Short Stories)* (Princeton, 1998)[17] employs biting satire, and Terry Farish's *Flower Shadows* (1987)[17] is a poignant novelization of the murder of Virginia Kirsch, a Red Cross recreation worker in Cu Chi in the summer of 1970.

Films include *Special Services: Where the Action Is* (1970)[17], a film made by Army Special Services to recruit women to serve in Vietnam, Mitch Wood's *No Time for Tears: Vietnam: The Women Who Served* (1993),[17] and the ABC News/Learning Channel documentary, *Women at War: Vietnam: The Soldier's Story* (2000).[17] Patricia A. Sweet Brimeyer's master's thesis, *Mother 6* (1990),[17] is a play about women who worked in Army Special Services service clubs. The playwright served with service clubs in Vietnam in 1967-1968. Perhaps the best-known and most produced play dealing with women in Vietnam is Shirley Lauro's *A Piece of My Heart* (1988).[17] Two of the characters in this play are civilians in morale and recreation, a Red Cross worker and a commercial entertainer.

Internet web sites have become increasingly popular for dissemination of information about women in Vietnam. Two reliable ones, with numerous links to other online resources are Marilyn Knapp Litt's "Women in Vietnam",[17] and Bill McBride's *Vietnam Veterans Home Page* "In-Country Women."[17]

Conclusions

When a woman says she served in Vietnam, the usual response is: "Oh, you were a nurse." People react with surprise and amazement to the idea that women went there employed as librarians, recreation specialists, and entertainment directors. Even without accurate statistical information, it is clear that the women who worked in morale and recreation in Vietnam were a small minority, in terms of both gender and occupation.

Ranking officers clearly described the importance that recreational activities and other creature comforts played in building and sustaining troop morale. Yet the role that this small group of civilian women played in accomplishing that mission is little known and seldom acknowledged by anyone other than themselves and the soldiers whose lives they touched. This lack of recognition extends to all of the women who served in Vietnam, even the nurses, whose live saving mission is the most well-known.

This is partially explained by the fact that the women who served in Vietnam refused for many years to talk about their service because of negative attitudes toward anyone who participated in the Vietnam conflict. Now, with the passage of time, the climate is different. People are more willing to listen, and the women are more willing to talk. Their voices, however, are not reaching the historians and other researchers whose scholarship can best record their experiences and place them in historical context.

A good deal of the scholarship that does exist is the work of the women themselves. Even these women, though, who would seem to have a vested interest, have not moved to the next level of attempting to publish their research. This is also true of their fellow scholars who did not go to Vietnam. Perhaps this is because the few people who have done scholarly research on the women who served in Vietnam have either chosen not to pursue a career in academia or are independent researchers with other commitments and obligations which do not permit them to devote the time and effort required to transform a thesis or dissertation into a published scholarly work. Perhaps some level of negativity and prejudice still exists against those who went to Vietnam. Such attitudes on the part of individuals in academe may influence choice of research topics, as well as the selection of manuscripts for publication by academic presses. These are areas that require additional research and study in order to determine why there is so little scholarship, and what can be done to encourage scholars and researchers to take advantage of the array of research opportunities available in history, women's studies, sociology, psychology, and medicine for those with the interest and scholarly curiosity to pursue them.

In conclusion, we must not forget that women have been a part of America's wars since the Revolution. At a time when both military and civilian women are routinely in harm's way, it is important to study women's roles in previous wars and conflicts in order to establish historical context for the history women are making now. The history of the civilian recreation workers, and all American women, who served in Vietnam, is an essential link in this chain. It must be collected, studied, and analyzed so that it may contribute to a better understanding of women's roles in war and how those roles ultimately affect the women themselves and their society.